Hollywood
on
Hollywood

By the same author:

The Unkindest Cuts: The Scissors and the Cinema
Susan Hayward: The Divine Bitch
Down the Yellow Brick Road: The Making of the Wizard of Oz
The Golden Age of "B" Movies
Hollywood on Ronald Reagan:
    Friends and Enemies Discuss Our President, the Actor

Hollywood
on
Hollywood

Tinsel Town Talks

by
Doug McClelland

faber and faber

Boston · London

Published by Faber and Faber, Inc.
39 Thompson Street
Winchester, MA 01890

Printed in the United States of America

Library of Congress Cataloging in Publication Data
McClelland, Doug
   Hollywood on Hollywood
1. Moving-picture industry—California—Hollywood—History.
2. Hollywood (California)—Social life and customs. I. Title.
PN1993.5.U65M37   1985   384'.8'0979494   84-28678
ISBN 0-571-12530-1 (pbk.)

This book is dedicated to my friend
JOAN HACKETT
1934–1983

CONTENTS

FOREWORD

My previous and recent book was titled *Hollywood on Ronald Reagan: Friends and Enemies Discuss Our President, The Actor.*

When it came out, my friends along with family and media members invariably said, "Congratulations! . . . What's your next book going to be?"

I tossed a few subjects around to several people to get their reactions, and once again their responses were invariable: a decidedly lower-case "oh."

The implication was that, at least in the eyes of those consulted, it would require quite a subject to follow the most famous man in the world.

Eventually, the obvious became clear.

My book of comments on President Reagan had been my most successful in every way, so why, as Hollywood has said (and said), tamper with success? I would continue to mine the lucky vein I had struck and do another book of comments by the Hollywood great and near-great on a particular topic. Furthermore, what better topic than the "Sunkist Pompeii" itself, HOLLYWOOD, whose shimmering name is known (and fantasized about) in as many far corners of the globe as Mr. Reagan's. And has been for generations.

"The greatest dream factory in the history of the world—Hollywood," certified *New York Times* film critic Vincent Canby recently.

Voilà:

Hollywood on Hollywood: Tinsel Town Talks!

For the record, Hollywood was founded in 1886 by Horace Henderson Wilcox, a Methodist prohibitionist and land developer from Topeka, Kansas. His purchase: a one hundred and twenty-acre fig tree ranch near Los Angeles on which he laid out streets and sold lots. His wife Daida named the area Hollywood after a friend's Illinois summer home.

Hollywood's first mayor was a retired millionaire meat-packer from Indiana who forbade "the driving of more than two thousand sheep, goats or hogs through city streets at any time unless accompanied by eight competent men." Drinking was banned in 1904, but only for a few years, and a bank opened in 1905.

Around 1907, Francis Boggs, a director with the Selig Polyscope film studio in Chicago, was shooting *The Count of Monte Cristo* when, beset by particularly bad weather, he remembered a stay in sunny Hollywood and moved his entire company there to finish the production. His star, Hobart Bosworth, who had suffered from consumption, flourished in the warm climate. Not wanting to return to cold, wintry Chicago, Bosworth convinced Boggs to write boss Colonel William Selig and suggest he move his entire film operation to Hollywood. And this Selig did, setting up quarters in the Silver Lake area.

Boggs is generally believed to be the first director to complete a film in Hollywood. His promising career as the potential father of Hollywood film production ended three years later when he was murdered by a Japanese gardener, thus probably providing yet another first: the first of many lurid scandals that would plague Hollywood through the years.

In 1910, Hollywood, anxious to share in Los Angeles' proposed Owens Valley water supply, allowed itself to be annexed by that city. Meanwhile, additional film studios sprang up in barns, bungalows and even saloons, as well as on vacant lots (hence the term "movie lots"), eventually spreading out over several L.A. communities. The city-within-a-city called Hollywood today comprises about two percent of the territory allotted to the City of the Angels.

The hundreds of often spontaneous quotations and interviews in this book cover all aspects of life in the Southern California fig ranch-cum-film capital, from the first decade of this century when other moving picture pioneers, escaping the unstable Midwestern and Eastern climates, sought a more reliable year-round temperance in the West; to now, when, as one star reveals, the big trip is from party livingroom to the bathroom, from whence much sniffling is heard.

In between, the screen traveled from lowbrow pastime to art form. Esteemed historian Arthur Schlesinger, Jr., has said, "Film is *the* American art." When I was in high school in the 1950s, on Friday afternoons teachers were still admonishing students not to waste their weekends reading comic books and going to the movies. Now those early comic books—so unceremoniously dispatched to garbage cans by equally disapproving parents—are selling to collectors for hundreds, sometimes thousands of dollars, and film study courses are common in seats of learning.

The film medium went from "flickers" to "photoplays," from "movies" to "film." Ring Lardner's 1920's appellation was "leaping snapshots."

As movies grew up, however, they—like children—began to lose much of their charm. Television took over. The tinsel was replaced by styrofoam. Today, a much smaller percentage of the feature films released are made in Hollywood.

Happily, Hollywood's untarnished glory can still be seen in revival theaters and on (very) late-night television, if only occasionally in a contemporary film.

Hopefully, some of Hollywood's excitement and fascination and wondrous achievement will also be conveyed on ensuing pages in the often passionate words of the remarkable individuals who have made Hollywood great. The stars prevail, unsurprisingly, but the directors, writers, producers and cameramen, among others, have their say as well.

Comments include the good, the bad and the ugly, the proud and profane, the serious and the facetious.

But . . . How in the world does a writer follow both the most famous man in the world *and* the most famous place in the world?!

As I have done in the past, I go to the movies for my answer, this time from the redoubtable Scarlett O'Hara:

"I'll think about that tomorrow."

For their exclusive comments and interviews in this book, I am indebted to the following:

Ed Asner. This actor, much-honored for the television series *The Mary Tyler Moore Show* and *Lou Grant*, appeared in the feature films *El Dorado, Change of Habit, Fort Apache, The Bronx* and *Daniel* and is President of the Screen Actors Guild.

Janis Carter. A glamorous blonde Hollywood actress of the 1940s and early 50s, she played in *One Way to Love, The Fighting Guardsman, Framed, My Forbidden Past, Flying Leather-necks* and *The Half-Breed*, among others.

Marguerite Chapman. In 1940's Columbia pictures, this brunette leading lady appeared opposite George Sanders (*Appointment in Berlin*), Glenn Ford (*Destroyer*), Paul Muni (*Counter-Attack*), Fred MacMurray (*Pardon My Past*), Robert Young (*Relentless*) and Larry Parks (*The Gallant Blade*).

Paul Clemens. The son of actress Eleanor Parker, he has been acting since adolescence in television's *Quincy* and the "docudrama" *A Death in Canaan*, as well as in the films *The Passage*, *Promises in the Dark*, *The Beast Within* and *They're Playing with Fire*.

Jeanne Crain. This top box office star, in films since 1943, won an Academy Award nomination for *Pinky*, adding to her laurels in such popular 20th Century-Fox productions as *State Fair*, *Leave Her to Heaven*, *Margie*, *Apartment for Peggy* and *A Letter to Three Wives*.

Rosemary DeCamp. A revered character actress, she is best known as screen mother to Sabu (*Jungle Book*), James Cagney (*Yankee Doodle Dandy*), Ronald Reagan (*This is the Army*), Robert Alda (*Rhapsody in Blue*) and Doris Day (*On Moonlight Bay*, *By the Light of the Silvery Moon*).

Gloria De Haven. The singer-actress, a Los Angeles native, left her mark on the screen in *Best Foot Forward*, *Two Girls and a Sailor*, *Step Lively*, *Summer Holiday* and *Three Little Words*, and was a regular on the television daytime serial *Ryan's Hope*.

Hector Elizondo. This actor of Hispanic descent has been prominent in the films *The Taking of Pelham One Two Three*, *The Fan*, *American Gigolo*, *Young Doctors in Love* and *The Flamingo Kid*, as well as in the television series *a.k.a. Pablo*.

Eddie Fisher. This singing star has headlined in all media, most relevantly in films with former wives Debbie Reynolds (*Bundle of Joy*) and Elizabeth Taylor (*Butterfield 8*), and not long ago wrote his autobiography, *Eddie: My Life, My Loves*.

Nina Foch. Nominated for the best supporting actress Academy Award for *Executive Suite*, her films also include *My Name is Julia Ross*, *The Dark Past*, *An American in Paris* and *The Ten Commandments*, as well as her activities with The Nina Foch (Acting) Studio in Beverly Hills.

George J. Folsey. A cinematographer since 1919, he was nominated thirteen times for the Academy Award and has photographed such MGM films as *The White Cliffs of Dover*, *Meet Me in St. Louis*, *The Clock*, *The Green Years*, *State of the Union* and *Seven Brides for Seven Brothers*.

Joan Fontaine. The best actress Oscar winner for *Suspicion*, this prestigious star who began films in 1935 has also scored in *Rebecca*, *The Constant Nymph*, *Jane Eyre*, *The Affairs of Susan*, *Ivy* and *Letter from an Unknown Woman*.

Beverly Garland. This pioneer television actress has done the series *Decoy*, *My Three Sons* and *Scarecrow and Mrs. King*, was a best actress Emmy Award nominee for a performance on *Medic* and has appeared in such features as *It Conquered the World*, *The Joker is Wild* and *Pretty Poison*.

Betty Garrett. On Broadway in *Call Me Mister*, this musical comedy actress went on to vintage Technicolor Hollywood musicals like *Take Me Out to the Ball Game*, *On the Town* and *My Sister Eileen*, plus the television series *All in the Family* and *Laverne and Shirley*.

Robert Getchell. An Academy Award nominee for his first screenplay (original), *Alice Doesn't Live Here Anymore*, the screenwriter next wrote *Bound for Glory*, *Mommie Dearest* and *Sweet Dreams*, and is creator of the long-running television series *Alice*.

Harry Goz. Once starred in Broadway's *Fiddler on the Roof*, this actor's films include *Marathon Man*, *Looking Up* and (as Joan Crawford's husband Al Steele) *Mommie Dearest*, while on television he was in *Bill*, starring Mickey Rooney, and the sequel *Bill: On His Own*.

Jane Greer. The ex-band singer's long acting career has included the films *Out of the Past* (the 1940s), *Man of a Thousand Faces* (the 1950s), *Where Love Has Gone* (the 1960s), *The Outfit* (the 1970s) and *Against All Odds* (the 1980s).

Butterfly McQueen. This actress, beloved for her portrayal of Prissy in *Gone with the Wind*, has also acted on Broadway, television and in other films like *The Women*, *Cabin in the Sky*, *I Dood It*, *Mildred Pierce* and *Duel in the Sun*.

Virginia Mayo. At home in all genres, the erstwhile "Goldwyn girl" starred in *The Best Years of Our Lives*, *The Secret Life of Walter Mitty*, *Colorado Territory*, *White Heat*, *Captain Horatio Hornblower* and *She's Working Her Way Through College*.

Alan Napier. A prolific English character actor in Hollywood's *The Song of Bernadette*, *The Uninvited*, *Three Strangers*, *Johnny Belinda*, *Joan of Arc* and many more, he is known to later audiences as Alfred, Bruce Wayne's butler in the television series *Batman*.

Jane Powell. The petite soprano starred in a number of MGM's best-remembered musical films, among them *A Date with Judy*, *Two Weeks with Love*, *Royal Wedding*, *Seven Brides for Seven Brothers* and *Hit the Deck*, as well as in *Irene* on Broadway.

Anthony Quinn. In films since the 1930s, this two-time best supporting actor Academy Award winner for *Viva Zapata!* and *Lust for Life* was graduated to star roles in major productions like *La Strada*, *Requiem for a Heavyweight*, *Zorba the Greek* and *The Shoes of the Fisherman*.

Ann Richards. This Australian star graced the 1940s American films *An American Romance*, *Love Letters*, *Badman's Territory*, *The Searching Wind* and *Sorry, Wrong Number* and is the author of *The Grieving Senses*, a book of poetry.

Ann Savage. The blonde actress had bits in the "A" films *What a Woman!* and *The More the Merrier* but was most conspicuous as female lead in melodramatic "B"'s such as *Passport to Suez*, *Apology for Murder* and the classic 1945 Edgar G. Ulmer-directed *film noir, Detour.*

Natalie Schafer. This veteran character actress has appeared in such films as *Marriage is a Private Affair*, *Keep Your Powder Dry*, *The Snake Pit*, *Anastasia* and *40 Carats*, but may be best known for her role as Mrs. Howell on the television series *Gilligan's Island*.

Robert Wise. He edited *Citizen Kane*, going on to direct *The Set-Up*, *The Day the Earth Stood Still*, *Somebody Up There Likes Me*, *I Want to Live!*, *West Side Story* and *The Sound of Music*, winning four Academy Awards as producer–director of the latter two films.

My gratitude, also, to Patrick Agan, John Cocchi, Kirk Crivello, Carl Del Vecchio, George Eells, Film Favorites, Lee Graham, James Robert Haspiel, Richard Hegedorn, Dorothy Horton, The Library of Lincoln Center: The Theater Collection, Eduardo Moreno, Movie Star News, Clifford, Janet and Thomas Nowland, Eleanor O'Sullivan, James Robert Parish,

David S. Rode, Bea Smith, Charles K. Stumpf and Lou Valentino.

Special thanks go to Charlie Earle, Beverly Linet and Jim Meyer, who are invaluable to me on all books.

My deep appreciation to *all* the Tinsel Town folk for talking (and talking) and providing the words that comprise this book. Even Hollywood could never have dreamed of gathering together such an impressive cast—who said actors couldn't speak without their writers?

Among those few movie people who declined to cooperate, my favorite refusal came from Ava Gardner. The disaffected film capital expatriate wrote me from her London home that she wished me well with my book about Hollywood, but then added her own emphatic (and pointed) interpretation of mogul Samuel Goldwyn's classic entreaty:

"Include me OUT!"

Doug McClelland
Summer, 1984

GROWING

Faraway Place
Hollywood, what a place it is! It is so far away from the rest of the world, so narrow. No one thinks of anything but motion pictures or talks of anything else. And, I, too, am getting like the rest. I have not read anything for a year. I do not know what is happening in the world.

Dolores Del Rio
The 1920s

Castles of Cardboard
In Hollywood, nothing is what it affects to be. What looks like a tree is really a slab of wood backed with barrels. What appears on the screen as the towering palace of Haroun-al-Rashid is actually a cardboard model occupying four feet by three of space. The languorous lagoon is a smelly tank with a stage hand named Ed wading about in it in a bathing suit.

P.G. Wodehouse
The Saturday Evening Post, December 7, 1929

Advice Never Sought
I have been in show business for 12 years. They have known me in Hollywood but two. Yet as picture–making goes, two years is a long time. Nevertheless, my advice has never been asked about a part in a picture. I found out I was going into *Susan Lenox* in Del Monte. Read it in the paper. When I walked on the set one day, they told me I was going to play *Red Dust* in place of John Gilbert. I have never been consulted as to what part I would like to play. I am paid not to think.

Clark Gable
1932

★ ★ ★

Money Mad
I don't want to go back to Hollywood if I can help it. I want to go back on the stage. The trouble with Hollywood is everybody is crazy for money. The producers are trying to make pictures cheaper and faster. They do not realize the public is becoming more critical, and can see the cheapness.

Ann Dvorak
July 18, 1932

Chain Gang

Hollywood is a chain gang and we lose the will to escape; the links of our chain are forged not of cruelties but of luxuries: we are pelted with orchids and roses; we are overpaid and underworked.

Clive Brook
1933

★ ★ ★

Vulnerable Joan

Hollywood was capable of hurting me so much. The things about Hollywood that could hurt me (when I first came) can't touch me now. I suddenly decided that they *shouldn't* hurt me—that was all.

Joan Crawford
Photoplay, the 1930s

★ ★ ★

Challenge Met

Taste has improved a hundred per cent in the last five years. Hollywood was too isolated, too provincial, before talkies brought a great number of New York stage people to the West Coast. They came with their Fifth Avenue fashions, and the movie colony accepted the challenge.

Travis Banton
Photoplay, April, 1934

★ ★ ★

Spare a Dime?

Most actors, you know, come out here with contracts from New York. They have gone through their hardships back East, and, once in Hollywood, everything is easy on them. But I can remember standing outside little one-arm restaurants along Hollywood Boulevard and wishing I had an extra dime—for a couple of doughnuts to go with my coffee.

Boris Karloff
Movie Classic, 1936

★ ★ ★

World Peace

Hollywood brings the world to the United States and the United States to the world. This interchange—of writing brains, talent, music, traditions—is important to world peace. It is equally important to good entertainment which knows no geography and has no international boundary lines.

Louis B. Mayer
Hollywood, October, 1937

Profit from Past

We are trying to profit by certain examples of profligacy in the past. Until now, no one has been in a position to benefit by such examples. Until now, Hollywood hasn't been old enough. Failures and successes were contemporary and therefore too close to each other to be able to judge. But a generation has come and gone and we young ones can see what has happened to some of the older ones; can see the one-time great stars dying in poverty; can see fame and fortune melt away like mist in the sun.

John Payne
Movie Mirror, October, 1939

A New Fondness

They asked me many questions about Hollywood over there (in the French Army). About Greta Garbo, Bette Davis, Irene Dunne and Norma Shearer. The only questions that troubled me were those that made Hollywood a phony place. It is too bad that the little part that is, perhaps, lurid should be what people hear about and believe. I tried to tell them that Hollywood is not like that. In defending it, there in the line of war, I felt a fondness for it and its people I did not know before.

Charles Boyer
Picture Play, June, 1940

The Hand of Man

The beauty of Hollywood is due entirely to the hand of man. For once man has not brought destruction, but grace and charm where there was nothing but waste.

George Arliss
My Ten Years in the Studios, 1940

Been Around

In Hollywood, those stars who have been around a long while and seem to grow better with time are the ones who regard "stardom" merely as an opportunity to grow.

Joseph Cotten
Photoplay, July, 1945

★ ★ ★

The Quiet Men

The picture business has grown up since I got into it fifteen years ago, has acquired a dignity that is beyond reproach. Hollywood is, today, a quiet town compared to other places I have been and can, moreover, be pretty proud of itself, having pushed more charities, given more time to selling war bonds and more talent to entertaining servicemen than any other town in any other part of the country.

John Wayne
Screenland, January, 1946

The screen's two great profiles, Greta Garbo and John Barrymore, teamed for the only time in *Grand Hotel* (MGM, 1932), the all-star first screen version of Vicki Baum's oft-filmed play.

Stars Clark Gable and the ever-wondrous Claudette Colbert both took home Academy Awards for the comedy classic *It Happened One Night* (Columbia, 1934), as did director Frank Capra, screenwriter Robert Riskin and the film itself.

Survival Kit

To survive in Hollywood, you need the ambition of a Latin American revolutionary, the ego of a grand opera tenor and the physical stamina of a cow pony.

Billie Burke
The 1940s

What's Lacking

England has been praised for turning out intelligent, adult pictures whereas Hollywood has been severely censured for turning out junk. I don't think the criticism is a valid one because, in defense of Hollywood, we have censorship problems England doesn't have. I'm not speaking of the license to do sexy stuff. I'm speaking of the license to present adult ideas and viewpoints, which we lack and which means in turn that many of our pictures lack intelligent content.

John Garfield
Screenland, September, 1947

Everything But Happiness

I am amazed at the desperate, violently unhappy people in our town, those who seem to have everything including the traditional minks and swimming pools. I don't mean to imply that everyone is frantic and unhappy; that's far from true. But many are, because of their careers and lives as actors and actresses.

Coleen Gray
Screen Guide, June, 1949

Bad Billing

Hollywood has come a long way since its infancy, when signs on for-rent apartments warned, "No dogs or actors!" We didn't even have the doubtful distinction of first billing!

Gloria Swanson
Silver Screen, November, 1949

More Traffic

Hollywood has grown, of course. There's considerably more traffic, but otherwise it's the same comfortable, friendly town it was before.

Vivien Leigh
Screen Guide, November, 1950

A Real Tribute

There is one thing I do want to say about Hollywood. It's thrilling to see firsthand the extra-ordinary reach of American films. It's so touching to have people in the smallest villages of

France and Italy come up to me—except when I'm painting!—and, as if they were seeing a dear friend again, wish Madame or Signora Colbert godspeed. This is a real tribute to all those who've worked so hard to make America the entertainment center of the world.

Claudette Colbert
Screenland, November, 1953

★ ★ ★

Flaunting It
Those were the years (the 1920s) when Hollywood was notorious for its willful flaunting of convention, and I leaped eagerly into that heedless life. I became flippant and superficial, and I was satisifed that I was following the prescribed Hollywood pattern.

Mary Astor
My Story, 1959

★ ★ ★

Hot Seat
Back in the forties everybody went to the movies. There were houses open twenty-four hours a day where the seats never cooled. Soldiers, war workers on the swing shift, housewives, school children, couples on a date, pensioners—they all packed in to see the dreams Hollywood printed on celluloid, preferably in gorgeous Technicolor.

Keenan Wynn
Ed Wynn's Son, 1959

★ ★ ★

Golden Era
Hollywood became a kind of Athens (in the 1930s). It was as crowded with artists as Renaissance Florence. It was a golden era. It has never happened before. It will never happen again.

S.N. Behrman
The 1950s

★ ★ ★

Kid with the Tuba
When you grow up in Hollywood, people always see you the same way as when they first worked with you. You're not allowed to grow up. This industry types actresses, categorizes and files them. To some of those guys I'm still the kid who played the tuba in the high school band.

Debbie Reynolds
The Saturday Evening Post, the 1960s

Aiming High
It can be frankly said about Katharine Hepburn that she has not grown up to Hollywood. Hollywood has grown up to her.

George Cukor
Films and Filming, July, 1962

★ ★ ★

They Had Faces
Realism. Being yourself. These are the things the big stars were made of in the early days of Hollywood. It's like that great Billy Wilder line in *Sunset Boulevard* where Gloria Swanson said: "In my day we had faces."

Barbara Stanwyck
Sunday News, August 15, 1965

★ ★ ★

Helping Out
As Jews of the German theater fled before Hitler, many of them came to Hollywood with talent, without much money, and with a message. "Call Ernst Lubitsch," Max Reinhardt, who was still in Germany, had told them. "He will help you."

Mickey Rooney
i.e., An Autobiography, 1965

★ ★ ★

Charitable Town
I am very proud of today's Hollywood, where all the stars work for some charitable or civic or cultural endeavor. In my day hardly anyone but Mary Pickford did a thing.

Colleen Moore
Silent Star, 1968

★ ★ ★

Hollywood Scorned
The public eagerly fed the lavish tastes of the Hollywood community. It allowed the stars and studio bosses to live in total comfort, in Roman splendor in sections developed by the small Hollywood community in Los Angeles. It was interesting, I think, that while a nation drooled with envy for the Hollywood set, the same set was shunned and looked down upon by the natives of Los Angeles. It was so bad at one time that local merchants wouldn't even honor a check from some of the top money-makers in Hollywood. They came around, of course, and there is a fairly stable relationship these days. But Hollywood in its growth years was scorned by Los Angelenos.

Veronica Lake
Veronica, 1969

Scarface (United Artists, 1932), featuring Paul Muni as a gangster of Borgia-Capone derivation and the neglected artist Ann Dvorak, was directed and produced by the Howards Hawks and Hughes, respectively.

No Part, No Way

The Hollywood of *Sunset Boulevard* was never part of our lives. Mr. (D.W.) Griffith's players simply had no time to get into mischief even if they had wanted to.

Lillian Gish
The Movies, Mr. Griffith, and Me, 1969

★ ★ ★

Swinging Sisters

Constance (Bennett) and I had a lot of fun in the Hollywood of the nineteen-thirties. The industry was at a peak of excitement with the advent of sound, and almost daily there was a new technical development or an exciting new personality to keep things interesting.

Joan Bennett
The Bennett Playbill, 1970

★ ★ ★

Family First

I think the old Hollywood was more fun. It was like a repertory company, particularly at Warners. We worked so hard, but we loved doing it. We had the publicity men working overtime, creating lies for us, and I just wouldn't go along with them. I ran away from (the publicity). My family was always most important. Talking about myself really embarrasses me.

Eleanor Parker
Ft. Lauderdale News, March 27, 1970

★ ★ ★

In Shock

On the historic night of October 23, 1927, Al Jolson's shadow sang from the silent screen. The sound waves of "Mammy" were as devastating as seismic waves. A major earthquake rocked the film world. The silent screen had grown a larynx! Hollywood shook. The inmates took over the asylum.

Frank Capra
The Name Above the Title, 1971

★ ★ ★

Golden Ghetto

Hollywood, at the time, was a small strangely remote enclave on the outskirts of Los Angeles—professionally and socially inbred and self-preoccupied—a weird mixture of goldmining camp and ivory ghetto.

Joseph L. Mankiewicz
More About All About Eve, 1972

Sharpest Thorn

Out of this trial and error, the (Fatty) Arbuckle case, came the sharpest thorn in Hollywood's side: the forming of a Censor Board.

Frances Marion
Off with Their Heads, 1972

Painted Skies

At rare intervals Hollywood paused long enough to discuss the European war, and these were moments of clouded uncertainty. Suppose President Wilson didn't hold to his promise that he would keep America out of the conflict? But why worry? Interest in the movies was increasing daily, especially in the rise of new stars who rode their steeds in a steeplechase across the painted skies of every studio.

Frances Marion
Off with Their Heads, 1972

Love at First Sight

I fell in love with the movies, Hollywood, everything! I arrived in Hollywood at a completely fascinating time, the climate was a mixture of confidence and chaos. The theater was going into one of its periodic low ebbs, the theater-going habit was dwindling, and road companies had almost disappeared. The movies had taken over both, just as television took over B movies many years later. And you couldn't make a failure in Hollywood in those days. The producing companies owned the movie theaters as well, people were hypnotized by sound, and any picture with sound would do business—rather like the nudies now.

George Cukor
On Cukor, 1972

Picking Poppies

Hollywood was a small hick town when I arrived in 1910. I used to take a streetcar to work and get off to gather poppies at what is now Hollywood and Vine. The first impression southern California made on me was one of great and novel beauty. From a car window at Pasadena I saw the palm trees in the moonlight. I have come since to dislike the palm trees and it was not till I had been out here three times that I began to like California. The first winter I found it difficult to adapt myself to work under the changed conditions. I longed to go back East.

Mary Pickford
Sweetheart, 1973

Filled with Phonies

If there's anything I hate it's a goddamned phony and Hollywood's filled with 'em, pretending to be what they're not and some of them never were.

Barbara Stanwyck
It Was Fun While It Lasted, 1973

Seven Duchies

Hollywood in the early thirties—and stretching out until perhaps ten years ago—could best be compared to the Holy Roman Empire or Germany prior to the unification and Bismarck. It consisted of seven duchies (Fox, MGM, Warners, Columbia, RKO, Paramount, United Artists), each reigned over by a feudal lord in battle with each other and yet bound together by their common interest, which was simply to get as much talent as possible and pay as little as possible for it. Or, if it served their purpose, to pay as *much* as possible for it.

To help them, they had created monsters known as agents.

Edward G. Robinson
All My Yesterdays, 1973

★ ★ ★

Racketeer Chic

In the Hollywood of the 1940s, top-level racketeers were quite chic. Stars and producers liked to brag of their friendship with Benny Siegel. The moguls of the studios pulled strings to invite him to parties in their homes. These men had a great rapport with gangsters: they were self-made dictators who'd come up the hard way; they had the same relentless drive, the disdain for others' feelings and lives, the calculating minds for ruthless deals. The racketeers were well entrenched in gambling, loan-sharking, movie unions. I don't think they bothered with prostitution because there were so many sweet young freelancers, looking for a break in films.

Phil Silvers
This Laugh is on Me, 1973

★ ★ ★

Plague of Agents

In the early 1920s, the agents descended on Hollywood like the proverbial grasshoppers. They signed up actors, directors, writers and anyone else connected with the motion picture industry whom they could coerce or run down. Agents became the fashion. Everybody who was anybody had to have an agent. If you did not have one, you became a pariah.

Raoul Walsh
Each Man in His Time, 1974

★ ★ ★

A Writing Tradition

It is inevitable that the writer be subservient to the director. In the early days of Hollywood, films were made by a small team which included only a director and the man with the camera. As filmmaking became more complex and sophisticated, people were hired to write scripts, but never were they considered other than hired talent. It was not unusual on the lot to hear directors refer to a screenwriter as "my writer." This tradition exists to this day.

Garson Kanin
Films in Review, November, 1974

★ ★ ★

Bring on the Censors

I brought the censors on in Hollywood, but I saved the industry—Paramount and seventeen hundred theaters. When I got out here the movies were doing so bad, during the Depression,

Shirley Temple danced with Buddy Ebsen, later of TV fame as star of *The Beverly Hillbillies* and *Barnaby Jones*, in the film *Captain January* (20th Century-Fox, 1936).

Frances Farmer, whose tragic life has been much-chronicled, made her greatest impact on screen in *Come and Get It* (United Artists, 1936), with Joel McCrea.

that you could fire a cannon in the theaters. My pictures broke all kinds of records, and I made a lot of money in Hollywood.

Mae West
The First Time, 1975

★ ★ ★

Putting Up a Front
I think Hollywood was full of more temptation (in the 1920s, 1930s, 1940s). It was a more seductive town, and lots of young players fell under its spell. An actor would get a foot in the door of a studio. He'd be there maybe two–three months and suddenly he'd show up on the lot with a Rolls–Royce and a driver. There was more emphasis on putting up a front. Most of the young players were not terribly economical, they didn't have the business managers of the caliber that are around today. I know several young stars who owned trunks full of gold mining stock . . . all worthless. They didn't find out until it was too late!

George J. Folsey
The Hollywood Reporter, 1976

★ ★ ★

More Innovative
A lot of the adventure of movie-making is gone. In the old days, if we wanted something we'd have to improvise. I also feel that working in "Old Hollywood" was a lot more glamorous, more creative and certainly more innovative, particularly for the cameraman.

Lee Garmes
The Hollywood Reporter, 1976

★ ★ ★

"City of Sin"
On my five-foot shelf of Hollywood novels are a number of fifth-rate fictions, sexually lurid and anti-Semitic, which paint Hollywood as Sodom and Gomorrah, where executive satyrs with exaggerated Jewish names prey on innocent teenage hopefuls who have come to the city of sin fresh from middle-American farms. The fact that immigrant Jews, excluded from this nation's established industries, were willing to gamble on the unproven medium, in which the film literally flickered in the Nickelodeons and the Penny Arcades, clearly accounted for the ascendancy of Jewish pioneers in the field of motion pictures in the teens, twenties and thirties. But it is doubtful whether sex played a more vital role in Hollywood than it did in any large department store or Eastern advertising business.

Budd Schulberg
American Film, May, 1976

★ ★ ★

Birth of an Industry
(D.W.) Griffith hired three or four directors who had been with stock companies and traveling shows. Under his supervision, they turned out eight or ten pictures a week. It was the birth of Hollywood.

Raoul Walsh
Films in Review, May, 1976

First Lady
You can really call Irene Dunne the first lady of Hollywood, because she's the first *real* lady Hollywood has ever seen.

Leo McCarey
Close-Ups, 1978

★ ★ ★

No Rating
(In 1930s) Hollywood there was an exclusive clique, and no matter how big a name you were on Broadway, until you had made it in the movies you didn't exist. I was just another Broadway star and didn't rate.

Ethel Merman
Merman, 1978

★ ★ ★

They Took Chances
The tycoons who dominated Hollywood in the first half of the century were adventurers in a competitive jungle. They might socialize together, but during business hours they were ready to cut each other's throats, along with anyone else's. Yet despite their questionable ethics and their despotic methods, these men possessed certain attributes lacking in those who hold the purse strings in filmmaking today. Gamblers by nature, they were willing to take risks and make personal decisions.

Howard Koch
As Time Goes By, 1979

★ ★ ★

True Story
People tell you that the reason a lot of actors left Hollywood when sound came in was that their voices were wrong for talkies. The truth is that the coming of sound meant the end of all-night parties. With talkies, you couldn't stay out till sunrise anymore. You had to rush back from the studios and start learning your lines, ready for the next day's shooting at 8 a.m. That was when the studio machine really took over. It controlled you, mind and body, from the moment you were yanked out of bed at dawn until the publicity department put you back to bed at night.

Louise Brooks
Show People, 1979

★ ★ ★

Living Well
From a letter in 1939:

People do seem to live awfully well out here (in Hollywood) and it's all so different from London and New York: nobody seems to take their acting very seriously and they all seem to be on long-term contracts and half the time they don't even know which film they're doing, but they are apparently never out of work.

Gladys Cooper
Gladys Cooper, 1979

The Magic Word
Seldom does Hollywood shake off its self-satisfied superiority and remember its beginning as a non-descript village of nickelodeon salesmen. But it took only one word to do it: *Garbo!*

Robert Stack
Straight Shooting, 1980

★ ★ ★

Let's Do It Again
For movie buffs remakes are themselves an interesting study in Hollywood history. Once the studio had found a winning story formula, they dressed it up in a thousand different ways and told it over and over again. Then, after a period of ten or fifteen years, when they had other stars in the stable and a new generation of filmgoers, they would package the story as a remake. The remakes were rarely as good as the originals and were a constant source of annoyance to movie buffs.

Sammy Davis, Jr.
Hollywood in a Suitcase, 1980

★ ★ ★

The Place to Be
A lot of actors who shared my "big" years in Hollywood, or even some of those years, are inclined to be very critical about the way the studios were run. But I was at MGM, and that was the best place to be. (L.B.) Mayer wanted a sort of family feeling, and in a way he got it. There was a definite morality, which could be a pain in the ass, but it was a lot better than being under contract at another studio. At Warners they had Jack, who really didn't like actors at all, and did his damnedest to humiliate them, and at Columbia they had Harry Cohn, who thought every actress on the lot owed him sex, ditto (Darryl F.) Zanuck at Twentieth, ditto Joe Kennedy and then Howard Hughes at RKO. At MGM we had a certain dignity; we didn't feel like whores.

Joan Crawford
Conversations with Joan Crawford, 1980

★ ★ ★

Racism Ignored
Yes, there was racism in Hollywood in the 1930s and 1940s. I dealt with it as I deal with it in my own race; I ignore it and concentrate on non-racism. I have no regrets about my years in Hollywood. I loved the weather there.

Butterfly McQueen
March 16, 1984

★ ★ ★

Growing Up Zorba
My grandmother was a great, great movie fan and started taking me to them from the age of two. She made me promise to get into the movies when I grew up, but I never considered it seriously. I wanted to be an architect.

I was born in Mexico but moved to Los Angeles at age four. I more or less grew up with the film industry in Hollywood. My father became an assistant cameraman at an early studio

Hollywood's dance team supreme Fred Astaire and Ginger Rogers perform "Let's Face the Music and Dance" from *Follow the Fleet* (RKO, 1936).

called Selig, which was also a zoo. (Today, people say *all* the studios are zoos!) Everyone came to Selig to do pictures that had anything to do with animals. Many of the beasts were trained, although my father was almost killed by one that wasn't. As a youngster, I used to go to the studios and became friends with many of the stars, such as Rudolph Valentino, who wanted to adopt me.

I still wanted to be an architect, but started doing extra work in the movies around the age of twenty to make some money. When I trained with the great architect Frank Lloyd Wright, he said my primitive Los Angeles speech needed polishing, that if I was going to convince clients I would have to speak well. So I exchanged janitor work at a drama school for some speech lessons, and I guess they were successful because I soon found myself doing theater work in the L.A. area, including a play produced by Miss Mae West called *Clean Beds*.

In the mid-1930s, some agents saw me and I began to get acting parts in films. Then Paramount Pictures, at the urging of my friend Carole Lombard, signed me. I was seduced away from architecture and never looked back.

When people talk about Hollywood, they always bring up things like the Fatty Arbuckle scandal. But we were workaholics in Hollywood then. (I still am.) We had to be at the studio at six in the morning and ready for the first shot at nine a.m. "B" movies were made in nine days, "A"s in a month. There was no fooling around. Everyone was much better organized in those days.

As for the much-publicized nightlife of the great stars of Hollywood, I don't think anyone ever saw Garbo out at night, and Clark Gable was rarely seen. During the thirty-odd years that I was married to Katherine DeMille, the daughter of the famed director Cecil B. DeMille, I don't think we went out to five cocktail parties.

True, in Hollywood we found plenty of time to play. There was the hunting group, headed by Wallace Beery and Gable. There was the yachting group, headed by Errol Flynn and Humphrey Bogart. Then there was the tennis group. But you couldn't drink all night and then work in the morning. And believe me, if you didn't know your lines, you were called into the front office and perhaps put on suspension. The moguls were very, very tough. The actors had twelve weeks vacation each year (without pay), and they usually went off on their boats or whatever then. I was a beach and mountain man myself.

The actors were much more serious than you hear they were today. Take that most infamous of Hollywood playboys, Errol Flynn, for instance. He used to have a yellow pad on the set and wrote books on them.

The studios were very rah-rah. It was as if you were going to an exclusive college or club, and you felt proud.

You see so much about the women stars doing exercises today. The studios had gyms then, as well as acting classes, schools, everything. There was the writers' building, the producers' building, the directors' building, the actors' building. You could go and find help and stimulation whenever you needed it.

Where did we go wrong? I'll tell you. We were creating a kind of Hollywood reality and morality promoted by the censorship board which was unreal. Only rarely did we portray human beings. Like the thing about a couple, even a married couple, being in bed for a scene —you had to keep one foot on the floor! In the 1950s Hollywood faced a crisis when audiences said "That's a lot of crap. People don't behave like that" and stopped going to the movies.

Neo-realism came in from abroad.

And the McCarthy Communist witch-hunts were tremendously destructive. Hollywood lost many gifted writers then, and still hasn't recovered. Because of their political beliefs, a lot of wonderful people were no longer able to work here and had to go overseas. They felt they were taxpayers and couldn't understand why they weren't allowed to work.

Now Hollywood is in the *Star Wars* era; it's still escaping its responsibility to say important, real things. I realize that sometimes the film business can't face our problems till they have passed. Like the Viet Nam war—no one in Hollywood wanted to touch it till it was over. The feeling is that the problem could be over in the morning and who knows how the public will react, anyway? So filmmakers do the trivial things. The only place we can deal with contemporary problems, strangely enough, is on TV. And the stage, of course.

Where, too, are the great Hollywood producers today? Men like Sam Spiegel, Hal Wallis and Henry Blanke who could lead a team to victory.

I've filmed all over the world, and I can tell you that what happens is amazing. Movies are the greatest ambassador ever: the cooperation everywhere is so great that the whole world becomes one. I hope someday we'll be able to go into Russia, China and other currently inaccessible countries and make movies. It could accomplish miracles.

Anthony Quinn
March 16, 1984

★ ★ ★

Home Girl
What was it like growing up in Hollywood? It was home. I was born at Good Samaritan Hospital in Los Angeles, and raised in town, so I have nothing to compare it to. I was strictly a California girl and loved it. My parents were vaudeville headliners who had done pictures, so going into the movies as a child seemed a natural progression for me.

Being at the prestigious MGM during the forties and early fifties was the greatest. It was a marvelous time for the contract player. They groomed us and prepared us for work. It was more glamorous, no question about it. In today's Hollywood there are discos, but there were big, elegant nightclubs then and they were extremely popular with the Hollywood set. (Having married very young, I didn't get around too much myself.) A lot of home entertaining was done, too; this still exists there.

If you were single and going to some special event like a premiere or the Academy Awards, the ever-publicity conscious studio might pair you with another young contract player of the opposite sex whom you didn't even know. The famous Howard Strickling of MGM's publicity department was always dreaming up something for us, so there was much more publicity for you then.

In the 1940s, a Hollywood star never went to a restaurant in jeans. Even if you were only going to the market or a department store, you dressed like the glamorous star the studio was trying to make you. We were kept aloof and isolated from the public. Audiences were supposed to think of us as something special, not just the boy or girl next door.

On the other hand, you didn't have the freedom as a performer that you have now. Our boss, L.B. Mayer, didn't believe in rocking the boat, so if an actor was successful at one kind of role MGM tended to keep him or her in that mold. I was the ingénue who also sang and that was that. When Dore Schary succeeded Mayer as head of production at Metro, we were allowed to break the pattern a bit. But I have no complaints about Mr. Mayer. It was a super time, those last years of Hollywood's heyday, and I feel so fortunate to have been part of it— and still working!

Overall, we had it so much better than show biz kids today, who have to wait on tables and drive cabs to pay for their lessons. At MGM, we had everything right there on the lot for free—drama coaches, dance teachers, school, even dentists. Of course, the money we got wasn't as good as it is today. I think television soap operas are among the great training grounds we have now.

I can't pinpoint the exact year that things began to change in Hollywood, but it probably started with the post–World War II popularity of films from Europe, which were so much more permissive than ours. Then film-making began leaving the studios, with more and more features being made on location. Styles of film changed. Musicals, in which I worked much of the time, went out. For a while it was either a great mass of Westerns or cops-and-robbers movies—when one type of picture was successful, ten more were sure to follow. Now Hollywood is diversifying, at least, and I love many of the films being made there today, from *Body Heat* to *Terms of Endearment*.

My favorite among my own films? I'd have to mention a couple: *Two Girls and a Sailor*, because it was so successful and launched me as a movie name, and *Three Little Words*. I only had a cameo in *Words*, but it was important to me because I played my own mother, Mrs. Carter De Haven. Has anyone else ever done this in pictures? Little girls dress up like their mothers all the time, but getting paid to do it in front of millions of people—only in Hollywood!

Gloria De Haven
March 20, 1984

★ ★ ★

Loyal Subjects
In those days in Hollywood (the 1930s), studio loyalty was a factor of your life. If you were a Warner employee, or a Fox employee, or a Metro employee, that was your home, your country. You voted en bloc for your company's films at the Academy Awards. You played baseball against the other studios. You had T-shirts with your studio's name on them. It was just like being a subject, and a patriotic subject at that. People who lived and worked beyond the studio walls just didn't belong, and you were prepared to fight them off, like the Philistines.

Milton Sperling
Zanuck, 1984

Joan Crawford on the set of *The Gorgeous Hussy* (MGM, 1936) with cinematographer George J. Folsey, who photographed many of the star's 1930s vehicles.

Born to Dance (MGM, 1936) starred Hollywood's premier female tap-dancer, Eleanor Powell, and (not shown) a singing James Stewart.

WORKING

Stage Struck
I don't want to have anything more to do with pictures. The stage is what I want. With luck I can make good on Broadway some day. But why waste my time and MGM's money? I've tried movie work often enough to become convinced I have nothing Hollywood wants.

Clark Gable
1927

★ ★ ★

Ordinary People
Hollywood was a flat, unlovely plain, inhabited by a group of highly ordinary people, all of them quite at sea and usually in a mild state of panic in their chosen work, turning out a product which, except for certain mechanical excellences, was as unimportant and undistinguished as the mass product of any plant grinding out rubber novelties or automobile accessories.

Robert Benchley
1930

★ ★ ★

New Girl in Town
I'm not a little girl from a little town makin' good in a big town. I'm a big girl from a big town makin' good in a little town.

Mae West
1932

★ ★ ★

Minds of Their Own
Hollywood? It doesn't do anything drastic to people. Certainly not to those who have strong personalities and firm minds of their own.

Marlene Dietrich
Modern Screen, the 1930s

★ ★ ★

Cutting Remark
The acting in Hollywood wasn't done in front of the cameras. It was done in the cutting room.

Sidney Howard
1936

No Kicking Allowed

We can't afford to be timid. We can't stand back and be pushed off the rungs of the ladder we have already climbed. Once you let Hollywood push you around, you might as well give up. You are beaten. Your prestige as an artist is gone, your importance and value as a personality somehow damaged. This business is not famous for its second chances. Once you arrive at the top, you've got to fight every moment to stay there. Which is why I never have and never will allow Hollywood to kick me around.

Merle Oberon
Photoplay, the 1930s

Horrible Hullabaloo

I still hate making pictures! And I don't like Hollywood any better. I detest the limelight and love simplicity and in Hollywood the only thing that matters is the hullabaloo of fame. If Hollywood will let me alone to find my way without forcing me and rushing me into things, I probably will change my feeling about it. But at present Hollywood seems utterly horrible and interfering and consuming. Which is why I want to leave it as soon as I am able.

Margaret Sullavan
Photoplay, the 1930s

The Living is Easy

Working in Hollywood may not be an actor's idea of Heaven, but the guy who says he wouldn't rather live here—aside from the work—is plain nuts.

Helen Broderick
Photoplay, May, 1938

Hash-Slinging "King"

Hollywood no longer awes me. If worse came to worse, I could go back to slinging hash!

Clark Gable
Screenland, the 1930s

Push-Button Mentality

It's nice to get away from the impersonal machinery of Hollywood. In the theater if you want to buy a fur coat, you go to your manager (producer). Suppose it's Al Woods. You tell him. And he'll say, "Baby, tell the auditor it's OK for an advance of $500. Pay it back each week. Fix it up with him." Suppose you went to a movie producer, if you could catch him outside of a conference. You say you wanted a coat. He'd say, "So what?" And push all the buttons on his desk.

Glenda Farrell
Silver Screen, November, 1939

Deep Are the Roots
I've never disliked Hollywood. I can't actually say I like it now, because my roots are still pretty deep in New York. But I am becoming accustomed to it and I've found a lot in it to admire. It can do fine and big things in a fine and big way.

John Garfield
Silver Screen, November, 1939

★ ★ ★

Plenty of Character
In Hollywood, they seem to have a hard time deciding what I am. Sometimes they call me a "character juvenile," sometimes it's "character lead." Sometimes it's just "character!"

James Stewart
Silver Screen, November, 1939

★ ★ ★

Pin-Up Girl Down
Hollywood has a way of letting you down that is rather discouraging. I guess the only reason I'm in a Broadway show now (*DuBarry Was a Lady*) is that films didn't want me. It comes something like a shock to you after you've worked in several studios and have been publicized around the country for years, suddenly to realize there are no available roles for you.

Betty Grable
1940

★ ★ ★

Show and Sell
Americans don't seem to realize that Hollywood is America's show window. This country is known the world over for the splendid pictures your movie-makers turn out.

Charles Laughton
Hollywood, January, 1941

★ ★ ★

Mixed Blessing
I laugh every time I think of the first interview I had here in Hollywood. The article about me said I had been a landscape engineer and a specialist with mixed-drinks. That's Hollywood! My landscape engineering amounted to digging ditches for the WPA. My specializing in mixed-drinks amounted to swabbing beer-puddled bars and, later, mixing drinks.

George Montgomery
Motion Picture, October, 1941

Nelson Eddy and Jeanette MacDonald, Hollywood's outstanding operetta stars, appeared together in eight films, reaching their zenith in the sumptuous *Maytime* (MGM, 1937).

Brazil Nott

Een Holleewood where I joos make two peecture dey geev me some songs I should seeng in Eenglish. So I stoddy very hard and seeng in good Eenglish. Den wot? Dey holler at me and tell me to seeng in Souse American like I talk! Dey must be notts!

Carmen Miranda
November, 1941

★ ★ ★

Army Discipline

There is more discipline in Hollywood than people believe. Rigid discipline. This business of the stars shouting for their own sweet way belongs to mythology. The place is run like the Army or like Big Business.

Rosalind Russell
Screenland, November, 1941

★ ★ ★

Late Bloomer

Why can't they start making pictures at noon and work until nine in the evening? That's the only thing I don't like about Hollywood.

Gene Kelly
Motion Picture, January, 1943

★ ★ ★

Kinky Character

At the close of the first day's shooting I was certain I was going to hate the place. They woke me up at 5:30 a.m., which was the earliest I had been up since I had been up that late. On the set, I was taken in tow by two business-like young ladies who put kinks in my hair with curling irons, after which I waited all day before being called to stand in a crowd scene where villagers gathered to watch a boat come in. When the "rushes" of the day's work were run and I could barely recognize the top of my head, I began counting the days until I was shed of Hollywood.

Charles Coburn
Screenland, December, 1943

★ ★ ★

Killing Time

People in Hollywood treat you as if you were a commodity, not a human being. I don't like it. I was being killed in Hollywood. I went to work at 6 a.m., got home at 7 p.m. and never saw my husband or baby. I couldn't bear recording songs and then mouthing them for the camera. That drove me crazy.

Mary Martin
Motion Picture, March, 1944

Colossally Modest

Whenever people laugh at Hollywood for its use of superlatives—such as words as "colossal," "epoch-making," "stupendous" and so on—I am always driven to reflect how modest Hollywood is. For it laughs with the people who laugh at it.

James Hilton
Lion's Roar, 1944

★ ★ ★

What Price Beauty?

Why be beautiful in Hollywood, for the love of Pete? With every car-hop in town a sensational looker, Hollywood is strictly a bull market when it comes to beauty. So if you're asking Walker, she's telling you that she'll struggle along with what she's got for the next fifty years or so. It's done all right for Walker so far.

Nancy Walker
Motion Picture, March, 1944

★ ★ ★

Rude Shocks

There are times when the Hollywood attitude toward the down-on-luck could be improved. A person whose option has been dropped by a major studio, and who has failed to score in Manhattan, is due for some rude shocks. I was astonished to discover how many myopic "friends" I had made; I was further hurt to discover how short were the memories for faces of those "friends." It would seem that I had acquired a quaint ailment distinguished by two symptoms: either I was quite invisible; or, when visible, I was quite unrecognizable.

Carole Landis
Movieland, November, 1944

★ ★ ★

Qualities for Success

I'm convinced the qualities that make people a success in Hollywood and the way they get to the top are exactly the same as they are for any job.

Cornel Wilde
Motion Picture, November, 1944

★ ★ ★

Color Factor

I hate to say it, but color is a factor in every field. A singer will be accepted when an actress is not. Hollywood, however, has been very nice to me and has presented me to the best of its ability.

Lena Horne
Circa 1944

Serious Puzzle
The thing that puzzles me about my career out here is that, though I made my reputation on the Broadway stage playing farce, in Hollywood I am mostly asked to do serious things.

Hume Cronyn
Motion Picture, March, 1945

Just a Business
I still have a high appreciation of my job in pictures. I like to work in them. But now I see it as a business, not a glamorous profession. Hollywood isn't a beautiful, glittering, exciting Christmas tree to me anymore.

John Payne
Motion Picture, March, 1945

Stardom Terrifying
I was appalled to find that when one has come (to Hollywood) from the theater, she is supposed to know all about "acting." In the theater—actually—it is supposed to take you years and years to learn the rudiments. You don't expect, in your most optimistic moments, to be recognized as a "star" until you have served a long, grueling, earnest apprenticeship. Here I found that you were a "star" because someone said you were. It was terrifying.

Dorothy McGuire
Photoplay, June, 1945

No Never-Never Land
I was scared when I came out here, but this is a business, and I intend to know it before I'm finished in Hollywood. That, most of all, is what one has to learn to succeed in Hollywood— that you are in a business, not in some wonderful never-never land of dreams.

Mona Freeman
Motion Picture, October, 1945

Deceitful? Yup
Hollywood personalities are really partly applesauce. We deceive the public, and get paid for it. I get paid pretty well so I deceive the public good.

Gary Cooper
Motion Picture, January, 1946

Work Open Sesame
So many girls think that just being pretty is open sesame in Hollywood. But, believe me, it isn't. It will get you just a little way up the ladder. You have to work. You have to dance until your legs feel like posts and say, "How now, brown cow" over and over and over. Then they

C. Aubrey Smith, David Niven and Ronald Colman were among the players in that most elegant of Graustarkian romances, *The Prisoner of Zenda* (United Artists, 1937).

Deanna Durbin (right), whose youthful musicals saved her failing studio, had one of her biggest successes in *Three Smart Girls* (Universal, 1937), with Binnie Barnes, Barbara Reed, Charles Winninger and Nan Grey.

give you scripts to take home and study. It isn't just glamour and posing before a camera. Of course, you're supposed to have some talent to begin with, but after that it's mostly labor.

Lina Romay
Screenland, January, 1946

★ ★ ★

More Than Meets Eye
You know, I was actually afraid of pictures at first. The camera seemed so emotionless. And I'd heard those rumors about studios being nothing more glamorous than factories of celluloid. Well, that's all hooey. I've discovered there is a lot more than glamour in Hollywood.

Kirk Douglas
Movieland, April, 1946

★ ★ ★

Semi-Screwball
I'm tired of that smart New York set who blast Hollywood calling it an intellectual void. Plenty of silly things are done here, but Hollywood isn't so very screwball. They do fine things in the theatre and splendid things out here, too. Baddies crop up on both coasts. I dislike it when critics sell Hollywood short.

Lizabeth Scott
1946

★ ★ ★

Some Other Racket
I'll give Hollywood thirty-five years and not a year more. If nothing happens, I'll try some other racket.

Marshall Thompson
Screen Stars, February, 1947

★ ★ ★

I Know the Face
If you and your husband both work (in Hollywood) you hardly have time to say hello. You just wave in passing. Actually, I have driven home after working all night to see Desi (Arnaz) passing in a car going to work. "That face is familiar," I say. "Oh, yes, my husband I haven't seen for days" and I wave. In Hollywood too-young people see too much, do too much, go too much. They see others getting divorces and they think nothing of trying it. In a small town they are restrained by example and opinion.

Lucille Ball
Photoplay, March, 1947

Heroes Short-Lived

Of course, everything about *The Killers* was important to me. It was to be my first independent production. If it turned out a hit, I would probably be a hero for a couple of months, which is about as long as any hero lasts in Hollywood.

Mark Hellinger
Photoplay, March, 1947

Fancy Footwork

Many's the time I looked at those other hand and foot prints (in the forecourt of Grauman's Chinese Theater) and wondered if mine would ever be there, too. I guess every newcomer to Hollywood has this thought when he first arrives here. The actuality seemed remote at the time—but I never lost hope.

Ray Milland
Screen Stars, March, 1947

Sing Out, Sweet Land!

I have thought, since my tours, that we in Hollywood run a great danger of becoming too insular. I know I was near it when I left. Hollywood is such a tight unit in the American scene that a Hollywoodite's map of the world is apt to show one large eastern seaboard area labeled "New York," and one west coast section labeled "Hollywood." There are a few pin dots scattered over the map reading, "Sun Valley," "Palm Springs," "Miami Beach," "Bermuda." The space between is arid waste. There are no dots reading "Cincinnati," "Sioux City," "Augusta," "Spokane."

Jeanette MacDonald
The Hollywood Reporter, September, 1947

Two Ways

There are only two ways to get ahead in Hollywood. You either have to get one great picture a year—these propel you forward—or your impact has to be made with a lot of pictures.

Rosalind Russell
The 1940s

Hard Ball

Hollywood has taught me that Cinderella's toughest job wasn't in the kitchen. It was at the ball!

Helen Walker
Motion Picture, March, 1947

Yardstick is Talent

There's a side of Hollywood I love. Here, it doesn't matter whether you come from a fine old socially prominent family or are discovered in a drive-in. If you have any talent, you can succeed. Talent bestows itself on anyone. It doesn't matter whether your ancestors came over on the Mayflower. It's what *you* are that counts.

Esther Williams
Movieland, May, 1947

★ ★ ★

Kowtowing Character

When you're an actor in Hollywood and under contract to a studio, it's supposed to be good form to stick around. Even if you're not working in a picture, if you're a *real* Hollywood character you drop in on the studio every day and visit with the right people. "Oh, Mr. Blotz," you say, sticking your head into some brass-hat's office. "I just happened to be in the studio, so I stopped by to say hello."

Robert Mitchum
Motion Picture, June, 1947

★ ★ ★

Imported Lady

I brought Ruth Warrick out to play Mrs. (Citizen) Kane because the part calls for a lady. I have not been able to find a lady in Hollywood.

Orson Welles
Motion Picture, June, 1947

★ ★ ★

Perfectly Profane

All the stars I've worked with have certainly conducted themselves perfectly. Oh, there were a couple examples of stars who used profanity, but they were the exception in Hollywood—exceptions you'd find in any town. When I was a little girl, there was an actor who swore a lot, so I asked my mother what the words meant. She simply said he was a sick man and it didn't matter what he said. I then felt sorry for him. Another time a director used profanity in front of me. He actually blushed and made himself stand in a corner for ten minutes.

Shirley Temple
Screenland, August, 1947

★ ★ ★

Smoking Sawdust

If Hollywood can package cigarettes and fill them with sawdust, it isn't going to fill them with tobacco.

Robert Mitchum
Screenland, September, 1947

The inimitable Marx Brothers (Groucho, Chico and Harpo) clown it up for romantic leads Maureen O'Sullivan and Allan Jones in *A Day at the Races* (MGM, 1937).

The Good Earth (MGM, 1937), Pearl S. Buck's story of poor Chinese farmers, was one of the last productions of legendary producer Irving G. Thalberg and co-starred Paul Muni and Luise Rainer, who won an Oscar.

Winning Bet
I'll bet I'm the only woman in Hollywood who will concede she is underworked, overpaid and likes her agent!

Florence Bates
Motion Picture, October, 1947

Confined to Cafés
I'm "in" Hollywood, but not "of" Hollywood because I'm Negro. I'd like to do a good serious role in a mixed-cast movie instead of being confined to café singer parts.

Lena Horne
Circa 1948

No Cheesecake
Hollywood has a queer way of taking an individual and fitting her into the American mold. I have worked hard to develop my style and I don't want anything to do with bathing suits and plucked eyebrows.

Ingrid Bergman
Silver Screen, February, 1948

Room for Improvement
You know how it is out here in Hollywood. When I told them my name was Flanagan, they turned it over in their minds for a bit and finally guessed they'd change it to Dennis O'Keefe. Why? Flanagan, they said, was too Irish!

Dennis O'Keefe
Motion Picture, March, 1948

Shopworn Superlatives
These Hollywood people are fantastic. Their conversation is a mess of shopworn superlatives interrupted by four telephone calls to the sentence.

Raymond Chandler
The 1940s

Early Bird
The thing that kills me about Hollywood is getting up so early. You have to go to bed by midnight because you get up at dawn. If you stay up any later, when you go to the studio they scream because your eyes are falling down to your chin.

Frank Sinatra
Silver Screen, March, 1948

Old-Fashioned Types

Hollywood is not an easy place for two people to work. When you leave your house, you're both sleepy, since it's the crack of dawn. When you come home, you're exhausted. All you want is an Old-Fashioned and some peace and quiet. The two of you, as a result, are so full of your own problems that you can't help each other at the time when you most should.

Cornel Wilde
The 1940s

★ ★ ★

The Green Promise

Money must be, I guess, what took me to Hollywood. When I first went out I certainly had NO ambition to make pictures.

Henry Fonda
Silver Screen, September, 1948

★ ★ ★

Chairman of the Bored

Pictures stink. Most of the people in them do, too. I don't want any more movie acting. Hollywood won't believe I'm through but they'll find out I mean it.

Frank Sinatra
1949

★ ★ ★

Seven-Year Wonder

Because a lot of people still think I am an overnight wonder, it might be noted that in seven years after coming to Hollywood I played in more than 30 pictures. And if anyone wonders why I got a little impatient, why I'm a bit finicky about my roles—well, in some of those 30 pictures there were animals with whom I would gladly have exchanged parts. Their roles were better and longer!

Larry Parks
Modern Screen, January, 1949

★ ★ ★

Work Gets Breaks

I put very little stock in the one thing people say a girl needs most of to get ahead in Hollywood, and I'm talking about luck. Anyone who amounts to anything naturally figures he has a lot of it, but it is something you simply can't count on. I have always figured that luck never comes by itself. It usually is accompanied by work, which creates the break in a right direction.

June Haver
Screenland, May, 1949

Accent Grave

It's not that I'm bitter about Hollywood, but I have had four years of loneliness in the tinsel city. I soon discovered that the struggle for a career isn't worth it. It was during the war, and they told me that I couldn't get any parts because of my accent. Now isn't that ridiculous? Why, many of Hollywood's greatest actresses are foreign-born.

Linda Christian
Screen Guide, June, 1949

All the Difference

I tell you something which very few people like to hearing (sic). Everything we do has been done before, even though we present it in a different way.

Michael Curtiz
Hollywood without Makeup, 1949

Battle Against Baloney

People outside of Hollywood don't understand how it is here. It's a battle to maintain a basic integrity; a scrap against bull and baloney. You've got to fight all the time.

Burt Lancaster
Hollywood without Makeup, 1949

Pressure Cooker

There's more pressure on you in Hollywood than in New York. On Broadway you do your performance every night and that's it. Here you have to get up at five in the morning—which is tough on me—in order to get ready in time at the studio. Then you have to rehearse, do your scenes, and you get home late where you have a relaxing dinner and start studying until bedtime. There's no let-up. There's also so much fussing about costumes and makeup and hair all day on the set. That's plausible, I guess, since the camera is on *you*—if you're lucky enough to get a close-up. On the stage your audience is at least twenty-five feet away.

Vera-Ellen
Screenland, September, 1949

Robert Knows Best

It's amazing to me that so many stars in Hollywood keep their heads as well as they do! There are pitfalls scattered all over the place. Bad ones that are constantly waiting to gobble you up. Probably the most difficult one to avoid is the sudden way fame hits you. One day you're walking up and down in front of a studio hoping for any kind of a job, just an ordinary Joe, and then Fate steps in and you're a star overnight. That's a pretty overwhelming situation and can easily send a guy topsy-turvy. Maybe I escaped the pitfalls because I was never an overnight sensation or a big star. I've kept my head in Hollywood because it never occurred to me to act any differently from the way I always did. Fame is a fickle lady anyway. Honest

Perhaps the screen's greatest swashbuckling romance, *The Adventures of Robin Hood* (Warner Brothers, 1938) found Olivia de Havilland and Errol Flynn at the peak of their youthful beauty and verve.

In 1939, Paramount Pictures designated its young contract players "The Golden Circle." They were, top row (from left): Louise Campbell, Betty Field, Joseph Allen, Ellen Drew and Judith Barrett. Middle row: Robert Preston, Patricia Morison, Susan Hayward and William Henry. Bottom row: Joyce Mathews, Janice Logan, William Holden and Evelyn Keyes.

happiness and right living are your steady companions. That's my motto for life in Hollywood.

Robert Young
Screenland, September, 1949

★ ★ ★

Nothing Smaller
There's a caste system in Hollywood, you know, and it just isn't good to take a smaller part than one you've done before.

Boris Karloff
The New York Times, October 30, 1949

★ ★ ★

Slap-Happy Mam'selle
In Hollywood, they call you always "darling" and "honey" and they do not mean anything by this but I do not know this. I think those who are calling me "darling" and "honey" are the wolves and I am slapping my head off! No man likes to be slapped, especially when for no reason. But I have no English to explain why I am slapping, to right and left, and no way to understand that because I am slapping, I am not getting a very good reputation, with no one liking me and no one giving me a picture to make.

Corinne Calvet
Silver Screen, December, 1949

★ ★ ★

Primal Scream
In Hollywood you've got to scream or they'll shove you around.

Betty Hutton
Look, January 3, 1950

★ ★ ★

Career Goes Swimmingly
It was funny: I didn't seek a career in pictures in the beginning. I was rather afraid of Hollywood and what the industry would do to me. But then, when Mr. (Louis B.) Mayer let me play my career as I wanted to play it, when he let me take it easy and learn what I was about gradually, I began to like the idea of making movies. And, as time went on, I liked it more and more.

Esther Williams
Silver Screen, February, 1950

Swept Off Feet

That first year (in Hollywood) was terribly exciting to me. Naturally, I knew nothing about the making of motion pictures or the technique involved, but I was so anxious to learn that the janitors practically had to sweep me off the sets at closing time.

June Allyson
Screenland, March, 1950

Starving Talent

Hollywood is one of the few places on earth where a person with absolutely NO talent can make a million dollars, and where a guy who is loaded with talent can starve to death.

Dan Dailey
Movieland, April, 1950

Know-All Mecca

It has been said that Hollywood is the Mecca of know-it-alls. I've found (such people) filling jobs in Hollywood in which they were actually supposed to be know-it-alls—and weren't. They *all* gave me advice which would have led to exactly where I *didn't* want to go, back home a failure perhaps—or at best somewhere in the outer fringes of the show world I wanted to enter.

Ruth Roman
Modern Screen, November, 1950

Clash of Commodities

In Hollywood, the girls have false hair, teeth and calves on their legs. The men have shoulders built up and wear toupees. So when two stars make love on the screen, it's a lot of commodities getting together.

Fred Allen
No People Like Show People, 1951

Chip on Shoulder

I did have a chip on my shoulder when I came out. I was used to New York's particular speed and system. I never guessed a huge business could be built almost wholly on the personalities of the people involved, so I was intolerant for my first year here, I'm afraid. I didn't see the cause for Hollywood customs. You have to be in a business to comprehend it. For instance, interviews appalled me. I'll never forget the shock I felt at my first one here. I was confronted with so many personal questions I was horrified. "Was I a great lover, actually?" Now what could you reply to that?

Richard Widmark
Silver Screen, March, 1951

Youth Must Be Served

Young love deserves a better break on the screen. The over-age stars get all the clinches, while the young actors in Hollywood today—if they're lucky—get the meaningless kiss or two.

John Derek
Motion Picture, June, 1951

Wife Liberation

We actresses are so conscious of the way Hollywood likes to present wives, that when we are offered the role of one we immediately shy away from it. No matter how long the part, or how good it may sound on paper, we know that in the picture itself we will get the raw end of the romantic and dramatic deal. We will not be allowed to look glamorous or wear fashionable clothes. And we take it for granted that the "other woman" will steal our husband. If we get him back at the finish, it's only because some catastrophe has befallen the charmer.

Anne Baxter
Movies, August, 1951

No Grooming

When I first went to Hollywood I just naturally assumed I would be given the grooming which, I'd always heard, was part of the star system. I didn't get it. For me there was no dramatic training, voice training, dance instruction, diction lessons or anything of the sort and I was not in a financial position, at that time, to afford these advantages myself. The result was that I went from one picture to another picture without learning anything.

Vivian Blaine
Screenland, April, 1952

Goes with Territory

Monumental success in Hollywood is sometimes accompanied by monumental loss of memory.

Loretta Young
Screenland, April, 1952

Tallulah Not Timid

In Hollywood you do nothing for yourself. You don't even apply your own make-up. You are awakened, taken to the studio, made up. You play your roles in snips and driblets, harassed by delays, interruptions and stupidities. Over the proceedings hangs the pall of indecision, the fear of the studio swami that the work may in some fashion upset a coal miner in West Virginina, a lama in Tibet. Timidity was the screen's curse. It still is.

Tallulah Bankhead
Tallulah, 1952

Butterfly McQueen tells Vivien Leigh she doesn't "know nuthin' 'bout birthin' babies" in *Gone with the Wind* (MGM, 1939), which earned Leigh the best actress Oscar and many other honors for the film, including best picture.

They Shoot Horses

You know about horses, don't you? When they get sick, they shoot 'em. When Hollywood's sick and tired of me—they'll have to shoot me!

Barbara Stanwyck
Movie Stars Parade, March, 1953

Dottyville

So you're coming out to Dottyville-on-the-Pacific, are you, boys? Poor lads, poor lads! Well, let me give you a word of advice. Don't try to escape. They'll chase you across the ice with bloodhounds. And even if the bloodhounds miss you, the pitiless California climate drives you back. The only thing to do is to stick it out. But you'll suffer, my unhappy young tenderfeet, you'll suffer.

W.C. Fields
Bring on the Girls!, 1953

Seclusion Sought

Seclusion is helpful to most players in the midst of a difficult picture, but it is one of the hardest things to find in busy Hollywood.

Judy Garland
Cue, March 6, 1954

Home to Rest

Yes, I am glad to be back (in Sweden), but not, as you might think, because I hate Hollywood. People talk a lot of nonsense about Hollywood. Let me tell you there are just as many temptations in Gothenberg or Stockholm as there are over there. In Hollywood you think mostly about working. I have had to work harder than most, and I am very tired now. I have come home to rest.

Greta Garbo
Garbo, 1955

Not Worth Two Cents

I wouldn't give you two cents for most of the actresses in Hollywood. Someone like Deborah Kerr, yes. She's really great. But most of them take two hours to make up and then they can't act worth a damn.

Dewey Martin
1955

Backward Business

This is the way we do things in Hollywood. I've done this death scene (for *Miracle in the Rain*) umpteen times now and it's finally been okayed. In a little while I have to go outside and stroll around in the rain for more re-takes of the sequence *leading up* to my demise. Everything's backward in this business.

Jane Wyman
Newark Sunday News, July 3, 1955

★ ★ ★

Ho-Hum Hugs

There are no more great love scenes in movies. Actors have that let's-kiss-and-get-it-over-with attitude and audiences sense this. Maybe it's because Hollywood has become too close-knit as a society. Most leading men know most leading women. They see each other often and it's as if they've all done too many pictures together.

Anne Baxter
The Milwaukee Journal, January 8, 1956

★ ★ ★

Exit Crying

I left Hollywood six years ago in tears. I was given a runaround (by Howard Hughes) and never appeared in front of a camera. Now I'm grateful Hollywood didn't want me. I became a star *despite* Hollywood. Perhaps producers there would have tried to change me . . . to make me look like *any* Hollywood actress.

Gina Lollobrigida
Picturegoer, April 21, 1956

★ ★ ★

Funny Thought

It seemed funny to think of going to Hollywood and acting in movies when I'd only seen a couple of them in my whole life.

Audie Murphy
Hollywood Life Stories, 1956

★ ★ ★

Only Marilyn?

We've been soft-pedaling on sex here in Hollywood, and now who've we got besides Marilyn Monroe who as a single feminine star-attraction can pack the house? This Hollywood habit of frowning on out-and-out sex appeal in an actress is costing the industry some much-needed star power for its pictures. In former times in developing and exploiting our actresses, we placed the accent on sex, and it paid off in dividends at the box-offices. In recent years we have gone almost puritanical, and now, outside Miss Monroe, we haven't a single new actress who on sheer strength of feminine appeal can attract, unfailingly, huge throngs at the theaters.

Charles Schnee
1956

The Late Good Sport
Everything happened so fast. I was in high school and the next thing I knew I was being groomed by Hollywood. There was this terrific mountain of work and no time to catch up with myself. It was that way for ten years, always a sense of pressure and no time to think, to relax, to take stock. I didn't know how to be temperate. I was afraid the executives would think I was a bad sport.

Gail Russell
The 1950s

Studio Property
Being a property in Hollywood means that when a person has signed a contract with a major studio, he (in this case she) ceases to be an individual and becomes instead a possession of the studio. With millions of dollars invested in me, it was to the studio's financial advantage to keep me neat and clean and photogenic—and to some extent, they hoped, happy. But my primary function was to work.

Judy Garland
McCall's, April, 1957

Who Was That Lady?
In my last film I played a nymphomaniac, a dipsomaniac and a kleptomaniac—which is not terribly lady-like even by Hollywood standards.

Arlene Dahl
The Seven Deadly Sins of Hollywood, 1957

Go Bag a Tiger
To bring a sense of perfection to Hollywood is to go bagging tigers with a fly swatter.

Ben Hecht
Charlie, 1957

She's Still There
I knew I was not good enough for Hollywood. I couldn't last there. I'd be back on Broadway as soon as film producers discovered that I had absolutely no talent.

June Allyson
The Saturday Evening Post, December 21, 1957

Preoccupied
The people I have met in Hollywood are completely sincere in their interest in their work, intense in their desire to improve. It isn't all tinsel and glamour here, believe me. The very young actors, especially, are almost suffocatingly intense about their work. I will admit,

At the Hollywood premiere of *Wuthering Heights* in 1939: producer Samuel Goldwyn, First Lady Eleanor Roosevelt, star Merle Oberon and Mrs. Roosevelt's son James.

Producer Mervyn LeRoy and director Victor Fleming flank Judy Garland on a Munchkin-overrun set for *The Wizard of Oz* (MGM, 1939), for which Judy won a special juvenile Oscar.

however, that I think a lot of Hollywood people overdo this preoccupation with acting or whatever they are doing in pictures. When they get together, they can't talk about anything but shop and, frankly, that gets a bit boring.

Claire Bloom
Silver Screen, the 1950s

★ ★ ★

Deanna Meant It
Press people must be sick and tired of quoting former Hollywood personalities as saying such things as "I don't plan a comeback . . . I'm not bitter with Hollywood, but I was never happy making pictures," and so on. But I mean it.

Deanna Durbin
1958

★ ★ ★

Hot and Bothered
I never saw the scripts of my first two movies in Hollywood. They would say, "Don't bother with that, just go out there and do as you're told."

Kim Novak
The New York Times, the 1950s

★ ★ ★

Starving at the Banquet
Being a failure in Hollywood is like starving to death outside a banquet hall with the smells of *filet mignon* driving you crazy.

Marilyn Monroe
The 1950s

★ ★ ★

Raised Ruckus
To be an ingénue in Hollywood is to be a nothing. And that's what they wanted me to be. Then one day they handed me a new script. I read it and threw it into the fireplace. I wasn't going to do it. *Period*. I kicked up so much fuss the studio (Universal) let me out of my contract.

Piper Laurie
TV Guide, June 27, 1959

★ ★ ★

Unhappy Endings
The worst effect of the legend of stardom overnight has been in the lives of uncounted numbers of young girls who have come to Hollywood hoping to be "discovered." Few have any experience in acting. Many are quite pretty, but they are coming to a place where there is a surfeit of prettiness. They stand little or no chance of getting inside the gate of a studio, and

less of being seen there or anywhere by a producer. They are fortunate if their fate in Hollywood is no worse than bitter disappointment; many of their pathetic stories have had more tragic endings.

Cecil B. DeMille
Autobiography, 1959

★ ★ ★

Magnificent Obsessions
Hollywood is obsessed with sex and sin. They don't stop talking about it or thinking about it or making movies about it.

Olivia de Havilland
National Enquirer, 1960

★ ★ ★

Wicked Bitchcraft
I'm fortunate. I've seen very little temperament—even of the Hollywood type of skulduggery and bitchcraft.

Celeste Holm
Theatre, December, 1960

★ ★ ★

Perfect Void
How many young actors would give their teeth to work in Hollywood today, and live here. Me, I like to work here. But living here—no. Maybe it's because there's nothing to search for. It's pretty, Hollywood; it's all manicured and lovely. It's perfect, easy on the eyes—and there's nothing to find.

George Peppard
Modern Screen, February, 1961

★ ★ ★

Dumb Like Hound Dog
I'm not a dumb animal and people think I am. I'm treated like a performing seal without the slightest sensitivity (in Hollywood). A seal gets a fish when he does a good job. I get a pat on the shoulder and a stab in my back. It gets discouraging after a while.

Elvis Presley
Modern Screen, April, 1961

★ ★ ★

Not Wanted
For years, I couldn't get myself arrested in Hollywood.

Clark Gable
The King, 1961

Last Picture Counts
In Hollywood, you're only as good as your last picture. If you haven't got a last picture, you're no good.

Erich von Stroheim
The Fifty-Year Decline and Fall of Hollywood, 1961

★ ★ ★

Now You See Them
Hollywood was a terribly lonely place for me. I had wonderful associations with Humphrey Bogart, Gregory Peck and all the others while I worked with them, but after they left the studios at night, they retired to their own circle of friends.

Ingrid Bergman
The Real and the Unreal, 1961

★ ★ ★

Decisions, Decisions
When I first went to Hollywod, naturally I wanted to get ahead. But I never realized all the involvements and details that being a star entails. Decisions, decisions and decisions. I became so immersed in thinking about my career that I miss things that are going on in life. If I could live and breathe a little more lightly at times rather than be dragged down about my work, I think I'd be a better wife to someone.

Kim Novak
Modern Screen, November, 1961

★ ★ ★

Fought Type-Casting
I had to fight type-casting in Hollywood. I remember after *Magnificent Ambersons* I was up for another picture but the producer said, "I'm afraid there are no hysterical parts in this film, Miss Moorehead!" Luckily, nowadays different producers seem to type-cast me in their heads in different ways: one sees me as eternally sitting on a front porch in a man's hat and shirt with a gun on my knees; another thinks I make a very good Chinese; while yet another said, "Oh, she's so regal she can only play queens."

Agnes Moorehead
The Christian Science Monitor
November 14, 1961

★ ★ ★

Myopic View
Hollywood has artistic myopia. If they see you acting they think of you as an actor. If you direct, you're thought of as a director. And if you're an actor *and* you direct something, they say "I saw Joe Blow, the actor, directing. Guess he's not working much as an actor." They fail to remember that some of the best directors at one time were darn good actors.

Cliff Robertson
December 31, 1961

The gag (?) feud between radio comedians Fred Allen and Jack Benny continued on screen in *Love Thy Neighbor* (Paramount, 1940), Mary Martin refereeing.

Mae West and W.C. Fields were paired for the only time in *My Little Chickadee* (Universal, 1940), also written by the terrific twosome.

Too Much

Isn't this pretty good for somebody Hollywood thought was too old, too fat and too undependable to offer a job? For an "undependable," I certainly made a lot of pictures. The only time I was undependable was when I was ill and couldn't work. Everybody is undependable when they're ill.

Judy Garland
Look, April 10, 1962

Modest Producer

I single-handedly brought Hollywood back to itself.

Ross Hunter
The Dreams and the Dreamers, 1962

Means to an End

Hollywood is a place to be used, as a means to an end, no more.

Sterling Hayden
Wanderer, 1963

Reason for Broadway

Basically I love Hollywood. The only reason anyone goes to Broadway is because they can't get work in movies.

Bette Davis
The 1960s

Legal Ladd

The things you settle with a handshake in Hollywood are things you have to take legal action to achieve overseas.

Alan Ladd
The 1960s

Dinner at Six

If you say, "Why do you like working in Hollywood?", I would say, because I can get home at six o'clock for dinner.

Alfred Hitchcock
The Cinema of Alfred Hitchcock, 1963

Growing Scars

Hollywood is a jungle and you hear a lot of atrocity stories from ex-child stars, but I don't go along with that. Nobody made them become stars. I have scar tissue still from public exposure, but I think growing up anywhere leaves scars.

Darryl Hickman
Daily News, March 8, 1964

★　★　★

Rich Rewards

Hollywood to me is like a marvelous dessert every day. It has given me a life I'd never have had otherwise. I've worked with talented people, met kings and queens, famous writers, Nobel Prize winners and scientists and distinguished political personalities. Rewards are rich in Hollywood. But there is hard work behind those rewards.

Debbie Reynolds
July 19, 1964

★　★　★

Helping Hands

Hollywood is full of these watching, waiting helpers, who look for pretty girls in distress. Mostly what they want is to help take your clothes off in their apartments. Many of them do have valuable connections, and will use them—but the asking price is rather high.

Mamie Van Doren
My Naughty, Naughty Life!, 1964

★　★　★

Exhilarating

I've always enjoyed working in Hollywood. They are so efficient. And it's so exhilarating.

Vivien Leigh
1964

★　★　★

Only Virgin in Town

They chose me to play the Virgin Mary in *The Song of Bernadette* because I was the only real virgin in Hollywood at the time.

Linda Darnell
1964

★　★　★

Who Needs It?

Hollywood just loves people who don't need Hollywood.

Ronald Reagan
Where's the Rest of Me?, 1965

TV Downfall
You don't go on television and compete with yourself, just to pick up a little pocket change. It's ridiculous. All the Hollywood stars going into television have contributed enormously to Hollywood's downfall.

Olivia de Havilland
Louisville Courier-Journal, April 11, 1965

★ ★ ★

All Together—Slam!
One bad film in Hollywood and, as if there were a giant conspiracy, the doors are slammed shut.

Josef von Sternberg
Fun in a Chinese Laundry, 1965

★ ★ ★

What's in a Name?
I went by my complete name (Rodney Taylor) when I first arrived in Hollywood, but shortened it after a couple of years. Now it annoys me a little when people ask me what my *real* name is. I guess "Rod" sounds like something I picked out of The Guaranteed Guidebook of Names That Lead to Hollywood Success.

Rod Taylor
1966

★ ★ ★

Gilded and Gelded
I was never able to cultivate a fondness for (L.B.) Mayer, sneaking or otherwise. To me, he contained in his small person with his marble eyes and rigid lips, the large faults of Hollywood —the power drive, the reactionary views, the false tears and values, the gilded and gelded hangers-on. Give him his due: he knew glamour, how to exploit it and how to create stars and impose their images on a pliant nation.

George Oppenheimer
The View from the Sixties, 1966

★ ★ ★

S.S. Mickey Rooney
There are at least a dozen agents around Hollywood who should have their yachts named after me.

Mickey Rooney
The 1960s

★ ★ ★

No Problem
I think our experience in Hollywood at that time (the 1940s–1950s) remains almost unique. It happened almost as in the theater. We could give our opinion about everything and to everyone. Everybody knows that screenwriters are generally mistreated in Hollywood. Scripts

Musical queens Alice Faye and Betty Grable became a sister act for *Tin Pan Alley* (20th Century-Fox, 1940), concerning the growth of America's popular song business.

pass from hand to hand and in the end forty authors have worked on the same story. For our part, we never knew these problems.

Betty Comden (interviewed with partner Adolph Green)
Cahiers du Cinéma, 1966

★ ★ ★

Nowhere Town
I just packed my bags one day and left (Hollywood). I couldn't stand mouthing those inane words in that nowhere town.

Merv Griffin
TV Guide, November 19, 1966

★ ★ ★

Out of Touch
I do not think that an art can be organized like a commercial enterprise. In Hollywood, the entire organization aims at manufacturing amusement. Without any doubt there are people of fine quality who work there, often conscientiously, and sometimes with talent. In New York, life is there all around, you are inside it. In California, you are in a protected atmosphere, and at the end of a year, or two or three, you have lost contact with America, and even with everything that happens.

Elia Kazan
Cahiers du Cinéma, March, 1967

★ ★ ★

Elusive Legend
When I first came to Hollywood, I thought the press was asinine. The studios wanted me to give a lot of interviews, but the press didn't know where the hell I was, thank God, so they couldn't track me down, and I didn't see anybody. Actually, I wanted to see whether I was going to be successful or not before I gave a lot of interviews.

Katharine Hepburn
A Special Kind of Magic, 1967

★ ★ ★

Incredible Shrinking Rooms
There was a great caste system. You were put in your proper cubbyhole, as to whether you were making $100,000 or twenty-five. Although they still do it out there; Hollywood can't get over it. You see it even in dressing rooms; the dressing rooms get smaller and smaller, with a big one for the star. I was kind of a maverick; they knew that I didn't like Hollywood, and it wasn't as popular not to like Hollywood then as it is now.

Burgess Meredith
Film Fan Monthly, February, 1968

Plain Not Fancy
Hollywood always wanted me to be pretty, but I fought for realism.

Bette Davis
The New York Times, March 10, 1968

Quit in Time
I had toe-shoes on from 8:30 in the morning until six every night. I was constantly in agony. Ankles big as an elephant's. I was in very bad health, worked under impossibly bad conditions, had to dance on concrete floors and windy sound stages. I had bruises and sprains that couldn't heal. When I walked out of Hollywood, after years of unhappiness, Fred Astaire and Gene Kelley both told me, "Leslie, you're so smart to quit while you can still walk."

Leslie Caron
This Week, 1968

Clichés True
All the clichés about Hollywood are true. It's silly to knock it, because it is so obviously stupid. The movie business is run by blockheads who sit around long tables and pay out all the money to *people*, instead of putting it into their product.

Shirley Knight
Do You Sleep in the Nude?, 1968

Crazy Game
It's a game out there in Hollywood. The people who make the crazy demands and do the bizarre things are the ones who don't get kicked around.

Estelle Parsons
1968

More! More!
I been tellin' 'em in Hollywood for years there's more of us than Sidney Poitier.

Harry Belafonte
Women's Wear Daily, July 26, 1968

Bending Backwards
In Hollywood, they used to be able to take you and make you into their creation. They could bend you and make you into whoever they thought you should be. It's really frightening to think that they could do that.

Faye Dunaway
Modern Screen, August, 1968

All the Little People
When you start out in Hollywood, the important things are the money and the billing. After 10 years, you ask, "Who's the director?", "Where am I going to live?", "Where are they going to make the film?" Then the atmosphere for work becomes important. When you start out, who cares who's playing the little parts or who the cameraman is? But the longer you're in this business, the more you realize how important the supposedly "unimportant" people really are.

Glenn Ford
December 9, 1968

★ ★ ★

Offer She Couldn't Refuse
I thought of Hollywood as Babylon-on-the-Pacific, but I couldn't refuse L.B. Mayer's offer to come there and work.

Greer Garson
January 7, 1969

★ ★ ★

Couldn't Care Less
Hollywood doesn't really take care of you. Oh, I was a dumb girl in those days—only interested in myself, in a career. At first Hollywood was very exciting, I really loved my work. Not even two years after I started everything started breaking up, and everyone was leaving—people like John Huston. When I came to New York, I decided not to go back. You know, it was so hard to talk to anyone out there. After a while I wondered what I was becoming. Workshops and Off Broadway give you a chance to learn. Hollywood neither hinders nor helps you—it just doesn't care.

Viveca Lindfors
After Dark, March, 1969

★ ★ ★

Calls for Cunning
To get your way in Hollywood you have to be cunning. When I was offered a script (to direct) which I thought had a basically good idea, however mis-handled, I would say: "Yes, fine." Then I'd sit back while the preparations went ahead. About a week before shooting was to begin I'd go to the producer and say: "Look, this is a wonderful script, but there's one little point"—and suggest a small but vital alteration. Then, of course, other things would have to be altered to fit in with the change, and gradually the old script would start coming apart at the seams. By the time we started shooting everything would be so confused I would be starting with no definite script at all, and could do as I liked.

Robert Siodmak
Films in Review, April, 1969

★ ★ ★

Wrong Atmosphere
I have no criticisms of Hollywood as a place, but only as a place to work in. The atmosphere is

Una Merkel accompanied Dorothy Lamour, Bing Crosby and Bob Hope on the *Road to Zanzibar* (Paramount, 1941)—there were seven entries in the "Road" series with Crosby, Hope and Lamour.

Ziegfeld Girl (MGM, 1941) was a stunning dose of Metro-Goldwyn-Mayer glamour with Judy Garland, Hedy Lamarr and Lana Turner, who gave one of her finest performances as a dissolute show girl.

wrong for me. At the same time, anyone is at liberty to say that I am wrong for the atmosphere, and no doubt will.

Peter Sellers
The Bright Side of Billy Wilder, Primarily, 1969

Celluloid Detroit
It's a celluloid Detroit, a factory town for mass production out of which something good comes now and then.

Billy Wilder
The Bright Side of Billy Wilder, Primarily, 1969

Hail to the King
To Hollywood actors, the director is king. Not even a great director can make a bad film good, but a great director can make a good film better. And a bad director can annihilate the best story in the world and the best acting.

William Gargan
Why Me?, 1969

Craftsmen from Everywhere
There was a time when Hollywood had a monopoly. Pictures were made all over the world and some of them were good enough to attract world attention . . . but Hollywood didn't particularly like the idea and didn't give the European pictures very good bookings. But in recent years they've developed their own stars and they're now making very fine pictures and it's rather a good idea because I think pictures are a universal medium and belong to the world. As a matter of fact, when we made a picture here in Hollywood it was made up of craftsmen and artists from all over the world. I think competition is very good.

Edward G. Robinson
Conversations, 1969

Indian Getter
The facilities are so good in Hollywood. For instance, you have that Indian scene. We can get our Indians right from the reservoir.

Samuel Goldwyn
The Moguls, 1969

It Must Be Tuesday
Usually the Hollywood slogan is "I don't want it good, I want it Tuesday."

Ruth Gordon
Conversations in the Raw, 1969

Fiddle-Dee-Dee!
I loathe Hollywood, and for no other part (Scarlett O'Hara) would I have dreamed of signing a contract. All their standards are financial ones. The more I see of Hollywood, the less possible it becomes.

Vivien Leigh
Vivien Leigh: A Bouquet, 1969

Well Kept
I was like a kept woman during my twenty-one years at MGM. Hollywood was like an expensive, beautifully run club. You didn't need to carry money. Your face was your credit card—all over the world.

Walter Pidgeon
Confessions of a Hollywood Columnist, 1969

Prussian Perfectionism
I was something that is always hated in Hollywood—a perfectionist. Nobody likes a perfectionist, you know: "He is so difficult to work with"—because he knows exactly what he wants! "Who cares for the audience? The audience are idiots!" Which, by the way, I think they are not. But most motion picture producers think the audience are idiots.

Fritz Lang
Fritz Lang in America, 1969

Tall, Dark and Gruesome
"You will have the tallest, darkest leading man in Hollywood." Those were the first words I heard about *King Kong*.

Fay Wray
The New York Times, September 21, 1969

Cop-Outs
I think actresses who go around saying that they hate Hollywood are cop-outs. They're like the Broadway actors who hate Hollywood until they make it there.

Sandra Dee
Modern Screen, December, 1969

Caged Victim
I'm still a victim of my name. I'm still caged by the fact that I was a Hollywood product.

Tab Hunter
After Dark, March, 1970

Sexy Fake

I never felt like a blonde bombshell. I have a kind of earthy sexuality, but I'm no great beauty. All the time I was in Hollywood I felt like a fake. That's why the temperament I was known for. Temperament is just another word for terror, and I was terrifed at the time because I was being made into something I'm not.

Shelley Winters
Films in Review, March, 1970

★ ★ ★

Doesn't Compute

I hear it's madness in Hollywood now. Everyone's taking deferments just to keep working. I saw (director) Fritz Lang the other day and he told me they now have computers to tell them if the story and star are right. Now how can computers possibly know *that*?

Joan Bennett
June 21, 1970

★ ★ ★

Self-Absorbed

To maintain an actress' position in Hollywood, one must have an enormous preoccupation with self.

Alexis Smith
Films in Review, June–July, 1970

★ ★ ★

One of a Kind

They don't have a type like me out here in Hollywood, so if I can't learn to act they'll soon tire of me, I expect.

Greta Garbo
Stardom, 1970

★ ★ ★

Talking Trophy

In those days, it was fashionable in Hollywood, when a producer or an agent came over to Europe on a spree, to bring a famous person back to Hollywood. Mr. David Selznick and his brother, Myron, who was an agent, chose me as a trophy for MGM.

Fritz Lang
The Real Tinsel, 1970

★ ★ ★

Improved Relations

Hollywood has come a long way in the field of black–white relations. There was a time when the movies did not present Negroes with dignity. Negro leaders had good cause to resent this.

George Raft and Edward G. Robinson vied for the affections of Marlene Dietrich (on screen and off) in *Manpower* (Warner Brothers, 1941).

To L.B. Mayer's credit, he recognized the problem and carried on a largely unpublicized crusade to prevent offensive characterizations.

George Murphy
"Say . . . Didn't You Used to be George Murphy?", 1970

Choosey
They don't understand (when an actor rejects unsuitable roles) in Hollywood. When you're out of work they think you're a bum.

Gig Young
Films in Review, February, 1971

Red Cap, Red Face
At last Paramount could no longer ignore the inevitable, and I was brought to Hollywood with great fanfare. A man in a red cap met me at the station and showed me to the nearest streetcar.

Bob Hope
Films in Review, March, 1971

Down the List
I always got roles in Hollywood I didn't want, the ones everyone else turned down. (Warner Brothers) would start at the top of the list—first Davis, then Lupino, then Sheridan. If they didn't want it, I got it.

Alexis Smith
May 9, 1971

Back to Work
It'd do a lot of these Hollywood actors a lot of good if they had to get out and work at it again, fight the street for it again. They ought to take all their money away from 'em and let 'em fight for it again. You can find out who you are.

Huntz Hall
July 8, 1971

Easy Street?
Before I came to Hollywood I dreamed that movie people led lives of ease and luxury, that their wants were filled before they could mention them and that life was a smooth succession of pleasure. So what did I find? For one thing I didn't discover the true meaning of work until I got out here. I've never worked so hard or so steadily.

Linda Darnell
The Fox Girls, 1971

Sex Sell

The minute any woman has any brains in Hollywood, it's supposed to cancel them sexually. They didn't know how to sell them if they couldn't sell them sexually. They never really knew what the hell to do with me. The idea in those days was, "She photographs like two million dollars, now if we could only get her to act." Well, I didn't photograph particularly well, but I could act.

Anne Baxter
The New York Times, August 22, 1971

★ ★ ★

Viva Censorship!

Hollywood must never permit censorship to collapse—it's far too good for the box office.

Claude Binyon
The Wit and Wisdom of Hollywood, 1971

★ ★ ★

Enrico? Pinky?

They're a bunch of con artists (in Hollywood). They think they can pat me on the head and I'll kiss their asses. They just don't give a damn what is good or what is crap just so their lousy pictures make money. They're a bunch of peanut brains with no taste. They wouldn't know the difference between Enrico Caruso and Pinky Tomlin.

Mario Lanza
Mario Lanza, 1971

★ ★ ★

Hollywood Mercenary

I hated everything about Hollywood. The brassy lingo. The lack of sensitivity and individuality. The gristmill philosophy. The yes-men. The crude and influential giants. The Seventh Avenue intrigue. The cruel caste system. The fakery. I hated everything except the money.

Frances Farmer
Will There Really Be a Morning?, 1972

★ ★ ★

Perpetual Motion

Being French, I adore food. Yet, I never gain a pound. I think Hollywood did that for me. I always worked my tail off in pictures! I was never still a moment. There always was a broom or a vacuum cleaner in my fist, or I was at the sink, scrubbing away for dear life. Now, you take Garbo. She was always sulking on a sofa in her movies. Or Marlene Dietrich, languishing in the shadows somewhere. I was never idle.

Claudette Colbert
The Paramount Pretties, 1972

Cloning, Studio Style

Let me say this about the studios, and it's easier to say now because the whole Hollywood system has changed. When you were hired, you were thought of as another so-and-so, a possible replacement for whoever was popular. Your personality and style became almost the personality of the then reigning star. At Fox it was Alice Faye, then Betty Grable, and then me. We had a lot in common, they thought: we were blondes, we had pretty faces and we could sing.

Vivian Blaine
Film Fan Monthly, April, 1972

Pretties Pall

In Hollywood at that time (the early 1960s) you had to be a knock-out, like Jane Fonda, before they would even consider you for a big role. For us slow climbers that is all changed now. The public grew very tired of pretty faces and beautiful props. Hollywood has discovered that—along with being noble and controlled, pouring tea with a stiff upper lip—I can also be wild and attractive.

Lois Nettleton
After Dark, November, 1972

Here, Jack

When I first arrived in Hollywood, they told me to get a new name, so I thought back to the best times I had as a kid playing on the tidal land (in Wales). There was a tannery and old mills. It was really mill land. So I called myself Jack Milland but they said, "In Hollywood, only dogs are called Jack," so I looked down a list and picked the shortest name I could find—Ray.

Ray Milland
The London Express, December 8, 1972

Bucking the System

I didn't want to accept a yearly contract. Hollywood was at the top of its empire in that time. It was really disciplined. I was offered contracts by colleagues, but under a contract you are purely a slave to the studio. You shoot the picture they want when they want. And I never accepted. I worked more or less independently, which is against the system in Hollywood, and more difficult.

René Clair
Focus on Film, Winter, 1972

Under a Cloud

Too many in Hollywood were operating under this cloud that continually hung over them: if you weren't a good boy and toed the line you were through—and where is the money coming from for the next payment on the swimming pool? I never had to operate that way. If it ever

The screen's Dr. Kildare–Dr. Gillespie series is represented here by *Dr. Kildare's Wedding Day* (MGM, 1941), with Gladys Blake, Frank Orth, Marie Blake, Gus Schilling, Red Skelton, Eddie Acuff, Horace McMahon, Alma Kruger, Nell Craig and Lionel Barrymore.

Sometimes called the greatest film ever made, *Citizen Kane* (RKO, 1941) was the first, and best, work of twenty-five-year-old writer-director Orson Welles, here with Ruth Warrick.

started to rain on me from that black cloud, I would say, "I'm going to New York to do a show." And I would.

H.C. Potter
Action, January–February, 1973

The Great Dictator
L.B. Mayer and MGM created stars out of tinsel, cellophane and newspapers. But all the stars were born and built and died more or less at the whim of L.B. Mayer, who was an absolute dictator of the studio—and a good deal of Hollywood to boot. If you were not in favor, he could blackball you at all the other studios. I was too young to know why all of a sudden a young woman would be blackballed and never heard of again. Evidently the casting couch bit really did happen. Of course, I never even heard about it until years later.

Elizabeth Taylor
Movie Digest, March, 1973

The Green Years
Hollywood? Loved it. Those were productive, rewarding years.

Danny Kaye
Films in Review, May, 1973

Man of the People
I love Hollywood. I don't mean the higher echelons. I mean the lower echelons, and the grips, the technicians.

John Ford
Pieces of Time, 1973

Show Time
You show me a successful businessman in Hollywood and I'll show you a man who knows nothing about motion pictures.

William Holden
The Films of William Holden, 1973

Romance Gone
The saddest thing you can say about Hollywood today is that they've taken the romance out of sex.

Lana Turner
It Was Fun While It Lasted, 1973

Different Slant
The secret of success in Hollywood lies in being different from anyone else.

Lon Chaney (Sr.)
Karloff: The Man, The Monster, The Movies, 1973

Democracy Works!
They treat you so great in Hollywood, make you feel so important even if you really aren't. The technicians there, you could have them in your home. They're bright, they're alert, they're intelligent, they're trying to help you.

Paul Lynde
July 19, 1973

Busy Lady
I came out to Hollywood to do an Eddie Cantor picture with twelve to fourteen show girls, right? They had more experience, more money, knew their way around. Yet I made it and they didn't. Why? Maybe because they turned down more working jobs for social opportunities and I did just the opposite. As a result, I've never been out of work in this town except for two hours between contracts.

Lucille Ball
Lucy, 1973

No Union Then
I liked living in Hollywood very much; the weather's nice. It didn't rain, and I had a car to go to work with, where in London I went on the underground because I had no money. But you worked long hours; there was no union when I first came out. We just worked until we dropped.

Binnie Barnes
Film Fan Monthly, January, 1974

Lucky Idiots
I have known many Hollywood producers and studio heads. Some are literate, sensitive, intelligent men. Others are two-fisted, business-oriented politicians. Still others are lucky idiots.

Garson Kanin
Hollywood, 1974

Blacklisted

I turned down parts and they blacklisted me. It works in an odd way in Hollywood. Joe Schmoe would have lunch with his cronies and say, "That bitch—she's nothing but trouble—don't hire her!" and pretty soon I couldn't get work.

Carroll Baker
People Are Crazy Here, 1974

★ ★ ★

Uppity Agents

I shut myself up in the phone booth and started calling around trying to find an agent. It's a strange thing about Hollywood, it's sometimes easier to get a job than to get an agent, very uppity they are. After three days of trying I finally found a couple who condescended to handle me.

Ray Milland
Wide-Eyed in Babylon, 1974

★ ★ ★

Another One

It never fails. Sooner or later every newcomer to Hollywood is told he is "another somebody or other."

Paul Newman
Paul Newman, 1974

★ ★ ★

Industrious Hollywood

In Hollywood everyone seemed to work harder than we did in the English studios, and heaven knows, we worked hard enough.

Anna Neagle
There's Always Tomorrow, 1974

★ ★ ★

Sour Grapes

It has become fashionable to make jokes about Hollywood. Most of them were just jealous jokes. When outsiders can't get in anywhere, they protect their egos with that kind of snide humor. In this case, everybody, secretly, wanted to be a part of the Hollywood scene. Why not? The most beautiful women, the most handsome men, the most talented musicians, the most capable writers were all working in Hollywood in the 1920s, 1930s and on into the 1940s.

Mervyn LeRoy
Take One, 1974

★ ★ ★

Sothern Style

I'm always amazed at what a lousy actress I was. I guess in the old days we just got by on glamour. Hollywood sold its stars on good looks and personality buildups. We weren't really

Hold That Ghost (Universal, 1941), the haunted house apex of comedy team Bud Abbott and Lou Costello (second and fourth from left), featured Evelyn Ankers, Richard Carlson, Joan Davis, Edward Pawley, Nestor Paiva, Joe LaCava and Frank Penny.

James Cagney (third from right) won the Oscar as George M. Cohan in *Yankee Doodle Dandy* (Warner Brothers, 1942), with Walter Huston, Rosemary DeCamp, Jeanne Cagney, Richard Whorf and Joan Leslie.

actresses in the true sense. We were just big names—the products of a good publicity department. Today's crop of actresses and actors have real talent.

Ann Sothern
The 1970s

★ ★ ★

Only in America?
Actors are freaks in America, and Hollywood is all freaksville.

Vincent Price
Vincent Price Unmasked, 1974

★ ★ ★

The Sons Also Rise
Nepotism was then rampant in Hollywood, but it didn't actually affect the finished product. Films might be slowed up by having to go through the hands of various sons, daughters, nephews, nieces, cousins and in-laws, but by the time a movie went before the cameras, experts had always been called in to straighten out the snarls.

Anita Loos
Kiss Hollywood Good-by, 1974

★ ★ ★

Payment Deferred
I never really made it in the movies. I know damn well the public would have done it for me had Hollywood given me the right breaks. I could have paid off in the right movie.

Angela Lansbury
Daily News, September 22, 1974

★ ★ ★

No Man an Island
The longer I've been in Hollywood, the more I realize I need help—that everybody does, that I can't do it all by myself. There's a story they tell here in Hollywood (not true!) that before Tony Curtis was offered *The Defiant Ones*, the film in which a black prisoner and a white one were chained together, the film was first offered to Bob Mitchum. He said, "Me? Be chained to a black guy? Never!" Then it was offered to Marlon Brando. He agreed to do it if he could play the black man. *I* was the next in line. I supposedly agreed to do it if I could play *both* the black and white man. That will give you a pretty good idea of what my reputation was.

Kirk Douglas
Family Weekly, October 20, 1974

Into the Swamp
There's a dismal swamp out there in Hollywood where the money goes and it's never accounted for. I had 5% of *Patton*, which cost $10 million to make and grossed $40 million, and I've never made a dime.

George C. Scott
Sunday News, December 8, 1974

★ ★ ★

Came to Act
I came to Hollywood to act, not to charm society.

James Dean
The James Dean Story, 1975

★ ★ ★

Famous First Words
"Where are you?" always precedes "How are you?" in Hollywood. It means "Where are you working?"

Samuel Marx
Mayer and Thalberg, 1975

★ ★ ★

Cinema Sow
There I was on the screen, a pancaked, lacquered Hollywood purse made out of a Cincinnati sow's ear.

Doris Day
Doris Day: Her Own Story, 1975

★ ★ ★

Saturday Night Fever
I have many happy memories of Hollywood. The good old days did produce some marvelous movies, but often the working conditions were much too demanding. I'll never forget the long hours I put in for my first big picture in Hollywood, *Lloyds of London*. We just kept shooting. We never had a Saturday night off, and we worked on Sunday, too. We just kept going until the picture was completed. After *Lloyds*, I had a case of pneumonia, and wound up in an iron lung.

Virginia Field
Hollywood Studio Magazine, April, 1975

★ ★ ★

Garbo Watches
When I came out to Hollywood I was amazed at the people who came on the set and watched me practice (dancing). Mind you, while I was rehearsing I never saw anyone out there, it could have been I-don't-know-who. Garbo used to come and watch me for hours. And Joan

Crawford used to come and lay on her tummy and watch me for hours. And I'm thinking to myself these are the people who are *big* movie stars and here they are.

Eleanor Powell
Focus on Film, Spring, 1975

Prognosis Negative
My feelings about Hollywood had nothing to do with moviemaking *per se*. My dislike was solely for the system of binding a creative person to a particular studio for a particular length of time. What an appalling waste of money, time, and talent! . . . I have always had a feeling of gratitude toward MGM. If its management had tossed Larry and me a few more crumbs, we might have been lulled into staying longer, and that would have been the end of Larry Hart and Dick Rodgers. I'm sure I would have ended up as a neurotic, a drunkard or both.

Richard Rodgers
Musical Stages, 1975

Down You Go
In Hollywood they like you until you're standing on a pedestal and they hand you an Oscar. Then they say, "How did he get up there? Let's knock him down."

Yul Brynner
Don't Get Me Wrong—I Love Hollywood, 1975

The Real Thing
I was the property of Columbia Pictures and they kept me busy. Since I could sing, dance and act, I never felt like one of those movie queens they used to manufacture in Hollywood. I had sexy genes, I guess, and that helped. I was held back by what the studio thought I could do. But I made some good films, though never a lot of money.

Rita Hayworth
The Glamour Girls, 1975

Actors Take Charge
Would I like to direct? With most Hollywood directors you can do that anyway!

George Segal
The Christian Science Monitor, April 19, 1976

It's a Wrap
Hollywood . . . where a producer loves you to death until the end of the job and can't recognize you on the street the next day.

Raymond Chandler
American Film, May, 1976

The story of a British family facing war, *Mrs. Miniver* (MGM, 1942) starred Greer Garson and Walter Pidgeon; both received Academy Award nominations—Greer won, as did the film, supporting actress Teresa Wright, director William Wyler, etc.

Spencer Tracy and Katharine Hepburn, one of Hollywood's legendary teams in nine co-starring features, first acted together in *Woman of the Year* (MGM, 1942).

Big Load
If I had my way, I'd load all those Hollywood producers into a truck and drive them into the middle of the Pacific.

Tony Curtis
The Swashbucklers, 1976

★ ★ ★

It's a Living
The whole Hollywood bullshit is just amusing to me. I look at it and I laugh. Basically, it's just another way of earning a living, a very pleasant way, but nothing more.

Charles Bronson
Bronson!, 1976

★ ★ ★

Worthwhile—Almost
Making movies with Bing (Crosby) almost made Hollywood worthwhile.

Mary Martin
My Heart Belongs, 1976

★ ★ ★

Money Talks
I've grown somewhat unhappy over people constantly referring to me as "the designer of the clothes for *Gone with the Wind*." I did a film for Lana Turner in the '50s called *Diane*, and I consider that my best work. But it had a terrible script and nobody remembers. I thought my clothes for Elizabeth Taylor in *Raintree County* were better also. But you see you get the recognition for the big money-makers in Hollywood. It's a money town.

Walter Plunkett
Los Angeles Times, August 22, 1976

★ ★ ★

Dental Boost
Audiences were conditioned to expect an ingénue to be the Hollywood prototype. All leading ladies, however ordinary or drab or impoverished the character in the story, were coiffed and clothed immaculately, made up to the nines and had perfect teeth. The hero was of course just as gorgeous. The regular, gleaming white teeth of movie stars undoubtedly gave a big boost to dentistry.

Irene Sharaff
Broadway & Hollywood, 1976

★ ★ ★

Knew What She Wanted
Opinions, *my* opinions . . . they got me into trouble the minute I got to Hollywood. That's when it started, that shopworn line about my directing my own pictures. Not true. What *was*

true was that I knew what I wanted to do in *Funny Girl* because I had played it a thousand times, literally, on the stage.

Barbra Streisand
Ladies' Home Journal, November, 1976

★ ★ ★

Thinking of Trash
All the scripts that have been sent to me in the last 10 years have been trash. I read through them—just to see what in the world Hollywood is thinking of—and when I'm finished, I throw them across the room. And feel insulted.

Lana Turner
November 30, 1976

★ ★ ★

Feeding the Animals
In Hollywood, it's like being in a cage. They thrust the parts through the bars and you take what they give you.

Ingrid Bergman
The Selznick Players, 1976

★ ★ ★

Small Town Experiment
My first impressions (of Hollywood) were rather depressing. New York in those days was an enchanting city. By contrast, Hollywood seemed a small town. However, as soon as I began working, my whole world was the studio, and it was very exciting.

Rouben Mamoulian
The Hollywood Reporter, 1976

★ ★ ★

Passes President
Hollywood, where a guy with brains can make more money than the President of the United States.

Victor Mature
The Swashbucklers, 1976

★ ★ ★

Unfair Practices
Hollywood is full of fine, young actors who aren't working and young non-actors who are.

Victory Jory
Hollywood Players: The Thirties, 1976

Wrecking Havoc

Nobody ever found out what to do with me in Hollywood. I run like mad from the pictures I've made. I know when I'm bad and I know when I'm good and I haven't been even passable in the dozen movies I've made.

June Havoc
Hollywood Players: The Forties, 1976

★ ★ ★

Voice of Experience

My advice to young stars today is, make sure you have some othe skill to fall back on. Be prepared for the day Hollywood may reject you. I can still act, I can still sing, but no one, not even the people I helped, will even see me any more.

Gloria Jean
Who's Who in Hollywood, 1976

★ ★ ★

Organized Bedlam

In Hollywood, I was fascinated by the organization, the technique and the studio morale (which you don't have today anywhere). People were always there on time, and you could start shooting at nine o'clock. They were enthusiastic, and when you started a picture you were on it to the end. In Europe, actors were often making three or four pictures at the same time, which naturally led to all kinds of confusion.

William Dieterle
Close-Up: The Contract Director, 1976

★ ★ ★

A Kind of Affection

For a long time, I felt a real hostility about the things that happened to me in Hollywood, but now I look back on the person I was then with a kind of affection. I was inexperienced and lost, and I didn't know if I wanted to be a movie star or a really good actress. I wouldn't say that I had a nervous breakdown. I just had a disgust. But I *survived*.

Piper Laurie
The New York Times, December 3, 1976

★ ★ ★

Signing Cats and Dogs

I don't understand it. Out in Hollywood they're signing up trained dogs and cats and grand-opera singers and everybody in the world but me.

Will Rogers
Goldwyn, 1976

Rosalind Russell (center) received a best actress Academy nomination for her hilarious enactment of the aspiring Greenwich Village writer in *My Sister Eileen* (Columbia, 1942), with June Havoc and Janet Blair.

Brazilian bombshell Carmen Miranda, "The Lady in the Tutti-Frutti Hat," stood out, as always, in *The Gang's All Here* (20th Century-Fox, 1943), with Phil Baker, Eugene Pallette and Edward Everett Horton.

Accidental Advantage
I don't know to this day what shapes a career out in Hollywood. It's still rather mysterious. It has, I think, a lot to do with how you look, what's available, how you take off at the box office. Or sometimes they don't know how to use you, so you find yourself lost. I was never a classic beauty. I had no image, so I found myself in a lot of things accidentally, like *The Enchanted Cottage* and *A Tree Grows in Brooklyn* and *Gentleman's Agreement*, and they all worked to my advantage.

Dorothy McGuire
Sunday News, January 9, 1977

Pet Projects
They always have to have a pet project in Hollywood, something they're going to do next year when the crap they're doing now is finally finished.

Elia Kazan
American Film, May, 1977

Misnomer
The name Hollywood is, to this day, a misnomer—one very small section of an enormous area where many people work in the movie business, but hardly any people who work in that business actually lived in Hollywood, as such.

Deborah Kerr
Deborah Kerr, 1977

Two Kinds of Women
Women stars in Hollywood were invariably in one of two categories. One group was made up of women who were exploited by men, and the other, much smaller group was composed of women who survived by acting like men.

Otto Preminger
Preminger, 1977

Of Stars and Brushes
The big American dream for a few odd millions is to go to Hollywood and be a star. But the very nature of wanting to be a star—not an actress, I'm saying, but a star—means you are a product. The Fuller Brush. And you're in trouble right there.

Evelyn Keyes
New York Post, August 6, 1977

Wading Through

When I left, being from Hollywood was a handicap because it was a factory then. Anne Bancroft was playing Indian maidens and Piper Laurie was eating flowers. Living here is good, but only if you're working. People have a tendency to push relationships. You have to wade through the b.s. and weed out the garden constantly. It takes a lot of hoeing.

Tab Hunter
Los Angeles Times, October 1, 1977

★ ★ ★

Tackling the Truth

If you tell the press—or anyone in Hollywood—the truth, it throws them, they don't know how to deal with it.

Lauren Bacall
By Myself, 1978

★ ★ ★

Set Paralysis

There are two things that are absolutely paralytic to actors when you go on the set, particularly in your younger years in Hollywood. That is, number one, the behind-the-camera intimidation which is never meant personally, but it's just guys reading newspapers when you're crying your guts out. Well, they've seen it all before. Second is when a big famous star treats you badly, or goes home before your close-up, or something like that.

Bruce Dern
The Dick Cavett Show, March 7, 1978

★ ★ ★

Coddled in Movies

I discovered that I had forgotten how to act. I'd been coddled a great deal in Hollywood and had been catered to. It was difficult for me to simply stand on a stage, swoon, whatever. You don't have to do that in movies because they can stop a scene at any time and move into a close-up or pull back.

Sylvia Sidney
Close-Ups, 1978

★ ★ ★

Fear Stalks Stages

One outstanding quality Hollywood possesses is not the lavishness, perpetual sunshine, the golden opportunities, but *fear*. Fear stalks the sound stages, the publicity departments, the executive offices. Since careers often begin by chance, by the hunch of a producer or casting director, a casual meeting with an agent or a publicist, they can evaporate just as quixotically.

Joan Fontaine
No Bed of Roses, 1978

Out in Front

That was the particular Hollywood style. Behind your back in the office, on the telephone with agents, they could be brutal, but there would never be any one-on-one confrontation the way there is in New York. In the New York theater everyone is carrying his long knife right out in front of him so you know what to expect.

Elizabeth Ashley
Actress: Postcards from the Road, 1978

Big Deal

In Hollywood's heyday, a man's word was really his bond. An executive like Harry Cohn, for example, might have an unsavory personal reputation, but if he said, "You have a deal," you had a deal.

Edward Dmytryk
It's a Hell of a Life But Not a Bad Living, 1978

What's Doing?

On Broadway if you've ever done a hit play they remember that play. Here in Hollywood if you've ever had a hit picture they only want to know what you've done last.

Sidney Sheldon
Blueprint on Babylon, 1978

Best Shot

I realized that Hollywood was going to be a tough nut to crack, but as soon as I cashed in my return ticket I knew I'd give it my best shot.

Susan Hayward
The Decline and Fall of the Love Goddesses, 1979

Story is All

My mentor was my father, Darryl Zanuck, from whom I learned what makes a good motion picture. The most valuable lesson he taught me was to uphold the story as all-important. Sometimes out here in Hollywood we get so caught up with stars—actors and directors—that we lose sight of the story we're trying to tell.

Richard Zanuck
Cosmopolitan, August, 1979

Ingrid Bergman and producer David O. Selznick, who brought the Swedish star to America in 1939, are seen at the Academy Awards in 1944.

Slow But Sure

When I was 17 some guy in New York with a bald head and a cigar told me, "Listen, kid, you want to go to Hollywood? Okay. Four months my way or four years your way." He really said that. Twelve years later I arrived here.

Joan Hackett
The Sunday Record, December 9, 1979

★ ★ ★

That's Acting?

In newsreels I'd watch stars arriving at Hollywood premieres and *that's* what I thought acting was!

Anne Bancroft
Films in Review, January, 1980

★ ★ ★

Nothing Left

What has blown Hollywood apart is paying the superstars $2 million for a picture. There's nothing left over for anyone else.

Dennis Morgan
February 2, 1980

★ ★ ★

Taste Made Difference

Too many of today's movies are tasteless and disgusting. To make audiences sick to their stomach is not entertainment. Every other word is bad. I would never think of saying those things. I realize the world is different now. But I certainly don't think that people live in such a rotten, filthy way as portrayed in these movies. You shouldn't take a pervert and depraved human being and make a big hero out of him. Plots today show what is ugly in life. Back in the old days of Hollywood we made a few movies that had some shocking things. But we had taste and could get away with it.

Jeanne Crain
National Enquirer, March 4, 1980

★ ★ ★

Inhuman Belief

Certainly, there are good marriages in Hollywood, but to imagine that people who are beautiful, and glorified by the camera and publicity, wardrobe and make-up departments and who are thrown together in close proximity day after day; to imagine they don't get *involved* with each other, especially when the emotional requirements of their scenes are that they be in love with each other—I mean it's not human to believe they don't!

Shelley Winters
Films in Review, June–July, 1980

Left to Entertainers

I disagree with the thinking in Hollywood on the part of the producers that people don't want to think, that they only want to be entertained. People want to be led out of the morass or at least to have a little help in clearing away the confusion. The problem is . . . people who have a social vision haven't found a way to express it in a mass language. There's so much rhetoric and so much sectarianism. It gets manifested in the cultural field and I think that's why culture gets left in the hands of the entertainers.

Jane Fonda
Cineaste, Vol. VI, No. 4, the 1980s

★ ★ ★

Minorities Excluded

(In the 1940s–50s) 20th Century-Fox was not untypical of Hollywood studios in its almost complete exclusion of minority workers on all levels.

Sidney Poitier
This Life, 1980

★ ★ ★

Wanted Realism

I felt that Hollywood was wonderful, and I couldn't in any way complain because I had a wonderful time, and people seemed to like me, and I hope we made some good pictures. But I just wanted to do something more realistic, and when I saw *Open City* I realized that somewhere in the world they did a different kind of picture, and I left.

Ingrid Bergman
My Story, 1980

★ ★ ★

Busting Through

Hollywood was an experience I wouldn't have missed. In those days, just after the war, ''Glamour'' was the magic word. Everything had to be geared to what the producers thought the public imagined was the perfect romantic male, or ideal woman of perfection. If one of your eyebrows didn't match the other it had to be made identical. If your mouth was crooked, that had to be made straight. If you had no bust, they gave you one. Rotten teeth—they whipped them out.

Ann Todd
The Eighth Veil, 1980

★ ★ ★

Slaves to Glamour

It has been said that glamour left Hollywood with the demise of the star system. It is also true that the system meant virtual slavery for the stars themselves. The studio simply took control of one's life, dictating appearances, dress, social behavior, standard and style of living, even acceptable love interests. It was a well oiled machine, perfectly designed to produce, nurture and promote precisely the image of glamour and mild titillation the public would buy, and to cast aside anyone who didn't fit the mold.

Ruth Warrick
The Confessions of Phoebe Tyler, 1980

★ ★ ★

Stage No Risk
I don't agree that Hollywood actors risk their careers by doing theater here. For one thing, this town doesn't take theater seriously enough for that to happen. So if you're no good on stage, nobody really cares.

Richard Chamberlain
Los Angeles Times, February 24, 1981

★ ★ ★

Deep Throat
The camera is too intimate. It crawls down your throat and creeps up your nostrils and it tells you what you are. On that screen I never can successfully compete with some shop girl who, after being cursed by a director like von Stroheim, can weep real tears. In Hollywood I'm constantly being defeated by corny sincerity.

John Barrymore
The Barrymores, 1981

★ ★ ★

The Last Breath
You can't retire in Hollywood. Nobody gives up a job, even if he's ninety, or sick, or has money like Midas. Everybody works until the last breath, and when one day they die, they die like Napoleon's grenadiers, who died with the words *"Vive l'Empereur!"* Just so, the last words of a director or producer are "Make another take!"

Lionel Barrymore
The Barrymores, 1981

★ ★ ★

Joyless Jean
There are none of the friendly, family feelings (working in Hollywood) that I get when I work in France. In France, you know if you're making a movie, you're going to sit around waiting in a café, which is not disagreeable. Here, they give you some superb trailer with a Frigidaire and a stove. I keep expecting to find warmth to the work in Hollywood which doesn't exist. The unions have imposed so many people for each job there is no longer a sense of personal responsibility. Some of the joy has gone out of acting for me.

Jean Seberg
Played Out, 1981

Gathered together for the twentieth anniversary of Metro-Goldwyn-Mayer Pictures in 1944 were many of the actors currently employed by MGM plus studio chief Louis B. Mayer (bottom row, center). Top row: Ben Blue, Chill Wills, Keye Luke, Barry Nelson, Desi Arnaz, Henry O'Neill, Bob Crosby and Rags Ragland. Second row: Blanche Ring, Sara Haden, Fay Holden, Bert Lahr, Frances Gifford, June Allyson, Richard Whorf, Frances Rafferty, Spring Byington, Connie Gilchrist and Gladys Cooper. Third row: Dame May Whitty, Reginald Owen, Keenan Wynn, Diana Lewis, Marilyn Maxwell, Esther Williams, Ann Richards, Marta Linden, Lee Bowman, Richard Carlson and Mary Astor. Fourth row: Tommy Dorsey, George Murphy, Jean Rogers, James Craig, Donna Reed, Van Johnson, Fay Bainter, Marsha Hunt, Ruth Hussey, Marjorie Main and Robert Benchley. Fifth row: Harry James, Brian Donlevy, Red Skelton, Mickey Rooney, William Powell, Wallace Beery, Spencer Tracy, Walter Pidgeon, Robert Taylor, Jean-Pierre Aumont, Lewis Stone and Gene Kelly. Sixth row: James Stewart, Margaret Sullavan, Lucille Ball, Hedy Lamarr, Katharine Hepburn, Louis B. Mayer, Greer Garson, Irene Dunne, Susan Peters, Ginny Simms and Lionel Barrymore.

Security Blankets
The amount of security that the star had—Crawford, Gable, Tracy, Taylor—was wonderful. Two or three pictures a year written for them by the top writers. It was like a baby being bathed and all wrapped in a blanket. You were safe. Today it's catch as catch can. Today someone buys a book or a play and asks, "Who can we go to the bank with?" not "Who's right for it?" It was a good system for a while, but Hollywood today is like a series of Mobil or Standard Oil stations leased to a distributor.

Barbara Stanwyck
The New York Times, March 22, 1981

Personality Plus
The greatest moment in my life, the thing that makes me most proud is when, thanks to Hollywood, I became an international personality.

Maurice Chevalier
Maurice Chevalier, 1981

Man Alive?
Hollywood ain't dog eat dog; it's man eat man.

Wilson Mizner
Hollywood Red, 1981

Assembly Line Star
We were all like off an assembly line. I was being marketed as a future movie star. The roles that I played gave me no outlet for expression. When I was in New York at acting school, I was playing wonderful scenes and parts and just thoroughly enjoying the experience of acting. Suddenly, Hollywood had nothing to do with that, and I hated it.

Jane Fonda
American Film, November, 1981

Never Left Town
Can you believe I was on this lot (20th Century-Fox) 50 years ago? When I was signed to come to Hollywood, I had a five-year contract, and I told my mother after we left New York that five years seemed so long, and she said it *wouldn't* be five years—that there were all these six-month options to the contract, and, as luck would have it, I never left.

Claire Trevor
The Hollywood Reporter, May 27, 1982

Sweet and Helpless

I never had a vacation until I was 20, and in those days we worked six days a week. The Hollywood people in charge kept saying to me, "Never change. Stay as sweet as you are." And oh God, I did what they told me to. I didn't even make a decision on my own until I was 25 years old.

Jane Powell
1982

★ ★ ★

Home Again

The journalists who came to interview me were all intelligent men, and we talked about music in Hollywood and the "factory" methods (as I called them) employed there, whereby a number of composers collaborate on a score in order to shorten the composing period. I forgot I had to return to Hollywood.

Miklos Rozsa
Double Life, 1982

★ ★ ★

No Failing Allowed

Nobody is allowed to fail within a two-mile radius of the Beverly Hills Hotel.

Gore Vidal
Los Angeles Times, August 8, 1982

★ ★ ★

Studio Signs Thing

In February, 1937, my mother and I boarded the train for Hollywood. I was 5'9" tall, weight 169 lbs., wore a tailored suit, a little derby hat, a blouse from the dime store, high heels and carried a Pomeranian Spitz dog. I was an anachronism! Well, we got off the train, and there was Ida Koverman, Louis Mayer's right-hand lady—looking at this *thing* the studio had just signed.

Susanna Foster
Films in Review, February, 1983

★ ★ ★

A Shocker

I'm amazed about everything here. The way you have to live like a monk, and go to bed early. I mean, one expects "Holly-wood," that sort of thing here. Everyone works hard. And people are nice. I expected ego trips all around. All this comes as a shocker.

Joe Piscopo
The Hollywood Reporter, September 9, 1983

Improbable Mogul
There was an allegation that Albert Einstein wanted to take over Hollywood. Now how would you find someone with brains trying to run Hollywood?

Johnny Carson
The Tonight Show Starring Johnny Carson
September 13, 1983

Sound of Laughter
Sometimes I regret I went to Hollywood. Maybe I should have stayed here (on Broadway). I love to hear people laugh.

Eddie Albert
Midday with Bill Boggs, September 16, 1983

What Makes a Star
In Hollywood, of course, people liked to play, "Mirror, mirror on the wall, am I the fairest of them all?" The girls were very vain about their beauty, because they thought that was what got them in movies. But essentially, what matters is personality. That's what makes a star.

Louise Brooks
The New York Times, September 16, 1983

Wrongs Right There
What do I dislike most? Hollywood! For years I bummed around trying to get a job. It was the same old story. My voice was too soft; my teeth needed capping; I squinted too much. I was too tall. And I know that if I walked into a casting office right now and nobody knew I was Clint Eastwood, I would get the same old treatment. Everything they said was wrong is still here.

Clint Eastwood
National Enquirer, September 20, 1983

The Ring of Truth
When the phone stopped ringing, I didn't sit by it. A lot of my friends in Hollywood do that. Much better to do plays, even if you don't get paid for them.

Rip Torn
New York Post, October 8, 1983

The Doughgirls (Warner Brothers, 1944), Joseph A. Fields' Broadway comedy set in wartime Washington, was brought to the screen with Eve Arden, Alexis Smith, Jane Wyman and Ann Sheridan.

Laura (20th Century-Fox, 1944), the Otto Preminger-directed classic mystery from Vera Caspary's novel, had Dana Andrews, Vincent Price, Gene Tierney and composer David Raskin's mood-setting theme music.

Fear is Platform

Fear is a very big platform for how things operate in Hollywood. The stakes are so high, there's so much tension, that it's hard to work, even for me.

Robert Redford
The New York Times Magazine, October 23, 1983

★ ★ ★

LA vs. NY

Hollywood is a wonderful place to work. The conditions are terrific. It's a car town, so you don't have the traveling hassle of New York. The distance may be greater to get where you're going, but it's rather pleasant. You miss some of the personal contact, but make up for that in other ways. I mean, how bad can it be when you're sitting in your car and the stereo is playing some lovely Bach quartet or cantata and you're humming along. If it's terribly hot you turn on the air-conditioning.

The people in Hollywood are fine, but different, that's all. They're not as fast. Everything is at your disposal to a greater degree than in New York. It's easier to film, to get things done. But there is a little more imagination, speed and energy in New York. I think the crew there cares slightly more about the product than in Hollywood, where they care more about the cosmetic aspects. New York is a tougher town and breeds a tougher kind of person, and one who will automatically be more imaginative because there's less to work with there.

Hector Elizondo
October, 1983

★ ★ ★

High Flyer

I wish the young actors and actresses today had the studio star system we had in Hollywood in the 1940s. Out of that system came so many wonderful stars, brilliant screenplays and films that have no equal. How fortunate to have been part of that golden era. Today, I do my emoting in the sky, and have been ever since I earned my pilot's license in 1972. Flying an airplane gives me the same elation I felt when performing in front of that beautiful, critical camera.

Ann Savage
October 28, 1983

★ ★ ★

Street Wise

In those days Hollywood had no competition. Now the talent is spread. The demands of television are insatiable and our super stars run the gamut from films for television to selling soap. Although I was fortunate to have appeared in films like *Wuthering Heights*, *Dark Victory*, *Watch on the Rhine*, my own response to the Hollywood I lived and worked in was futile. Like a lot of young people at the time, I believed there was some control actors could exert on their careers. There wasn't, because the machinery of making movies is extremely costly. I couldn't adapt myself to not having any voice in my destiny. I fought it to a standstill —then decided I should get out. If you have a burning desire to perform, you don't even need a theater—do it in the street and you will find an audience. I did.

Geraldine Fitzgerald
November 16, 1983

Robert/Roberta
I've been making films in Hollywood since June 20, 1938, and no one cared about me until I wore Blake Edwards' wife's clothes (in *Victor/Victoria*).

Robert Preston
Daily Variety, November 21, 1983

★ ★ ★

Accent on Stereotypes
If you have an accent in Hollywood, you are very, very limited indeed. You are never thought of for parts as a lawyer or doctor. In Hollywood you are stereotyped, compartmented, and I was a Latin and that was it.

Ricardo Montalban
Hour Magazine, November 25, 1983

★ ★ ★

A Streetcar Named Retire
Hollywood is very much like a streetcar. Once a new star is made and comes aboard, an old one is edged out of the rear exit. There's room for only so many and no more.

Cary Grant
Parade, December 11, 1983

★ ★ ★

Forties Flashback
I still find things to get angry about. Sometimes, I think I'm back in 1940s Hollywood and the studio system still prevails. And so as soon as I finish working, I take off. Let them try and find me.

Debra Winger
December 31, 1983

★ ★ ★

Lumet Method
In Hollywood, actors learn to act from watching television. In New York, people learn to act by walking down the street.

Sidney Lumet
The 1980s

★ ★ ★

Producers Input
Most screenwriters tell me I've been extraordinarily lucky in Hollywood. My first screenplay, *Alice Doesn't Live Here Anymore*, was optioned three months after I wrote it, and was shot a year later. *Bound for Glory*, the second screenplay, moved even faster. Obviously, then, I've no cause for great complaint.

And yet. And yet. An old story says it well and quickly. A Hollywood producer and an actor, lost in the desert, wandered for days, their water supply gradually diminishing until both of their canteens were empty. They wandered on, growing weaker and weaker, but found nothing but a blank horizon and shimmering heat. One day passed. Then another. The sun was merciless, and, looking at one another, they realized they were dying.

Suddenly, the actor grabbed the producer's arm. Through blackened lips he screamed with joy and pointed: there, a hundred yards away, was a single palm tree. In the shade under it— a pitcher of iced lemonade and two glasses. The lemonade was so cold that beads of moisture ran down the pitcher's sides.

With the last remnants of their strength, the two crawled the hundred yards. They reached the tree and the actor picked up the pitcher with trembling hands. About to pour, he moaned, "Boy, this looks good!"

"Wait . . . wait," said the producer thoughtfully. "Let's piss in it first."

I like that story, and it has truth in it—not the whole truth, but enough to make it worth repeating. In contrast to the story, I've had producers who were brilliant, saving me weeks of work on a script with a single idea. And obviously many actors can illuminate a scene in ways a writer can never have envisioned.

So. I have two answers, really, on what it's like to be a screenwriter in Hollywood today. On one hand, I am treated courteously, paid well; sometimes, too, my scripts get made quickly and well. Other times, however, my scripts—just as good or bad as the others—are not made or are made by stupid or venal men. Then (to switch images wildly, from lemonade to children) people say, "Funny about Bob Getchell's last two kids—both are cripples—one was a hunchback and the other had a clubfoot." Then I want to wail that the kids were fine until deformed by pressures I had nothing to do with.

I suppose what I'm saying is that it all evens out in the end. God knows that's a hoary idea, and God knows it may sound as if I'm fence-straddling, but, ultimately, it's true: it all evens out in the end.

Robert Getchell
March 11, 1984

★ ★ ★

Star Grazing

My mother and I were the biggest fans of Hollywood ever. We could see three or four movies a day! My mother loved them so. Any number of evenings she'd say to me, "There's a very good movie playing. If you've finished your homework we'll go." I'd lie and say I had and then do it on the school bus in the morning.

Years later, I'd say to my three sons, "There's a very good TV show on at eight o'clock. If you've finished your homework, you can watch it with me." I'd go into their rooms just before the show, which I was anxious to see but they weren't, to ask if they'd finished their homework. They'd say no. So I'd watch it alone.

I guess my boys were right to stick with the homework, though. Today, they're all writers. My son Alex Lasker co-wrote the Clint Eastwood movie *Firefox*, and my son Lawrence Lasker co-wrote *WarGames*, for which he was nominated for an Academy Award.

I started in show business as a band singer. My mother and I were brought to Hollywood in December, 1943, by Howard Hughes who had signed me to a six-month optional agreement. We were beside ourselves. Mother and I would take the several buses from our hotel way over to the fabled Hollywood and Vine to look for stars. We'd walk up and down for miles and never see anyone. One day Mother said, "I know what we're doing wrong. We're both walking on the same side of the street. You take the left side and I'll take the right." This we did. After a while I heard Mother screaming, "Bettejane! Bettejane!" She had run into our first movie star: Lee Bowman.

Howard Hughes didn't want us to have any social life, but we managed to sneak around

The incomparable Irene Dunne starred as an American girl who married an Englishman and made his country her own in *The White Cliffs of Dover* (MGM, 1944), with an up-and-coming Van Johnson.

Exotic Maria Montez played twin sisters in the "camp" favorite, *Cobra Woman* (Universal, 1944), an early screenwriting credit of moviemaker Richard Brooks.

and get into trouble—I married Rudy Vallee briefly. The Mocambo and Ciro's were very big watering holes then, and I'd go and be thrilled to see the stars out on the town. I still am! I mean, I can't believe I know Cary Grant!

Around 1946, after I'd signed with RKO Pictures and was acting with Douglas Fairbanks, Jr., in *Sinbad the Sailor*, I was in the studio commissary one particular lunchtime when in walked Cary Grant, Claudette Colbert, John Wayne, Maureen O'Hara, Robert Mitchum and, for some reason, two Lincolns!

So, when a male friend from my hometown, Washington, D.C., came out to Hollywood, I couldn't wait to invite him to commissary. After we sat down, I whispered to him, "Don't look now, but Cary Grant is two tables behind you."

He said, "Am I supposed to fall down?"

I tried again. "There's Maureen O'Hara."

"I guess she's kind of pretty," he yawned.

That did it. I said, "I can't have lunch today. We'll just have coffee. Let me have your pass." Then I saw him to his car, rushed around to the back of the lot to the cluster of people always waiting there and grabbed a little boy fan. I took him to lunch in the commissary, and he was thrilled with what he saw. So was I.

The disappearance of the contract system had a lot to do with the changes that eventually took place in Hollywood. I felt very secure under contract, I felt they were building me. Of course, some actors felt otherwise and sued to be free.

But I adored RKO. It was a wonderful studio until Howard Hughes bought it. I had just married Edward Lasker, but I had dated Howard, too, and this caused a falling out between Howard and me. He decided I wasn't going to work there anymore.

The only reason I got *The Big Steal* at RKO opposite Robert Mitchum was because Bob had been in a drug bust, quite a scandal in the late 1940s, and all of the other actresses in town were afraid of what working with this pariah would do to their careers. I didn't like the script, and furthermore I'd just learned that I was pregnant. But Bob and I had co-starred in *Out of the Past* shortly before, and I was very fond of him. I loved his warmth and humor. (Years later, when our complicated *Out of the Past* became a favorite with movie buffs, Bob said it was because three pages from the script had been lost and people kept going back to try and figure the thing out.) So I pushed for *The Big Steal* to show him I was behind him.

I wouldn't have got *The Company She Keeps*, either, except that the screenwriter, Ketti Frings, went to Howard and said she'd written it for me and insisted I do the picture.

It's an odd thing about Hollywood, too, but your friends don't often hire you for pictures. It was always someone who felt he'd discovered me. Like Jimmy Cagney, who asked for me in *Man of a Thousand Faces*.

When I started, the standard time it took to make an "A" feature was three and a half months. When we got to the early fifties and *Down Among the Sheltering Palms*, which I did at 20th Century-Fox, it was twenty-nine days, with eighteen days of retakes. The studio boss, Darryl Zanuck, and the director, Edmund Goulding, were battling. Goulding was going to show him. When the film was completed, Zanuck fired everyone connected with it, including Goulding.

Moviemaking became less personal. When you were under contract at a studio, everyone knew you, nurtured you. When this system ended and you went to another studio, you didn't know much about them and they didn't know much about you. Today, some of my Hollywood friends tell me they find it hard going on a new picture because they have never met any of the people on it before. However, it was different working on my recent film, *Against All Odds*—a remake, by the way, of my oldie *Out of the Past* in which I play the mother of the character I played in *Past!* The director, Taylor Hackford, was wonderful. He met with us all a month before shooting began to go over our scenes and rehearse.

The first day on the set was a little strange, though. I hadn't made a film in years, and there were all these young men the same age as my sons with buttons in their ears—turned out they had walkie-talkies. And everyone was so *quiet*. I was used to the screaming assistant directors of the old Hollywood calling us for a scene by shouting, "GET OVER THERE!" But instead I got—in the softest, sweetest voice—"Jane, dear. Action, okay?"

Jane Greer
March 12, 1984

★ ★ ★

Warner Whirlwind

Hollywood was like fairyland. I'd wanted to be in pictures since I was a child back in St. Louis, Missouri, and when I finally got there in 1943 it was everything I'd dreamed.

I was signed by Samuel Goldwyn Studios, which was much smaller than, say, MGM or Fox where they made a hundred movies a year. Goldwyn made maybe one movie a year, but they were known for their painstaking care and quality, and I was usually in each of them for the five years of my contract. By contrast, Warner Brothers, where I signed in 1948, was a whirlwind of activity, and I really loved this. It was truly a golden age. Everything was going on at the studio. This was the most exciting period for an entertainer to be alive—it seemed almost preordained, fate, that all the most wonderful talents in the world had converged on Hollywood at that time.

Talk about seeing stars! You'd be walking along on the lot and there would be Cagney, Gable, Ladd, Peck, Lancaster or even Ronald Reagan strolling by. I got to co-star in films with most of them, too, including Ron. I did *two* movies with the President of the United States!

All the actors were so protected under the old Hollywood contract system. Different studio people tended to your needs for you. There were no worries except doing your work. If you were dedicated, as I was, you could really have a ball, just go in and do your job and enjoy the work and the camaraderie. Some actors like to knock the big studio era, claiming it was bondage, but not me. All departments worked together to achieve such miracles.

My one complaint is that we weren't paid enough. Even Clark Gable, "The King," only got $8,500 or $9,000. That may sound like a lot of money, but today the actors get millions for one picture!

I was always busy working (those musicals were grueling), so I didn't go to many Hollywood parties. In those days we worked Saturdays, too, so we had to get our rest. Saturday night was the only night we could go out. I remember that my boss, Jack Warner, gave fabulous parties at his huge mansion surrounded by acres of lawn, and my husband Michael O'Shea and I would go every Saturday night. When I turned thirty Jack gave me a birthday party there. At table, Jack Warner was on my right and Clark Gable was on my left!

Around the time I left Warners in 1958, the changes really began in Hollywood. All the studios started to fall apart. Up to then, the only warning signals I'd seen at Warners were economy factors—sometimes we'd have to wear costumes off the racks of the wardrobe department instead of having the clothes made for us. About 1960, all the contract players were being let go and the studios were retrenching, going into TV. Everybody was panicking.

Career-wise, I sort of went downhill then. I did a nothing picture in Europe and some low-budget Westerns, but the offers were few. I had a family and contented myself looking after them. After a while, I began doing stage work around the country which continues to occupy me.

I compare the palmy days of Hollywood to that period in France a hundred years or so ago when so many great artists were living there and creating their masterpieces on canvas. That's passed now in Hollywood. It was a group that was there at that point in time to create their masterpieces on celluloid.

These days, people don't have to go to the movies. They're not needed anymore. During the Depression, no one had any money: movies were all we had, they were a necessity then, they sustained people through the tough times. Then everyone escaped the horrors of World War II at the movies. After that, it was the post-war insecurities. Now, people have more money and freedom. They can go skiing, travel, do pretty much whatever they want. And, of course, with tape and cable they can sit in their own homes and watch whatever they want on TV. A film has to be a blockbuster today to lure audiences into theaters.

Mind you, in that bygone Hollywood we never knew that we were involved in an art form, which we are now told it is. We were just doing our jobs—and, for my part, loving every minute of it.

Virginia Mayo
March 14, 1984

★ ★ ★

Nicer in Oregon
It's nicer to be (directing a film) in Oregon or London. Here in Hollywood your money men can come on your set and give you crap, especially if you're on probation with the studio or don't have the hit films to back you up.

John Badham
American Premiere, Winter, 1984

★ ★ ★

How to Be Popular
In order to make it in this town and be really popular, you have to kind of go into the dumper every other year.

Burt Reynolds
The 10th Annual People's Choice Awards
March 15, 1984

★ ★ ★

Have Voice, Will Travel
Hollywood—I really wasn't there when I was *there*! I was in such a dreamworld.

I went to Hollywood in 1943 as an adolescent singing prodigy who was very guarded, and soon after that when I signed with Metro it was the same—not much time for anything but school and work. It was studio, studio, studio. I had very little social life. I made acquaintances at MGM but few real friends. It was like anyplace else—if you're wrapped up in your job, you don't have much time for other things. They were wonderful, busy, productive years for me, though. I quit MGM in the mid-fifties because I wanted to grow up, and the studio wouldn't let me, on screen or off. They weren't making musicals anymore, so they were probably getting ready to fire me, anyway.

There have been many changes in Hollywood since then, so many new people. The whole world has changed, so why should Hollywood be any different? The truth is, Hollywood is no longer Hollywood: films are made all over the world today. My home is still in Bel-Air, California, and my children (all grown) are out there, but now I go to whatever place on the map where there is work.

Jane Powell
March 21, 1984

Ann Savage and Tom Neal played the leads in *Detour* (Producers Releasing Corporation, 1945), a "B" melodrama directed by Edgar G. Ulmer today admired by *film noir* buffs.

Betty Smith's popular novel *A Tree Grows in Brooklyn* (20th Century-Fox, 1945) was memorably filmed by new director Elia Kazan and players Ted Donaldson, Joan Blondell and Peggy Ann Garner.

Good Crews

I never thought about Hollywood, certainly never dreamed of becoming a director. I was from a little Midwest town and was a journalism major in college on partial scholarship. It was the Depression, and when my father's business began to fail I had to drop out of school. My older brother had gone to Hollywood in 1928, working his way up in the accounting department at RKO Studios, so I came out here simply to make a living.

I arrived in July, 1933, and because of my contact there soon started in the shipping room of RKO's film editing department. My eyes were as big as saucers—I'd never been in a movie studio before. They were cutting *Flying Down to Rio*, the first Astaire and Rogers movie, and I'd hear "The Carioca" all day long. I loved it all from the word go, and still do.

After five years of apprenticeship, I became a full-fledged editor myself. One of the films I edited was *Citizen Kane*, which some have called the best of all time. No, we couldn't know while we were working on it that it would become so celebrated, but from looking at the "dailies" (the scenes just filmed) we knew something quite marvelous was happening. Everything went smoothly; it was very well planned by Orson Welles, who was extremely dedicated. The only problem occurred when the New York-based presidents of the different motion picture companies became worried that because of Kane's resemblance to the powerful William Randolph Hearst it might have a damaging effect on the whole film industry, and therefore might have to be put on the shelf. I made my first trip to New York to show the picture to them. We made a few minor cuts, nothing significant, and the film was released.

I got the chance to direct some second units and pickup shots and began to think: this directing—I can do this. My first film as a director was a well-received "B" picture called *Curse of the Cat People*.

When Howard Hughes bought RKO in the late forties, I became apprehensive because of his dilettante reputation. I had been set by the previous regime to direct the prizefight story *The Set-Up*, and was anxious that I be able to do that and just get out, which I eventually did. I had been at RKO fifteen years. *The Set-Up* turned out to be a big steppingstone for me.

The industry was in flux then. Television was stealing our audiences, "B" production was stopped, box office dropped drastically as the studio system as we had known it deteriorated. Luckily, it worked out all right for me and some others because, free of studio contracts, we were able to work successfully as independents, which gave us more say and control over projects. The last studio contract I had was at MGM from 1954 to 1957. However, I had no problems with the studio system: I grew up with it, it helped me get ahead. But I have always enjoyed my freedom.

Luckily, too, I wasn't affected by the Communist witch-hunts in Hollywood during the late forties–early fifties. I was very much on the liberal side, though, and was involved with certain organizations that were under scrutiny, but evidently not sufficiently involved for anyone to come after me. I was certainly sympathetic to the "Hollywood Ten," the group of so-called "unfriendly" writers (primarily) who were jailed around 1950 for refusing to cooperate with the House Un-American Activities Committee which was investigating alleged Communist infiltration of the film business.

Personally, I think my own strongest decade was the sixties, when I produced and (with Jerome Robbins) directed *West Side Story* and produced and directed *The Sound of Music*. Both films were voted best pictures of their years by the Academy, and I was named best director. I collected four Oscars for them.

I was never one for the Hollywood glamour life. I was a working stiff. Frankly, I don't think there was any more glamour during the so-called "golden age" than now. It was just that more was made of it then by the gossip columnists like Louella Parsons and Hedda Hopper. Actually, going by the stories I've heard, I have always looked back on the 1920s as the really fabulous times in Hollywood. The glamorous restaurants and nightclubs on Hollywood Boulevard were all gone by the time I got there, or at least by the time I was able to take notice of them.

Today, you have to include as part of Hollywood the television series like *Dynasty* and *Dallas*, whose stars seem to be as written-about and glamorous as the stars of yore. And the rock stars out here get plenty of attention as well. So all this plus the still going movie industry make it seem pretty much like business as usual to me.

Of course, there have been changes. The moguls like Mayer, Zanuck and Cohn who were giants and loved the movies are gone, replaced by lawyers and agents who, while capable, don't have the passion for the industry that the pioneers had.

Leaving RKO years ago, I had some trepidation about what it would be like at the other studios. But being on the set with the crews and shooting the film remained the same. The crews were expert at all of the lots, so you felt at home. The people in the front office differ, and sometimes there are problems here, but the crews are always the good, solid common denominators.

Robert Wise
March 29, 1984

★ ★ ★

Duvall Truth
The attitude with a lot of people in Hollywood is that what they do in England is somehow better than what we do here. To tell you the truth, a lot of these English actors, I don't like.

Robert Duvall
Daily News, April 5, 1984

★ ★ ★

Gotta Dance
God, I was ugly. I said, there's no way I'm going to make it in Hollywood. You're out of your mind if you think you're going to go to Hollywood and do anything. All I really wanted to do was dance.

Goldie Hawn
Interview, April, 1984

★ ★ ★

Schlock Waves
Once the Hollywood producers know you need money, they'll throw you all the "schlock," the bad parts. In this way, they grab a name actor for nothing, and if you have nothing to fall back on, you're in trouble.

Ernest Borgnine
The Saturday Evening Post, April, 1984

★ ★ ★

Like Mother Like Son
I was born in Hollywood in 1958 and raised here, but even though my mother is a movie star, Eleanor Parker, I had none of the problems that some other young people in my position have growing up in this town. It was when I started to work that I began to hurt.

I admit it was a little different for me growing up than it was for my older sisters Susan and Sharon and my brother Rick. Their childhood years were my mother's busiest; she was a star at Warner Brothers and then MGM and working much of the time, opposite actors like Bogart, Gable and Flynn. There was a lot of pressure on my sisters and brother because they were the kids of a big, visible movie star. By the time I came along, she was still active but not quite as much as before, so while I may have gotten a little teasing from some kids because my mother was "a big movie star," that was about it.

To Mother, family and the home always came first. She's a very private person who rarely gives interviews, has never appeared on a TV talk show and was never big on Hollywood parties. She gave me a lot of attention, so I had the benefit of having her around a lot. Occasionally, too, I'd go to the studios to see her, although she has a rule about not having family around while she's shooting a scene. We had a very secure home life.

There's a vast difference between my mother and ELEANOR PARKER. Mother's not at all ostentatious; she's a no-frills person. I remember when I was a little boy she took me to see her in *The Sound of Music* and I had a hard time connecting that glamorous lady up there on the screen with Mom.

Her work gives me a sense of great pride. Hollywood is crazy and should be ashamed for not giving her more work today. It's very rough out here for mature actresses. They wouldn't have to be star parts—good supporting parts would be fine with her, I know.

Being Eleanor Parker's son never got me any parts, but it did get me an agent at age thirteen—hers. We still share him. You know what they say out here now—changing agents is like changing deck chairs on the Titanic. At fourteen I got the first job I ever interviewed for, a TV "pilot" by the creators of *M*A*S*H*. Then I did a play in Illinois called *Finishing Touches* that was a real family affair. Mother was starred, and I played her son. My stepfather, Raymond Hirsh, played her husband and my brother Rick and my sister Sharon also had parts. My big break came in a 1978 TV dramatic special called *A Death in Canaan*. It was a true story, and I had the lead, a teenager accused of murdering his mother.

My mother always said, "Hollywood can be heart-breaking." She got that right. After *Canaan*, which was such a success, I accepted the first feature film offer that came along, because on paper it looked very good. It was called *The Passage*, starring names like James Mason and Patricia Neal, and was to be filmed in France. I thought, "My role's not that hot but I can't pass all this up." It died. On top of that, the people behind Bette Midler's *The Rose* called to ask me to appear in that, but I was already on *The Passage* and had to pass on it. Frederic Forrest went on to play the role they wanted me for, winning an Academy Award nomination.

I was second choice for the role which won Timothy Hutton his Oscar in *Ordinary People*. I almost had it—I'm still not over losing this! Later, I was told that Robert Redford, the director, wanted Hutton because he reminded him of his own son.

So far, the movies I did get haven't been big hits. *Promises in the Dark*, with Marsha Mason, received good reviews but its downbeat story about a dying girl did not attract audiences.

It's so difficult for a young actor in Hollywood today. It's not like it was in my mother's era, when you were under contract to a studio and they saw to it that you worked. Today, you're on your own. When you go up for a role you're either too old or too young, too fat or too thin, unless somebody already has you in mind. Just getting the interviews for roles is tough— as is making sure that the agent doesn't lose sight of you.

I keep seeing films where I say to myself, "I could have done that part." Or I see films starring big hunky-type actors who can't act. Frustration is your constant companion in Hollywood, but when things all come together as they did in *A Death in Canaan* you know why you've chosen the profession.

Paul Clemens
May 4, 1984

State Fair (20th Century-Fox, 1945), Rodgers and Hammerstein's only original movie musical, had Dick Haymes, Fay Bainter, ravishing Jeanne Crain and Charles Winninger in the foreground.

Natalie Schafer and Lana Turner worked together several times, including *Keep Your Powder Dry* (MGM, 1945), a bit of fluff about the Women's Army Corps.

Photography Means Folsey

I began my career as a movie cameraman in New York in 1919.

Her Bridal Night, starring Alice Brady, was my first picture. It was full of double exposures because she played two parts, twin sisters. Since no optical system had been developed for double exposures as yet, they had to be done in camera. The original camerman quit the very first week—perhaps because of the double exposure problem. "I quit. I go to France. I raise violets," he said. So the director asked me if I could do it. I am nineteen years old—I can move the studio if needed! I jumped at the challenge, made all the double exposures he wanted, the picture was successful and I was on my way.

The industry was young and so was I; it was a great learning experience. With optical and special effects unheard of, we had to use the resources of the camera itself to give the director what he wanted. John Robertson, who directed many of the top-grossing pictures then, hired me for *The Enchanted Cottage*, starring May McAvoy, and during filming asked me if she could change right on camera from the ugly duckling in the story into the beautiful creature she actually was. I won't go into all the details of how I managed this except to say that I made use of a still camera in order to maintain her exact size and position when she stepped out of frame and then back in for the makeup change.

John was pleased with the results and asked me for help again in a sequence in *Dr. Jekyll and Mr. Hyde*, where John Barrymore made the change from Jekyll to Hyde. When Jack drank the volatile potion, he clutched his stomach, grimaced and dropped out of frame onto the floor. Under the camera he shoved a grotesque set of teeth into his mouth, chewed on some soap and then suddenly reappeared in my frame, foaming at the mouth, as the hideous, twisted, malevolent Hyde—scaring me half to death! (During those years, the cameraman stood behind the camera dutifully grinding out by hand every foot of film.)

Another lasting memory of the silent era was working with Billie Burke, who was then a beautiful young leading lady and as nice as she was beautiful. She used to like to stand behind the camera and grind out the slate numbers for me. Just before I left for Hollywood in the early 1920s (I would travel back and forth for a decade), Flo Ziegfeld, Billie's husband, called me and said that he and Billie wanted to do something for me to show their appreciation for the work I had done for her—and would I kindly accept an automobile! "I'd give you a Rolls-Royce," said Mr. Ziegfeld, "but we can't afford it." I explained that I was moving to the Coast, and he solved the matter by presenting me with a sizable check to cover the cost of a new car, plus a lovely gold inscribed cigarette case—which I still have.

I joined Metro-Goldwyn-Mayer in 1932 and stayed twenty-seven years. Working in Hollywood in the 1930s and 1940s was plain hard manual labor. We'd start out at seven or eight in the morning and finish around eight or nine at night, sometimes later. We worked every single Saturday and Saturday night, often until sunrise and then some. I remember doing four pictures in a row with no time off in between and overlapping one another—each picture running six weeks in shooting. It meant twenty-four weeks of uninterrupted toil with only Sunday intervening as a brief respite in which to catch up on one's sleep. Talk about wild Hollywood! Who had any time or energy left for it?! Work and sleep—that's all there was to it.

Eventually, the unions changed the picture and imposed penalties where they hurt, which in turn put an end to unreasonable hours. Thank God.

In the 1950s and 1960s, while the unions prevailed it was still hard work, made even more intense by necessity in order to accommodate the same shooting schedules into shorter work weeks.

Of all the directors I worked with, Rouben Mamoulian was outstanding, an extremely imaginative fellow who was way ahead of his time. I photographed *Applause* for him. In my opinion, the most important man on the set is still the director. I have always felt it was my responsibility to work closely with him and deliver to the screen the mood and quality he was pursuing.

I photographed all the big MGM stars, and most of them were fine people. I made many films with Joan Crawford. Ollie Marsh had photographed her before me. He was a nice man but lazy: he'd sit underneath the camera and whittle all day long. One day, Clarence Brown, the director, asked me to do a test of Crawford. I did and they liked it, so I began our association by photographing her in *Chained*—which co-starred Clark Gable, who was a fantastic human being with this great animal quality that exploded off the screen. The key to how to photograph Joan came while they were rehearsing a boat scene with her for *Chained*. Inadvertently, a light high up in the rafters came down and lit her face. She looked gorgeous. I said that's how we're going to shoot her. When she saw the film, she fell down—she hadn't looked that good in years. We used that philosophy of lighting from then on in all our films together throughout the 1930s.

There weren't many problems with the stars about how they looked. Robert Taylor was a very nice guy, the handsomest man in the world who surely didn't have to worry about his looks; but he had a rather thickish kind of neck, and if you didn't throw it in shadow he was very unhappy. But he was never difficult.

Once, when Bob and I were on location in Colorado for *Saddle the Wind*, we were sitting on the steps of an old ramshackle barn and he said to me, "Well, how do you like it here, George?" I told him that I liked it fine except for the fact that I had to leave for the location very early in the morning and got home too late at night to go to the grocery store and buy the fruits I loved. That night when I got home, there on the bed were five bags of fruit from Bob.

I didn't see much temperament, though Hedy Lamarr could be a pain—more out of laziness, I think. She'd come in at nine in the morning and I'd say, "Where are you going to be?" and she'd stand there a minute and say, "Oh, I'm so tired." Nine in the morning and she was tired already! She must have been a beautiful child who was spoiled by everyone and she just grew up that way.

Spencer Tracy was the best actor I ever saw. But he was a drunkard. Katharine Hepburn, who was very protective of him, kept feeding him chocolates. There was one little quirk about my working relationship with Tracy: I could never get out of his line of vision when he was acting. He wanted me the hell out of the way, because, he said, seeing me distracted him. But I had to watch the scene. No matter where I moved to, though, he'd find me.

I loved Kate. One morning when I was photographing *State of the Union*, with Tracy and Hepburn, Kate came on this large exterior set at 7:30 in her long khaki pants and babushka. I had set up my shaving utensils right there on the stage and was shaving. "Oh, my, aren't you ashamed?", she said, adding, "Oh, dear, I forgot to cut my toenails!" She sat right down there, took off her shoe and began to chew on her toenail just to embarrass me! She was something. You wanted to hug her.

Another great artist was Irene Dunne, with whom I worked on *A Guy Named Joe* and *The White Cliffs of Dover*. She was an absolutely charming, delightful lady. Films like *White Cliffs*—which was set in England but was actually filmed on Metro's back lot—were a great credit to MGM's wonderful scenic artist named George Gibson. He'd paint a background for a certain picture, and afterward they'd pack it up and put it away until another picture came up they could use it in. Sometimes you'd get a part on one of these backgrounds that was a little dark for the current picture, so I'd call George Gibson and with absolutely no ego he'd call five or six scenic artists, they'd touch it up and soon the background would be singing with light.

The Green Years was a favorite picture of mine. It was directed by Victor Saville, an Englishman who was unpopular in Hollywood because of a rumor—untrue—that he had made anti-American remarks. I don't mean to sound immodest, but Saville would see the rushes and exclaim, "When I say photography, I say Folsey!" The picture had an enchanting performance by little Dean Stockwell, who was one of the most beautiful, curly-haired children I've ever seen. His mother had a restaurant in Culver City where some of us used to go to eat and talk. I remember she served pizza, which at that time in the mid-1940s I'd never heard of before.

I thought *Green Dolphin Street*, also directed by Saville, was a damn good show, too. It was the first time that I used reflected light to light a scene. I'd always looked at the great paintings and wanted to get the kind of light they had. On this picture, I got the idea to put big silks up and scattered the light around them. It starred Lana Turner, who, while not the greatest actress, did a good job, and she was very pretty. When I photographed Lana and Joan Blondell some years earlier in *Two Girls on Broadway*, Joan complained that I hadn't made her look as good as Lana. Now I have nothing against Joan, but who the hell could?! *God* couldn't!

Meet Me in St. Louis was a pet picture of mine, for the costumes and the colorful early 1900s period. And, of course, for Judy Garland. She was the greatest actress, singer and dancer of them all; she could do everything perfectly. Unfortunately, even as early as *St. Louis*, which was begun in 1943, she was showing signs of being troubled. There were many days when I would come on the stage and my electrical crew would say, ''Go play golf. She's not here.'' So we'd quit for the day and I'd play golf.

The Clock, with Judy again and Robert Walker, was started by director Fred Zinnemann. But Judy liked the way Vincente Minnelli had directed her in *Meet Me in St. Louis* and was going with him then, so she wanted him to direct the film. He replaced Fred. Like Judy, Robert Walker had problems, too: I don't think he ever got over his ex-wife, Jennifer Jones. He died tragically young five or six years later. But our relationship was very pleasant. When lunchtime came, those of us who had been on our feet for hours and didn't feel like walking here or there ate right on the set. One day Walker came by while I was eating and said, ''I see you're a hypochondriac.''

''Why do you say that?'', I asked.

''Because you eat everything that's good for you,'' he answered—I was in the habit of eating fruit and other goodies from my garden. I asked him if he'd like Mrs. Folsey to make him a similar lunch. He said sure, so the next day I brought him a very healthy lunch. He sent a nice thank-you note to my wife.

I also photographed Judy's ''Madame Crematon'' number from *Ziegfeld Follies*, as well as that picture's ''Limehouse Blues'' and ''This Heart of Mine'' segments danced by Fred Astaire and Lucille Bremer. In my unbiased opinion, these three musical numbers are among the best ever created for a movie.

My favorite film, however, is *Seven Brides for Seven Brothers*, a fabulous musical. It was comprised mainly of outdoor scenes, almost all of which were shot on stage indoors—day, night, winter, summer, spring. It was a big challenge to make it all look believable, but I had a great camera crew. We shot almost all of it simultaneously in the then new wide screen process called CinemaScope and in what we called ''poor man's CinemaScope.'' (The latter was a wide effect achieved without getting the anamorphic CinemaScope lens but simply by cutting off the top and the bottom of the picture and printing the section in the middle.) The famous director George Stevens said, ''CinemaScope is very good for photographing snakes, but not people,'' and he was right.

I got one of my thirteen Academy Award nominations for *Seven Brides*, but *Three Coins in the Fountain* won that year (1954). It was the only time a cameraman's award was lost to a song.

MGM was called ''the Cadillac of the Hollywood Studios.'' Why? Because of the great stars, great directors, great writers, a wonderful art department, wonderful crews in all departments—all very professional people. Also, Metro had the best back lot in the business for serving up its world to the movie fans. And I don't discount for one second the

Humphrey Bogart (right) perfectly embodied Raymond Chandler's sardonic gumshoe Philip Marlowe in *The Big Sleep* (Warner Brothers, 1946), with Lauren Bacall (Mrs. Bogart) and Paul Webber.

The Jolson Story (Columbia, 1946) was a surprise smash, with Evelyn Keyes as Mrs. Al Jolson, Larry Parks as the great entertainer and Jolson's own electrifying voice belting out the songs on the soundtrack.

contribution of our boss, Louis B. Mayer. He was the pulse of the whole studio; he knew the public and gave them what they wanted in the way of great musicals, comedies and dramas.

George J. Folsey
June 2, 1984

★ ★ ★

Epic Actor
I've got to go back to Hollywood and knock off an epic, then I'm coming back to Broadway and see if I can still act.

Spencer Tracy
Hot Times, 1984

★ ★ ★

Good Golly Miss Dolly
I just ain't going to take no s--- off of nobody. I know who I am. Hollywood ain't gonna give me no trouble. If they come to me and offer me big money, it's because they know who I am. They're not fools. But what's even better, I ain't either.

Dolly Parton
People, July 9, 1984

★ ★ ★

Peerage Pressure
To Richard Burton in the 1950s:
    If you want to be a star, go to Hollywood. But if you want to be an actor, stay here in England.

Laurence Olivier
The Hollywood Reporter, August 10, 1984

★ ★ ★

Salt Mine
When I enter the studios—be it in Hollywood or in London—and the heavy doors close behind me, there is no difference. A salt mine is a salt mine.

Alfred Hitchcock
Hitchcock, 1984

Based on Marjorie Kinnan Rawlings' novel about backwoods farmers in Florida, *The Yearling* (MGM, 1946) was beautifully filmed with Gregory Peck, Claude Jarman, Jr. (who won an Oscar as outstanding child actor) and Jane Wyman.

LIVING

Seeing is Disbelieving
Hollywood is a town that has to be seen to be disbelieved.

Walter Winchell
The 1930s

★ ★ ★

Looking Back
I looked back at Hollywood as I left on a plane trip. Now you would be surprised at Hollywood if you looked at it from both sides. As you come up to it and its people, you see the movie side, all the pain and glitter and make-up and make-believe houses; but as you look back at it, why a lot of those houses have backs to 'em, and people live in 'em, and they don't have any make-up and they eat and sleep and fret and worry about work and about their children and everything just like any other place. But you got to look back to see it.

Will Rogers
1932

★ ★ ★

The Hardest Things
The two hardest things I've had to learn in Hollywood are how to smile and how to talk about myself.

Jean Harlow
Screen Book, the 1930s

★ ★ ★

No Wastrels
Oliver (Hardy) and I have lived apart from the rest of the movie colony in Hollywood because the hardships of those lean years made too deep an impression on us to let us be wastrels now.

Stan Laurel
Photoplay, June, 1933

★ ★ ★

Won't Concede
Hollywood is a carnival—where there are no concessions.

Wilson Mizner
The 1930s

Hollywood Hiatus
How can a motion picture reflect real life when it is made by people who are living artificial lives? The only thing to do is to get a better perspective. I believe that any star will make better pictures if she will take six months of each year away from Hollywood.

Miriam Hopkins
1934

★ ★ ★

Legend Stays Home
Hollywood is the loneliest place I have ever lived in. Never in my life have I been so lonely nor stayed home so much. When I first came, I did not think I could stand it—I would not have stood it if I had not had my work.

Marlene Dietrich
Screen Book, the 1930s

★ ★ ★

Breathing Space
Into the community that lives and thinks film pictures I arrived, prepared to work very hard to succeed. I liked Hollywood. I like breathing space. I like green things growing around me. There isn't the feeling here of millions of people huddled together.

Ronald Colman
Film Pictorial Annual, 1935

★ ★ ★

Pack of Jackals
Hollywood is a dreary industrial town controlled by hoodlums of enormous wealth, the ethereal sense of a pack of jackals, and taste so degraded that it befouled everything it touched.

S.J. Perelman
The 1930s

★ ★ ★

Boring Boys
I think all the boys in Hollywood are terrific bores. If I couldn't stand my own company, I'd be the unhappiest girl in the world, because I'm alone morning, noon and night.

Frances Farmer
1935

★ ★ ★

Too Much Competition
You don't have real friends in Hollywood, there's too much competition.

Joan Blondell
The 1930s

Sans Fans

Hollywood? Don't ask me. All that I know about it I pick up from the syndicated columns. I'm a homebody and never go anywhere. You can check on that easily enough by referring to the film magazines where my name or photograph hardly ever appears.

Paul Muni
The 1930s

★ ★ ★

All Aboard

Hollywood is like an excursion boat and all my friends are on it.

Eric Blore
Photoplay, May, 1938

★ ★ ★

Late Marzipan

In Hollywood, everybody's home seems to be a kind of personal wish-fulfillment. The buildings are in the Spanish manner, the New England or English farmhouse style, the Tudor colonial or in what Charles (Laughton) and I call Late Marzipan. Naturally there are lovely houses, but on the whole the designs are not in harmony with each other. Only a few people seem to have taken a peep at the blue sky and decided how life should be lived underneath it. One feels it is all rather like a film set, or perhaps made of icing sugar.

Elsa Lanchester
Charles Laughton and I, 1938

★ ★ ★

Sewer Service

Hollywood is a sewer with service from the Ritz Carlton.

Wilson Mizner
The 1930s

★ ★ ★

Wives Give Support

I could never have caught on to Hollywood without my wife. I wonder how many of us here in Hollywood would be where we are without the help of some woman who loves us. Think of the tremendous influence Dixie Lee Crosby has had on Bing. Of the vast importance of Bella Muni to her extremely talented and sensitive husband, Paul Muni. There are dozens of cases—and you don't have to stop in Hollywood, of course.

Basil Rathbone
Photoplay, August, 1938

Dressed to Kill (Universal, 1946), with Basil Rathbone and Patricia Morison, was the final chapter in Rathbone's series of Sherlock Holmes features.

Alan Napier and Geraldine Fitzgerald were among the principals in *Three Strangers* (Warner Brothers, 1946), an offbeat melodrama written by John Huston and Howard Koch.

Rich, Full Lives
Perhaps in our hurried lives in Hollywood, where careers stretch over a span of but a few years and we try to juggle fame and popularity on the tips of our noses, we are too busy expressing life to live it. But if this is the price we have to pay, it is certainly worth it. For our lives are rich and full in their own way.

Norma Shearer
New York Journal-American, August 13, 1938

★ ★ ★

Unsound Reasoning
All over Hollywood they are continually advising me, "Oh, you mustn't say *that*. That'll get you in a lot of trouble," when I remark that some picture or director or writer or producer is no good. I don't get it. If he or it isn't any good, why can't you say so? If more people would mention it, pretty soon it might have some effect. This local idea that anyone making a thousand dollars a week is sacred and beyond the realm of criticism never strikes me as particularly sound reasoning.

Humphrey Bogart
Photoplay, September, 1938

★ ★ ★

Biggest Small Town
Hollywood is the biggest small town in existence. It is continually conniving ways and means through gossip and reports to break up a romantic friendship between two people. It has never left off trying to sever my going with Cary (Grant).

Phyllis Brooks
Movie Mirror, December, 1938

★ ★ ★

Simply Home
There is more brilliance, talent, beauty, sex AND ambition per square inch in Hollywood than I suppose in any other city in the world. I say "I suppose" because frankly, I don't know much about people living outside of Hollywood. I once took a trip to Europe and at another time went to Honolulu, and that's all the traveling I've done. I remember people in Europe often asked me, "Is Hollywood as bad as they say it is?" I told them I didn't know. I couldn't tell if Hollywood is worse than other towns, because what is Hollywood to others, is simply a home town for me. I grew up here.

Loretta Young
Silver Screen, July, 1939

Astonishing Challenge

I wanted adventure, and that's why I wanted to be in pictures. I saw that Hollywood was an unpredictable place, and that was swell. I want to be surprised. I couldn't stand anything cut-and-dried. Uncertainty is a challenge! That's why I've never been disillusioned about Hollywood. I counted on it being the most impulsive, astonishing place in the world.

Joel McCrea
Silver Screen, November, 1939

Mouthing Off

I've cracked Hollywood wide open, and you can tell the boys and girls that this fame isn't all it's cracked up to be—not by a long shot. Maybe I've made quite a bit of money, and maybe I've saved it—but the point really is that so many things have happened besides getting on a payroll that it hasn't been any fun.

Martha Raye
Circa 1940

Doug's Druthers

I like Hollywood, but there are other places I like every bit as well and some much more. If I had my "druthers," I'd like to live three months here, three in New York, three abroad and three in Virginia, my wife's home.

Douglas Fairbanks, Jr.
Modern Screen, May, 1940

Famous Last Words

Too many Hollywood marriages have smashed up because the husbands were Mr. Joan Fontaine. That will never happen in our marriage because I am, 100 per cent, Mrs. Brian Aherne.

Joan Fontaine
Movie Mirror, September, 1940

Can't Go On

Hollywood is dangerous. It can warp your point of view so easily. I wonder how players and writers and directors can go on out there, year after year, and expect to keep their balance. They can't, of course.

Paul Muni
American Theatre Magazine, 1940

Madness Required
Hollywood is goofy, but I like it. If you weren't a bit mad you wouldn't be there.

Charles Laughton
Hollywood, January, 1941

Pictures and Pews
Religion plays a bigger part in Hollywood that most people realize. I'd be willing to vouch that at least fifty per cent of our Hollywood population are regular churchgoers.

Irene Dunne
1942

Look, It's Jack Benny
I'm always afraid I'll wake up at twelve o'clock in Hollywood and find the place turned back into a pumpkin! I went to the Brown Derby while there. It's a popular café where people from Iowa mistake each other for movie stars.

Fred Allen
Liberty, February 28, 1942

That "Thing"
The Hollywood "graveyard" is studded with the headstones of men who were handsome and talented, and girls who were pretty and gifted. Somehow, they didn't have that "thing."

Robert Taylor
Modern Screen, the 1940s

Rara Avis
Next to privacy, the rarest thing in Hollywood is a wedding anniversary.

Gene Fowler
Silver Screen, January, 1943

★ ★ ★

Framed
I came here with a fine contract, was put to work immediately, and became a star in my very first picture. That should have made me very happy. But it didn't. It brought about the sort of life I wasn't prepared for, and I was miserable and confused. Success in Hollywood was not what I thought it would be. I am a simple person and love the quiet life. But I soon found out I was considered public property. I wasn't emotionally equipped for it. It was like having a picture frame put around me so that everyone could stare at me.

Luise Rainer
Motion Picture, July, 1943

Three Little Girls in Blue (20th Century-Fox, 1946) boasted tuneful songs by Mack Gordon and Josef Myrow plus the sprightly title leads, Vera–Ellen, June Haver and Vivian Blaine.

Rita Hayworth was at her alluring peak as the amoral *Gilda* (Columbia, 1946), singing ''Put the Blame on Mame'' and beguiling Steven Geray.

Normal Family Life

I like making films because in Hollywood I can live a normal family life. I can get up early, finish at the studio early and get home. I have a three-year-old daughter and I'm crazy about her. I just can't sleep late. A man's blood follows the day—it rises with the sun and sets with it. Working in pictures enables a man to follow his energy. But when you're working in a play, you start working when most other people are relaxing. You have to get up a noon-day vitality at night-time. And an actor cannot hold an audience without vitality.

Henry Daniell
Motion Picture, March, 1944

Put the Blame on L.A.

If this town ever gets down on me, it has only itself to blame, because it was Hollywood that looked me up, not the other way 'round.

Ann Sheridan
July 14, 1944

Fog, Slacks Must Go

Question: What don't you like about Hollywood?

Answer: The occasional high fogs that wash out the bridges. And the purple slacks you see sometimes on women who have no right to wear them.

Randolph Scott
Motion Picture, August, 1944

★ ★ ★

First Year Blues

I arrived in Hollywood with this wonderful contract. They had built this terrific publicity before I got here. And that was all I did for a year, just nothing *but* publicity. They took pictures, galleries of pictures, they arranged interviews, they partied and dined me. But no film roles. I finally could not look at my thumbs twiddling any longer. In addition, there was the war and I couldn't bring my little boy over, as I had planned. I had, then, a nervous breakdown. I asked for my release from the studio. They were depressingly willing. I then set out for Washington to try to straighten out my immigration permit which, I discovered, allowed me to work for RKO and no one else. A body blow. No work done, money running low, no work possible. I could have gone home (Sweden). My pride would not permit. That was a dreadful experience, my first year in Hollywood.

Signe Hasso
Silver Screen, September, 1944

Warm Welcome

There isn't an actress in the world, I am sure, who doesn't secretly hope sometime to find welcome and success in Hollywood. I did find a welcome and kindness at every hand.

Ann Richards
Lion's Roar, 1944

★ ★ ★

Untouched by War

It was a painful thing to come home to Hollywood, for it's still largely untouched by any of the things going on in Europe. Hollywood stands blessedly in the middle of a productive area, where foodstuffs are plentiful. Film-making goes on very much as usual. They make war films and go to see them, but still they don't realize.

Ann Dvorak
The Baltimore Sun, October 29, 1944

★ ★ ★

Plugging Away

Sure I'd like to click and become a box office tornado, but if I don't, I've got no kick coming. Personally, I like Hollywood, and I like pictures. But that doesn't mean I have any illusions about either. The way I look at it, when my time comes I'll know it. And until it comes, I'll keep on plugging.

Marjorie Reynolds
Screen Stars, January, 1945

★ ★ ★

Marriages Wrecked

Sometimes I wonder if I should give up the screen when I marry. Looking around, it seems that Hollywood marriages are wrecked when the wife is more prominent than the husband, or when her paycheck is bigger than his.

Shirley Temple
Movieland, January, 1945

★ ★ ★

Prop Smiles

Most of the girls in Hollywood overdo their eagerness to please by resorting to a prop smile. How men hate that! There is nothing more annoying or discouraging to a man in the process of unloading his thoughts than the sight of an on-again-off-again artificial smile. A girl who can't smile naturally, pleasantly and sometimes fondly should find other means to convey her reactions.

Judy Garland
Motion Picture, March, 1945

Tight Squeeze

All the sincerity in Hollywood you can stuff in a flea's navel and still have room to conceal four caraway seeds and an agent's heart.

Fred Allen
The 1940s

★ ★ ★

Ideal Climate—If

Question: Do you like the Hollywood climate?
Answer: It's ideal—if you're an orange.

Fred Allen
Motion Picture, May, 1945

★ ★ ★

Ignorance Bliss

I think probably the only man who can be happy all the time under contract to a movie studio is the dumb one, the really dumb one who signs up to act for five years and who does exactly that without a care or worry about the sort of thing that's handed him. There are some people like that in pictures and I think they are the only ones who have licked the problem of being happy, though in Hollywood.

Spencer Tracy
1945

★ ★ ★

The Happier Time

In New York money was something you bought a pair of shoes with. Out here it's an entirely different matter. In Hollywood money means superficialities, like excellent cars and a house that you like to show to people. It means security and a hedge against all the tough things that could happen to you again. Yet I was pretty happy in New York. Maybe happier than I'll ever be again.

Robert Walker
Screenland, July, 1945

★ ★ ★

The Good Earth

There's nothing the matter with Hollywood that a good earthquake couldn't cure.

Moss Hart
Silver Screen, August, 1945

Out of the Past (RKO, 1947), a complex crime drama starring Robert Mitchum and Jane Greer under Jacques Tourneur's direction, has acquired a cult following.

Dane Clark and Ida Lupino were touching in *Deep Valley* (Warner Brothers, 1947), the romance of a stammering farm girl and an escaped convict.

Loose "Darlings"
Question: What don't you like about Hollywood?

Answer: All those pink and yellow stucco houses, the boys with wavy locks who dash around in purple roadsters the length of a yacht and the loose use of the words "darling" and "terrific."

Dane Clark
Motion Picture, November, 1945

Bachelor in Paradise
I have been married, but if you wonder what I think of marriage in Hollywood—well, I am a bachelor. Doesn't that answer your question?

Fritz Lang
Movieland, December, 1945

Glamour Perishable
Hollywood glamour is a highly perishable coating which disappears after the first wash. Those who need glamour the most are the beginners and the has-beens.

Gary Cooper
Motion Picture, January, 1946

Race a Challenge
My first impressions of Hollywood? Too many people with too much money. Too many stars eating with their gloves on. What I like about it is the business challenge, the sharp race to get ahead.

Maria Montez
Motion Picture, January, 1946

Glad to be Back
I missed Hollywood (while in the Coast Guard). I love the town, my job, the people in it, even the occasional phoniness, and I'm glad to be back.

Victor Mature
Motion Picture, April, 1946

Scarlet Starlet
In Hollywood, starlet is the name for any woman under thirty not actively employed in a brothel.

Ben Hecht
The 1940s

Spoiled en Route

The old Hollywood idea is that pictures, when they leave here in the can, are all Academy Aware winners. When they turn out to be flops, the "know-it-alls" of the business say something happened to it en route to New York, probably around Kansas City. When I got used to it, I had to laugh.

Gregory Peck
Silver Screen, November, 1946

★ ★ ★

Came the Dawn

I decided I needed Hollywood when I realized Jimmy Stewart played to more people a week than I had done in two years (on the stage in *The Philadelphia Story*).

Van Heflin
Photoplay, January, 1947

★ ★ ★

Tinsel Town Vapors

When I first came to Hollywood, they gave me advice. They told me to be aggressive. Every time I tried to be aggressive, I got so tired folks had to find me arm chairs and bring me hot tea.

Mary Anderson
Screen Stars, February, 1947

★ ★ ★

First Base

You can be a talented actress, pretty as a picture and intelligent to boot, but if you don't play the old Hollywood game the right way, you won't get to first base on the road up. Believe me, I know! I've seen so many wonderful actresses in this town who were lost in the shuffle simply because they didn't know the ropes. Hollywood is full of taboos, and it's worth your career to buck any of them.

Joan Leslie
Screenland, February, 1947

★ ★ ★

Mildred Fierce

I know how witchy some women can be—and some of the worst specimens are right here in Hollywood. Hollywood is the mecca for some of the most beautiful girls in America. Unfortunately, there are about 200,000 more women than men in Hollywood. Because of that, most of the men in Hollywood are spoiled—and it's the women who do the spoiling. It's also true that some of the girls, in their eagerness to attach a male, will stop at nothing. Particularly they won't stop because the male is already married or believed to be in love with another woman.

Joan Crawford
Screen Stars, March, 1947

Goldfish Bowl

Sure, there's glamour in Hollywood, some of it very real and glittering and a lot of it very unreal and glittering. I'd be an absolute square if I didn't see that this town has more color, more excitement and more ambition than any other community on earth. When you click, even in three-minute bits, you are in the spotlight, you do begin swimming around in the eternal goldfish bowl.

Guy Madison
Photoplay, March, 1947

★ ★ ★

Female Prey

Hollywood women, especially, seem to be prey to men who want something—glamour, or publicity, or professional advancement.

Esther Williams
Photoplay, March, 1947

★ ★ ★

Cynical City

I've encountered much cynicism in Hollywood. I don't like it. Cynical criticism of myself or anyone else hurts me. I have a good sense of humor, so joking criticism, intelligent comment or kidding is all right. There's too much of the mean brand. I have learned how much ruthlessness is here.

Guy Madison
Screenland, June, 1947

★ ★ ★

Marital Misconceptions

I think divorces here generally are the result of a false sense of values: too often in Hollywood people enter into marriage with the wrong idea in mind. Perhaps they put their careers first, or perhaps they base their marriages on financial or physical attractions, or—as often happens—they get married with the idea that if it doesn't work out, there's something can be done about it. In any event, the marriage is a secondary consideration.

Rosalind Russell
Movieland, June, 1947

★ ★ ★

He Who Vegetates

Hollywood has everything that God has to offer. Beautiful surroundings and a beautiful climate. In Hollywood there are no daily obstacles such as people everywhere else in the world have—the obstacles of bad weather, difficult transportation to work, sharp changes of season. Hollywood also permits you to live too comfortably. With the result that in Hollywood one vegetates.

George Sanders
Photoplay, July, 1947

The Voice of the Turtle (Warner Brothers, 1947), from the long-running stage comedy by John van Druten, was among the best films of Ronald Reagan who co-starred with delightful Eleanor Parker.

Miracle on 34th Street (20th Century-Fox, 1947), the holiday staple about a man (Edmund Gwenn) who claimed to be Santa Claus, was well acted by Natalie Wood, John Payne and especially Gwenn, who won the supporting actor Oscar.

No Dividing Line

I don't think Hollywood morals are different. It's just that they get so much publicity that the code seems franker. Now, I used to live in Joplin, Missouri, and other small towns, and I don't see any difference. After all, there's no dividing line in morals. You don't pick out Los Angeles and say, "This is where you get moral," and then arrive in Hollywood and say, "And now let's get immoral."

Bob Cummings
Screenland, August, 1947

Ain't Misbehavin'

A lot of people misbehave in Hollywood, I admit, and a lot of them get caught at it, but think of the millions of people outside Hollywood who act badly but are never noticed. Really, I do get so mad at this fervent desire to slap Hollywood—*especially* when the same stars in this town are always called upon whenever there's a cause to be pushed. The way some of our big names helped in the unfortunate Texas City disaster is an example. Yet it still remains more fashionable to kick us than to give us a pat on the back.

Linda Darnell
Screenland, August, 1947

Woods Full

Hollywood is full of over-ambitious girls—they're around every corner. And phony girls. The woods are full of phonies.

Peter Lawford
Photoplay, August, 1947

New Perspective

I was the shy, studious, "arty" type as I grew up—and kept on habitually making a mountain out of mixing with strangers in Hollywood. I learned from my Red Cross work (in Washington during World War II) that I'd not only deceived myself, but that Hollywood had pampered me. Whenever I'd visited New York the studio had met me with a flanking bodyguard of three to seven men. Everything I did had to be a production I fancied, because the studio said so. Do you know what that had done for me? It had multiplied my self-consciousness so I was even afraid to stop and look at people. The Red Cross job broke down the barrier Hollywood puts around us out here, unless we get away for a perspective.

Myrna Loy
Screenland, September, 1947

Pastel People
There are too many pastel people—pastel characters—in Hollywood. They don't know how to portray a character because they don't know people. Some of them are just busy little people studying their lines. If they learned more about life, about people, about psychology, about acting and timing, their characterizations would be more believable. Pastel people can ruin a picture.

Robert Mitchum
Photoplay, September, 1947

Jean and Howard
He's (Howard Hughes) the only man I date in town. But I have no intention of marrying now. I just don't understand Hollywood. If a girl isn't married, everyone tries to get her marrried, and if she is, everyone tries to get her divorced.

Jean Peters
Screenland, October, 1947

False Impressions
Hollywood: A place where you spend more than you make, on things you don't need, to impress people you don't like.

Ken Murray
The 1940s

Frightening Sight
My only frightening experience in Hollywood was seeing myself on the screen. I look just like I look.

Henry Morgan
Photoplay, April, 1948

Manana Country
I like living both in New York and Hollywood, because I feel that if I stayed here (in Hollywood) I'd get in a rut. Southern California is a vacation land, a *manana* country. I used to spend my time between pictures sun-bathing, but how much sun-bathing can you get!

Gene Tierney
Screen Guide, July, 1948

Home Boy

Sometimes, you get periods out in Hollywood when you are terribly discouraged. You think it would be best to give it all up and go back home. Go back, and buy the folks a better house, maybe build one for yourself on a lot of acres and lead the sort of life that was yours to start with. Maybe a girl will turn up who belongs to that life. Maybe not. That's what you *think*. But you never do anything about it.

James Stewart
Modern Screen, January, 1949

★ ★ ★

An Education

I'm not even sure Hollywood as such exists. It's a name tied to it like an old hat. It's a dream world, a fairy story in many ways—and often not a very nice fairy story, mainly because so many have made fun of it. Yet, Hollywood is primarily a place to me made up of the people I love and the work I love. It has taught me all I know. It has given me everything I have—the good and the bad. We in this business are very lucky, for what we don't know at first is taught to us free of charge. If we have to dance in a film or if we have to speak French in a scene and we can't do either, we're given lessons. Hollywood can be a great education.

Joan Crawford
Screenland, May, 1949

★ ★ ★

Gender Bender

Ever since they found out that Lassie was a boy, the public has believed the worst about Hollywood.

Groucho Marx
Modern Screen, May, 1949

★ ★ ★

Going His Way

I prefer living in New York instead of Hollywood. Out there you start out with your own ideas but then you find yourself going the next guy's way. Before you know it you don't know what you think or want, or what you believe in.

Montgomery Clift
Screen Guide, June, 1949

★ ★ ★

Journey's End

When I came (to Hollywood) I had a Pomeranian dog and a white canary that had traveled with me on the road all the time. They stood the rigors of that kind of life but couldn't take Hollywood. They died shortly after I came here.

Vera-Ellen
Screenland, September, 1949

A tribute to the Variety Clubs charity, *Variety Girl* (Paramount, 1947) had a star-packed cast: 1. William Bendix. 2. Howard da Silva. 3. Macdonald Carey. 4. Barry Fitzgerald. 5. Cecil Kellaway. 6. Marilyn Gray. 7. Sterling Hayden. 8. Catherine Craig. 9. George Reeves. 10. William Demarest. 11. Richard Webb. 12. Johnny Coy. 13. Rae Patterson. 14. Roger Dann. 15. Billy DeWolfe. 16. Renée Randall. 17. Dorothy Barrett. 18. June Harris. 19. Patric Knowles. 20. Mavis Murray. 21. John Lund. 22. Mikhail Rasumny. 23. Frank Faylen. 24. Arleen Whelan. 25. Virginia Field. 26. Burt Lancaster. 27. Lizabeth Scott. 28. Bob Hope. 29. Olga San Juan. 30. Mary Hatcher. 31. Bing Crosby. 32. Janet Thomas. 33. Gary Cooper. 34. Dorothy Lamour. 35. Joan Caulfield. 36. William Holden. 37. Sonny Tufts. 38. Sally Rawlinson. 39. Alan Ladd. 40. Veronica Lake. 41. Lucille Barkley. 42. Nanette Parks. 43. Wanda Hendrix. 44. Mona Freeman. 45. Stanley Clements. 46. Andra Verne. 47. Gail Russell. 48. Pat White.

Wonderful News

They brushed me off in Hollywood. It's now rather amazing how people act since I opened in *Kiss Me, Kate*. People who wouldn't give me the time of day now come up to my manager and say, "Isn't it wonderful what's happened to Pat?"

Patricia Morison
1949

★ ★ ★

Quick Study

In forty-eight hours after I arrive in New York (from Europe) I learn not to swallow chewing gum. The second thing I noticed about America is that everybody in Hollywood is called "darling."

Michael Curtiz
Hollywood Without Makeup, 1949

★ ★ ★

Double Exposure

I was terribly afraid of exposing myself to heartbreak in Hollywood. Romances continually crash about you here, and that makes naturally shy persons doubly wary. I was terrified by the notion that something might go wrong as a penalty for daring to love someone as wonderful as Guy (Madison).

Gail Russell
Silver Screen, February, 1950

★ ★ ★

Today is Brief

You know, age has been abolished in Hollywood. Look at Marlene Dietrich, Gloria Swanson, Joan Bennett—all grandmothers, and not trying to hide it. Bette Davis, Joan Crawford, Claudette Colbert are not bemoaning their years, either. Why should they? None of us is lingering in the past. We know that yesterday is gone, and that today is brief.

Barbara Stanwyck
Movieland, April, 1950

★ ★ ★

Healthy Type

By French standards, I'm really too thin. In Hollywood, they want everybody to look downright meager. Why, I visited the Louvre Museum here (in France) and saw some of the most beautiful women in the world. All those women were much fatter than I.

Deanna Durbin
January 27, 1951

Less Cattiness

I know there are catty and vicious women, but among the girls and women I know in Hollywood there is less cattiness, less viciousness than I've known to exist in small towns. If women are busy and secure they have neither time nor inclination to gossip and my friends and acquaintances here are busy and secure.

Ava Gardner
Silver Screen, March, 1951

★ ★ ★

Good and Colossal

Nothing is just good in Hollywood. It's either colossal, terrific or stupendous. The enthusiasm and high gear sales talk goes on with everything, and it wouldn't be bad—except that almost no one means it. People come up to you and grab you and squeeze you and kiss you. They say, "Oh, darling, it's so good to see you," and, hell, they don't care if they ever see you, really. You get so you can't believe what people say. It's a make-believe world.

Audie Murphy
Motion Picture, June, 1951

★ ★ ★

Privacy Possible

There are over 500 correspondents writing about us in Hollywood. That must mean there is a lot of public interest in stars, how they live, what they think, what they do. Such minute attention to a group of people does make it difficult to maintain any degree of privacy, I admit, but I have found that even with this, a star's book is only as open as he permits it to be.

Gregory Peck
Silver Screen, June, 1951

★ ★ ★

Considering Candidates

Getting dates is no problem, but finding a suitable husband is something else again. In Hollywood your vista is sort of limited. More than in most businesses, you think, live, breathe and eat your career. Most people become very intense about it and somehow you feel that the man you choose for your husband must share this enthusiasm for show business, or it'll be no go. In finding a husband most girls in the movie industry are limited—since they gravitate naturally to men in the industry and almost automatically eliminate all others from consideration.

Lizabeth Scott
Motion Picture, June, 1951

Homeseek

In a letter from Paris to her American agent only weeks before her sudden death, Maria Montez wrote:

I am homesick for Hollywood, and very anxious to return to do a film there. I need very much to shoot a film there and get some Hollywood publicity, Now I am without any plans, but frankly what I want is to go back for a while to America.

Maria Montez
July, 1951

Divorced from Reality

Hollywood is wronged by the fact that rapes, illicit love and divorce within its bounds are front-page material while 50th wedding anniversaries are inside (the paper) or not used. Our divorce rate is lower than that of Bangor, Maine, but how many people know that?

Barry Sullivan
November 12, 1951

Questionable Associates

An associate producer is the only guy in Hollywood who will associate with a producer.

Fred Allen
No People Like Show People, 1951

She's Had It!

I've had it! All the glitter-trappings of Hollywood, I mean. The huge house, complete with enormous swimming pool, life against a fabulous background—just as you have read about and imagined it . . . And as for the swimming pool, the super-symbol of Hollywood success, I think that it is the thing we have "had" most thoroughly of all!

Jan Sterling
Screenland, April, 1952

People Like Sets

Hollywood's a funny place. I don't know whether I like it or not. The people are very strange. They all seem to have fronts and no backs. They're just like the sets.

Brandon de Wilde
Motion Picture, April, 1953

Danny Kaye and Virginia Mayo co-starred in the lush elaboration of James Thurber's droll short story about a daydreaming young man, *The Secret Life of Walter Mitty* (RKO, 1947).

Cary Grant played an angel and Loretta Young and Monty Woolley mere mortals in *The Bishop's Wife* (RKO, 1947).

Oil and Water

In my book glamour and home cooking just won't mix—not in Hollywood. (And I can cook when I have to.) I don't know who first started mixing the two, but whoever did made the mistake of his lifetime. Even my two boys, Tim and Gregory, have their own ideas about this Hollywood of ours: they expect their mother to be the Movie Star, even on Sundays. I tried to explain to them once, when they caught me without any make-up, that each morning of the week I spend two hours or so "getting beautiful" for pictures, and that on Sunday I like to rest. But I'm afraid my explanation didn't go over very well with Tim and Greg; they don't like gingham aprons, either.

Susan Hayward
Motion Picture, the 1950s

★ ★ ★

Dollars and Scents

Hollywood smells like a laundry. The beautiful vegetables taste as if they were raised in trunks, and at those wonderful supermarkets you find that the vegetables are all wax. The flowers out there smell like dirty old dollar bills. Sure, you make money writing on the Coast, and God knows you earn it, but that money is like so much compressed snow. It goes so fast it melts in your hand.

Dorothy Parker
New York World-Telegram and Sun, 1953

★ ★ ★

Beautiful Music

We (husband Fred Karger) knew each other casually. It's funny about Hollywood. You can know someone for years, see them at parties, meet them at previews. Then suddenly your work throws you together and you begin to discover that you have so many things in common. In our case, it was music.

Jane Wyman
Movie Play, November, 1953

★ ★ ★

Going Hollywood

As for those who fall by the wayside, don't blame Hollywood. No one *goes* Hollywood—they were that way before they came here. Hollywood just exposed it.

Ronald Reagan
Variety, January 6, 1954

William Powell, Myrna Loy, Keenan Wynn and Clinton Sundberg appeared in *Song of the Thin Man* (MGM, 1947), the last of six films in the popular Powell-Loy Thin Man mystery series.

Body and Soul (Enterprise, 1947) was a notable prizefighting drama with John Garfield, Joseph Pevney, Anne Revere and Lilli Palmer.

Double Whammy

Hollywood is a funny place. I like it. I've learned to get along with it. But there are some odd things about it. Like the golf clubs. No single woman can join a Hollywood golf club (the men will back them but the married women won't). It seems that when you get a divorce in Hollywood, you not only lose a husband, you also lose your golf club membership.

Vera Ralston
Picturegoer, March 20, 1954

★ ★ ★

Sitting Pretty

I sat around doing nothing my first year in Hollywood. I came from London with a fat scrapbook and a lean bankbook. After three years in good London plays, I was quite a topic there. But when I arrived here I was just a paragraph in the local trade papers.

Greer Garson
March 28, 1954

★ ★ ★

Royal Raspberry

At times I think I actually hate Hollywood. I have many acquaintances there, but few friends.

Grace Kelly
The Saturday Evening Post, the 1950s

★ ★ ★

No Match

You have to leave your country to get a perspective, to see what makes America great. Now I can say that nowhere in the world is there a match for what we have in Hollywood!

Kirk Douglas
May 30, 1954

★ ★ ★

Ants at Picnic

When I came to Hollywood I had a rather precious and coddled attitude about my own integrity. It was so stupid of me to resist so directly the prejudice that money is right. But just because the big shots were nice to me, I saw no reason to overlook what they did to others and to ignore the fact that they normally behave with the hostility of ants at a picnic. The marvelous thing about Hollywood is that these people are recognized as sort of the norm, while I am the flip. These gnarled and twisted personalities see no other way to live except on a pedestal of malicious gossip and rumor to be laid on the ears of unsuspecting people who believe them.

Marlon Brando
Time, the 1950s

Janis Carter had her best role as a scheming waitress in *Framed* (Columbia, 1947), with Glenn Ford as her victim.

Lost Cat

Don't get me wrong. I'm not one of the wise ones who try to put Hollywood down. It just happens that I fit to cadence and pace better here as far as living goes. New York is vital and, above all, fertile. They're a little harder to find, maybe, but out there in Hollywood, behind all that brick and mortar, there are human beings just as sensitive to fertility. The problem for this cat—myself—is not to get lost.

James Dean
The New York Times, March 13, 1955

★ ★ ★

Too Much Heartbreak

I've got to quit or blow my top. I just can't take the heartbreak anymore. Hollywood is not as glamorous as it seems.

Betty Hutton
Hollywood Yearbook, 1955

★ ★ ★

Broke the Mold

Hollywood is a small town. When you don't go out and buy a house with a swimming pool, drive a Caddy convertible, or go to Ciro's or Mocambo, they don't like it. When you don't kowtow to the powers of the town, they hate you. I am trying to do just two things—act, and live the way I want to live. Because I refuse to fall into the Hollywood mold, people think I'm a bum and a slob. Well, so be it! I've got nothing against Hollywood. But it is a business, and when you've made enough loot, the thing to do is to pull out.

Marlon Brando
That Guy Brando, 1955

★ ★ ★

Hello, Gary

Hollywood has a bad habit of changing good honest family names to something theatrically flossy, and I wanted no part of it. Frank Cooper I had been born, and Frank Cooper I would remain.

Gary Cooper
Saturday Evening Post, March 3, 1956

★ ★ ★

Slugger Susan

My life is fair game for anybody. I spent an unhappy, penniless childhood in Brooklyn. I had to slug my way up in a town called Hollywood, where people love to trample you to death. I married for security and love. I didn't get either.

Susan Hayward
Motion Picture, January, 1957

Superior Inferiors

The people who are superior about Hollywood are those who were too inferior to make it here. A dull place? You've got everything here. You've got sun, snow, golf, sailing, good conversation, gambling, terrific scenery—all within a couple of hours. I can't stand this idea that all the good actors are in the theeyetar and the movies are for jerks.

Humphrey Bogart
The Seven Deadly Sins of Hollywood, 1957

★ ★ ★

Looker

I don't really have any friends in Hollywood. I've been away from Hollywood a year and I've learned something, I hope. I want to develop. I just want to grow. And I don't mean where some people think I mean. I want to grow in stature, be a real actress. In New York I learned to make friends. Before, I never had any friends, only conquests. I didn't have the time to find real friends. I was always being looked at, had no chance to look. I am perfectly serious about wanting to act seriously.

Marilyn Monroe
The Seven Deadly Sins of Hollywood, 1957

★ ★ ★

Palmy Days

The first two weeks (in Hollywood), nothing but palm trees and sunshine. I'd never seen a palm tree in my life, nor had I ever seen the sun shine so steadily. It was magnificent. On the fifteenth day, I woke up; the sun was still shining, the palm trees were still there and I was bored to death.

Anne Bancroft
The New York Times Magazine
February 9, 1958

★ ★ ★

Opportunism Knocks

Opportunism. It comes in every form, shape and size—and is ever present in Hollywood.

Nick Adams
Modern Screen, June, 1958

★ ★ ★

That Old Feeling

Hollywood is Lonelyville to me. I always get that sick, lonesome feeling when I go there.

Sal Mineo
Modern Screen, August, 1958

Not Guilty—For Once

I was one of Hollywood's top box office names (but my) mental breakdown cannot be scored as another black mark against the West Coast film city and its frantic mores. My doctors say my career had absolutely nothing to do with my illness. They tell me I handled it as a mature person.

Gene Tierney
November 12, 1958

Strangers When Met

You can work in Hollywood for eighteen or twenty years and not get to know many of its leading figures and not ever meet, more than casually, many of its celebrated stars.

Errol Flynn
My Wicked, Wicked Ways, 1959

Dying Big Biz

Hollywood, we decided, was a nice place to die, but we wouldn't want to live there. Dying seemed to be the biggest industry. The California cemeteries make dying sound so attractive it's a real effort to keep breathing.

Jack Paar
I Kid You Not, 1959

Hairdos Have It

In Hollywood a girl's virtue is much less important than her hairdo. You're judged by how you look, not by what you are. Hollywood's a place where they'll pay you a thousand dollars for a kiss, and fifty cents for your soul. I know, because I turned down the first offer often enough and held out for the fifty cents.

Marilyn Monroe
The 1950s

Place of Business

I love the continuity of the seasons in New York. You can see and feel them change, unlike Hollywood where one month is almost like the next. I much prefer living here (in New York), anyway. To me, Hollywood is a business address, something functional, so it makes it much more palatable. But I'm not crazy about it as a resort or a permanent base.

Anthony Perkins
Theatre, May, 1960

Marguerite Chapman and Robert Young (in pre-*Father Knows Best / Marcus Welby, M.D.* days) were romantically paired in the western *Relentless* (Columbia, 1948).

New York Convert
New York is my home and I would never live in Hollywood again. In Hollywood if I'm not working I vegetate.

Roddy McDowall
New York World-Telegram and Sun, the 1960s

★ ★ ★

Monomania
People in the motion picture business in Hollywood are passionate about it. It's a mono-mania. It's wonderful to be with passionate people, but, if you are a certain type of person, you must be passionate about something else. If you stay in Hollywood, you become bored and unhappy. Another thing—I don't like the weather in Hollywood. It upsets me a little bit, the same sunshine every day. And it's too warm for my blood now.

Olivia de Havilland
1961

★ ★ ★

Prize Bull
Remember in the Bible where Ecclesiastes starts with "Vanity, vanity, all is vanity"? Well, that's what I think of Hollywood, except that for "vanity" I would substitute the word "bullshit."

Humphrey Bogart
The Real and the Unreal, 1961

★ ★ ★

What Price Pools?
I believe that God felt sorry for actors, so he created Hollywood to give them a place in the sun and a swimming pool. The price they had to pay was to surrender their talent.

Cedric Hardwicke
A Victorian in Orbit, 1961

★ ★ ★

Drastic Thoughts
If I had stayed in Hollywood, I would have killed myself. Or someone would have done it for me.

Piper Laurie
New York World-Telegram and Sun
April 21, 1961

★ ★ ★

Funny Feeling
I had a funny feeling that I wasn't smart enough for all the razzle-dazzle Hollywood people.

Jean Seberg
Modern Screen, October, 1961

Rouben Mamoulian directed *Summer Holiday* (MGM, 1948), the musical version of Eugene O'Neill's *Ah, Wilderness!* featuring Walter Huston, Frank Morgan, Agnes Moorehead, Jackie "Butch" Jenkins, Marilyn Maxwell, Mickey Rooney and Gloria De Haven.

Sorry, Wrong Number (Paramount, 1948) earned Barbara Stanwyck (left) an Oscar nomination as an invalid who hears her own murder planned; the company also included Burt Lancaster and lovely Ann Richards.

The Family Type
My family life is more important to me than my career. How many Hollywood marriages do you know of where the wife is an actress and the marriage still works?

Elizabeth Taylor
The Elizabeth Taylor Story, 1961

★ ★ ★

Just Another Pretty Place
Hollywood is too pretty. I like something that shakes me up. Hollywood is like a resort town. You get too complacent there.

George Maharis
Hollywood Yearbook, 1961

★ ★ ★

Success if Sued
This is a funny kind of town. If you're a producer, you're not really successful until someone sues you. If you're an actor, you're not really a star until the whispers begin that your interest in youth is not connected with the Boy Scout recruiting drive. If you're an actress, your name goes up in lights about the same time the stories start which indicated that Madame Du Barry, compared to you, was as unattainable as the moon. Generally, in this town, there is community-wide rejoicing only when a competitor fails. We seem to thrive, personally, on the catastrophe of others.

Kirk Douglas
Hello, Hollywood!, 1962

★ ★ ★

Picking Lemons
Hollywood is a place where you have a stand-in when you're a standout. But don't let it go to your head, because it's tough to find a double for an empty stomach. The sweeter part, though, is mighty sweet. What could be finer than getting up in the morning and picking oranges in your back yard! Then in the afternoon going to the track and picking lemons?

Bob Hope
Hello, Hollywood!, 1962

★ ★ ★

Sarong, Hollywood!
Listen, I don't want to talk against Hollywood. I've still got a couple of good friends there. But they're all very shortsighted. Toward the end the phone didn't ring. There weren't so many invitations. Some people never paid back a dime of what I loaned them—even crossed the streets to avoid me. That's when we decided to leave Hollywood and move to Baltimore, my husband's home town.

Dorothy Lamour
Motion Picture, the 1960s

Joan Fontaine did some of her finest work in *Letter from an Unknown Woman* (Universal, 1948), a remarkable evocation of Old Vienna with Louis Jourdan.

Moved to Work
You can't live (in New England) and work on a steady basis and since I have to work, I had to move. I can take Hollywood. I was never a part of the Hollywood colony when I lived there before, and I don't plan to be a part of it this time.

Bette Davis
The 1960s

★ ★ ★

Give Me the Simple Life
I wouldn't want to live in Hollywood all the time. It's like coming to a brilliant, creative dreamworld. I like a simpler kind of life.

Susan Hayward
The 1960s

★ ★ ★

Out of Use
When I look back now I see "Veronica Lake" as someone, or something, quite separate from me today—something that was invented by Hollywood and that ceased to exist when Hollywood had no further use for it.

Veronica Lake
Sight and Sound, the 1960s

★ ★ ★

Love's Labor Lost
Hollywood is so dull. It's not Sodom and Gomorrah. I've tried to like L.A., but it's akin to making love to a dormant woman.

Mort Sahl
Hollywood Screwball, 1962

★ ★ ★

Single Girls Vulnerable
I think single girls are very vulnerable in Hollywood. I've lived most of my life in New York; there's more protection there. Buildings are high and guarded by doormen. Here they're *out* with a million glass doors and French doors, and anything can happen.

Suzanne Pleshette
Modern Screen, March, 1963

★ ★ ★

Facing God
This is what my life in Hollywood is like (a quickly dismantled palace set close-by). It's all surface. Maybe that's what human life is like. We go through days and years of existence. And

Metro-Goldwyn-Mayer players assembled in 1949 for that studio's twenty-fifth anniversary. Top row: Alexis Smith, Ann Sothern, J. Carrol Naish, Dean Stockwell, Lewis Stone, Clinton Sundberg, Robert Taylor, Audrey Totter, Spencer Tracy, Esther Williams and Keenan Wynn. Second row: Peter Lawford, Jeanette MacDonald, Ann Miller, Ricardo Montalban, Jules Munshin, George Murphy, Reginald Owen, Walter Pidgeon, Jane Powell, Ginger Rogers, Frank Sinatra and Red Skelton. Third row: Katharine Hepburn, John Hodiak, Claude Jarman, Jr., Van Johnson, Jennifer Jones, Louis Jourdan, Howard Keel, Gene Kelly, Christopher Kent (Alf Kjellin), Angela Lansbury, Mario Lanza and Janet Leigh. Fourth row: Gloria De Haven, Tom Drake, Jimmy Durante, Vera-Ellen, Errol Flynn, Clark Gable, Ava Gardner, Judy Garland, Betty Garrett, Edmund Gwenn, Kathryn Grayson and Van Heflin. Bottom row: Lionel Barrymore, June Allyson, Leon Ames, Fred Astaire, Edward Arnold, Lassie, Mary Astor, Ethel Barrymore, Spring Byington, James Craig and Arlene Dahl.

it can seem glittering, like the palace. But the days and years go by. When the set is gone, we have to face our God.

Dolores Hart
Modern Screen, September, 1963

★ ★ ★

Rat Race
Hollywood is the rattiest place in the world.

Liza Minnelli
The 1960s

★ ★ ★

Garbo Lived Here
So many in Hollywood live in houses which used to belong to other personages, such as Greta Garbo or John Barrymore, and would identify their domiciles by the names of the great who had lived there. Nowadays it is the "Sinatra house" or the "Debbie Reynolds house," and I am puzzled to know just when the imprint of a personality ceases to exist as an attribute to the house and a new imprint occurs. *There's* impermanence for you. Perhaps we shall have to emulate London and put blue-and-white plaques on the houses, commemorating those who have lived in them.

Peggy Wood
Arts and Flowers, 1963

★ ★ ★

What a Dump!
Isn't Hollywood a dump—in the human sense of the word? A hideous town, pointed up by the insulting gardens of the rich, full of the human spirit at a new low of debasement.

F. Scott Fitzgerald
The Letters of F. Scott Fitzgerald, 1963

★ ★ ★

No Place for "Baby"
Hollywood can be a terrifying, disheartening and unrewarding place. It's no place at all for a woman alone, as I was during my blackest period right after Bogie died. I found out then who (and how many) my real friends were. I didn't want our two kids—who kept me going—to grow up with a death association there of a father who was so important in the industry.

Lauren Bacall
The New York Times, February 23, 1964

★ ★ ★

Nature-Kissed
Hollywood, the sunkist Pompeii . . .

Pat O'Brien
The Wind at My Back, 1964

Taking No Chances

I suppose the tolerance of Hollywood is best expressed by the burial of Mark Hellinger, the producer. A drinker, hard liver, always in dark blue shirts, a white tie, a bullet-proof Caddy, he wore out before fifty. A Jew, he was buried as a Protestant, with a Catholic medal around his neck.

Pat O'Brien
The Wind at My Back, 1964

★ ★ ★

Out of Sand

I have no life in Hollywood anymore. I'll miss my friends. Out of the twenty I thought I had, I'll miss the six I really have, narrowed down in the passage of time since Bogey's death. But I won't miss the idle chit-chat, the smiling, simultaneous hello and goodbye, the meaningless blown kisses and meaningless conversations, the constant scrutiny of one's private life. I won't miss the constant comment that everything is great, no matter what. I won't miss having my head in the sand.

Lauren Bacall
Films in Review, April, 1964

★ ★ ★

Boom Town

I drove to Hollywood, parked my car and took a walk down Hollywood Boulevard. It seemed that I had never been away. There were the same long lines of one-story shops, the stale-looking Army and Navy stores, the cut-rate drugstores, Woolworth's and Kresge's, all of it depressing and lacking sophistication. Hollywood had not outgrown the look of a boom town.

Charles Chaplin
My Autobiography, 1964

★ ★ ★

Likeable Place

What do I like most about Hollywood? It's convenient to the studio! (Sorry for the bad joke.) It's close to the beach (surfing), mountains (skiing), desert (riding and shooting) and movies and theater. Also my friends are here.

Richard Chamberlain
The 1960s

★ ★ ★

No Entanglements

I believe there are more promoters per square inch in Hollywood than anywhere else in the world. If all were put together, one thing is certain—their hands would not become entangled by reaching for the dinner check.

Mamie Van Doren
My Naughty, Naughty Life!, 1964

A Good Word
This town, Hollywood, and its people, have been very good to me since I waltzed in from the Middle West, saxophone in hand, quite a few years back.

Fred MacMurray
April 24, 1965

Loves Movies But
I may love movies, but I loathe Hollywood.

Mike Nichols
Cosmopolitan, 1965

Silence is Golden
The best way to get along in Hollywood is to smile sweetly and say nothing. Honesty about yourself isn't always the best policy.

Joanne Woodward
Hollywood Screen Legends, August, 1965

Runaway Star
My absence from Hollywood and residence in Switzerland have been a source of controversy, especially with labor unions who tag me "a runaway star." But I've been in this business 28 years and that's long enough to know that I don't want to put up with some of the nonsense that goes with it.

William Holden
August 9, 1965

Layered Tinsel
Strip away the phony tinsel in Hollywood and you find the real tinsel underneath.

Oscar Levant
Inquisition in Eden, 1965

★ ★ ★

The Gay Life
I was still a Midwest movie fan as far as the gay life of Hollywood was concerned. I had a feeling there must be an exotic night life going on into which I had not yet been initiated. I would be a long time finding out that the people of Hollywood are very much like the people next door.

Ronald Reagan
Where's the Rest of Me?, 1965

Romance on the High Seas (Warner Brothers, 1948) was the first movie for band singer Doris Day (second from left), and the instant-star was abetted by Janis Paige, Oscar Levant and S.Z. Sakall.

A Letter to Three Wives (20th Century-Fox, 1949), a marvelously fresh comedy with Ann Sothern, Linda Darnell and Jeanne Crain, won screenwriter-director Joseph L. Mankiewicz Academy Awards in those categories.

Bogie's Definition

I don't like the Hollywood definition of an actor. I like people who can act. The so-called Rock Hudsons and Tab Hunters are a dull bunch of cruds. I like the Lunts. I like Leslie Howard. I think they have to know a little bit more about something than just acting. Too many actors in Hollywood only think about their next part and about what Louella Parsons will say about them.

Humphrey Bogart
Bogey: The Good-Bad Guy, 1965

In There Pitching

I've played so many old hags most people think I'm 65 years old. I didn't want to play all those nasty ladies but in Hollywood you're either a member of the working group or not; and if not, you're very easily forgotten. I've had high spots, medium spots and a couple of low spots, but I've always been in there pitching.

Angela Lansbury
The New York Times, June 5, 1966

Babe in the Studios

I didn't have a very good time in Hollywood. I didn't know anything about acting. I was a ballet dancer. And if you don't know what you're doing in a pressure medium like movies, it tends to make your relationships bad all around. Now I can understand their hostility.

Janice Rule
Sunday News, June 19, 1966

Equal Time

I have to put in my pitch for Hollywood. It gripes me—so often the industry doesn't get credit for all the good it does. It's commendable what performers do—directors and producers, too—on an adminstrative level—in giving freely of their services for charitable causes. I wish more were said about what's good about Hollywood than what's bad—which is such a small percentage anyway. Hollywood's not Goody-Two-Shoes, but let's have equal time.

Janet Leigh
Los Angeles Times, August 1, 1966

Boring Problem

My educated guess is that boredom has caused most of the problems with Hollywood personalities. I know when I'm working I seldom get into trouble.

Hedy Lamarr
Ecstasy and Me, 1966

A Lady's Prerogative

I used to loathe Hollywood. It seemed miles from anywhere. The papers seemed just local gossip, and I felt unconnected with the rest of the world. But now I think that Hollywood is as real as New York or as real as London or as real as Venice. There's no place I'd rather be. When I'm away for very long, I can't wait to get back.

Julie Andrews
Time, December 23, 1966

★ ★ ★

Fancy Facility

Hollywood is like Picasso's bathroom.

Candice Bergen
February 14, 1967

★ ★ ★

I Happen to Like N.Y.

Hollywood? It's rather like living on the moon, isn't it?

Cole Porter
The Life That Late He Led, 1967

★ ★ ★

Chock Full O' Talk

New York is live, not on tape. I'd rather run a Chock Full O' Nuts in New York than a studio in Hollywood. At least the talk would be better.

Mel Brooks
Newsweek, May 29, 1967

★ ★ ★

Big Charge

The Eastern Seaboard has every kind of location, Europe, the South—I'll find you everything here but desert. There is no age in (Hollywood); they have sets but not the genuine thing. Even the lampposts are wrong—they're made of Styrofoam. I hate being separated from other life— there is nothing organic about Los Angeles. When it rains, the soil slides down; when it's dry, there's fire. The history of art is the history of great cities. When you shoot here (New York), it's like sitting on a big lid ready to blow off. And this energy reaches the screen.

Sidney Lumet
Newsweek, May 29, 1967

★ ★ ★

Showing the Crowd

I'm going to show that crowd. You just watch. It may take a year; it may take five years. But I'm going back there one day, and when I do, I am going to bring Hollywood to my feet.

Grace Moore
King Cohn, 1967

Closer to the Stars

When we made *Gone with the Wind* we were, as stars, a million miles from the public. The colony of Hollywood was absolute and we never talked to anybody outside our own gilded circles. Hollywood does not exist anymore. The industry that created people like me has gone, and I think it is a very good thing that, because of TV, the public should be much closer to its stars.

Olivia de Havilland
1967

★ ★ ★

Lovely Time of Year

It's lovely this time of the year—the fake snow on Hollywood Boulevard, the fakes on Sunset Boulevard and the studios bursting with pictures that can't be released.

Groucho Marx
The Groucho Letters, 1967

★ ★ ★

Swinger

These New York guys come to Hollywood and see all the lights and say, "It's phony." I hate to tell you but the cultural swing is to the West. I love Los Angeles—the temperance, the weather, the girls.

Warren Beatty
Do You Sleep in the Nude?, 1968

★ ★ ★

Three-Time Loser

It's a big bore. Who ever said I liked it there? . . . All I've got (from Hollywood) is three lousy ex-husbands.

Ava Gardner
Modern Screen, May, 1969

★ ★ ★

Place of Worship

Our town worships success, the bitch goddess whose smile hides a taste for blood.

Hedda Hopper
The Moguls, 1969

★ ★ ★

Fast Year

The year you win an Oscar is the fastest year in a Hollywood actor's life. Twelve months later they ask—"Who won the Oscar last year?"

Cliff Robertson
June 27, 1969

Eleanor Parker deserved her Academy nomination for a magnificently-shaded starring performance as the young girl corrupted by prison in *Caged* (Warner Brothers, 1950), with Hope Emerson.

Working Stiff

I like to work in Hollywood, but don't like to live there. I'm too young to die.

Claire Bloom
July 22, 1969

Sick—Sick—Sick

I'm fed up to the teeth with people making Hollywood the stepchild of show business—with those who say our industry is sick-sick-sick. What could be more sick than the legitimate theater?—and I speak from experience. There always *has* been something *wrong* with Hollywood. But there are just as many things that are still *right* and no one will ever make me believe they can kill this place off! I expect to see Hollywood regain its rightful place in the sun and, if it is the last act of my life, be a part of it—I hope.

Bette Davis
Motion Picture, the 1960s

Too Good to be True

So here I was, in Hollywood at last! Warm sunshine, flowers in the garden outside my window, attentive voices from Paramount Studios on the telephone, a limousine and chauffeur awaiting me; why, I wondered, had I any hesitation about coming before? It all seemed too good to be true—and it was.

Brian Aherne
A Proper Job, 1969

House Not Home

I've been knocking Hollywood so long it's become a joke out here. I don't like it and that's all there is to it and I don't really know why. Maybe I'm perverse. Life is pleasant, but it's just not me. It will never be home. This house is not me. It's rented out all the time. The kids went to a school that was very proper, all straight A's and Debbie Reynolds was head of the Girl Scouts, you know what I mean? I couldn't wait to get them out of there.

Joanne Woodward
Conversations in the Raw, 1969

Suffering Populace

Hollywood is the only community in the world where the entire population is suffering from rumortism.

Bert Lahr
Notes on a Cowardly Lion, 1969

Smart and Gifted

The smartest, most gifted people in the world live in Hollywood. Those who knock the town, one, never made it; two, have no chance to make it; or three, made it and blew it.

Billy Wilder
The Bright Side of Billy Wilder, Primarily, 1969

★ ★ ★

Get Giesler

Whenever trouble arose in Hollywood, the first cry for legal help that went up was, "Get (Jerry) Giesler!"

Joan Bennett
The Bennett Playbill, 1970

★ ★ ★

Of Cesspools and Sewers

Hollywood is an intellectual sewer, a cesspool of folly!

Richard Bennett
The Bennett Playbill, 1970

★ ★ ★

World Influence

Hollywood has influenced the world. I used to find, on going to Europe, that Hollywood had infiltrated every culture in the nation. I remember when stars had to put on black glasses because of the Hollywood sun and suddenly black glasses became the rage all over the world. And they're still worn by people who don't need them.

Anita Loos
The Real Tinsel, 1970

★ ★ ★

Sunny Soporific

Oh, gosh, did I hate Hollywood. You see, we came out of the bitter cold of New York into the terrific warmth of California, and it was all I could do stay awake. I'd get on the set, and if I could stand still for two minutes, I'd doze off.

Conrad Nagel
1970

★ ★ ★

Unpardonable Sin

I've committed the unpardonable sin in Hollywood. I've grown up.

Nelson Eddy
Motion Picture, the 1970s

Cruel Business

They came rushing out to Hollywood, long on ambition and short on talent and luck, hoping to make it big but unable in many instances to get through the front gate of a studio. The movie business can be cruel.

George Murphy
"Say . . . Didn't You Used to be George Murphy?", 1970

Wonderful Years

People ask me if I came to the (Hawaiian) islands because I was bitter about Hollywood. Of course not. I had 30 wonderful years in Hollywood. But I found out there are other things in life besides facing a camera.

Richard Denning
The 1970s

Squinting Toward Mecca

We saw our first inhabitants of Hollywood. They were bronzed, had capped teeth and wore huge dark glasses. They had faces but were minus eyes. Sunshine bled from every corner and the dazzling white buildings gave me a permanent squint.

Shirley MacLaine
Don't Fall Off the Mountain, 1970

Kicked Out

Hollywood kicked me out. Although I was suicidal at the time, it was the best thing that ever happened to me. I've never been happier. Frankly, I don't know how I survived the Hollywood rat race as long as I did without going completely nuts.

Carroll Baker
Sunday News, February 14, 1971

Retirement Town

Hollywood is now a place to retire to. Even the producers are itinerant there—they have no home base . . . The past bores me. I don't remember many movies and certainly not my own. I lived in Hollywood long enough to learn to play tennis and become a star, but I never felt it was my home. I was never looking for a home, as a matter of fact. I collect Egyptian cats— I have a collection larger than the Metropolitan Museum's—but I don't like to collect anything I can't pack.

Paulette Goddard
Life, February 19, 1971

Olivia de Havilland won her second Oscar for *The Heiress* (Paramount, 1949), the affecting drama of a wealthy but plain and unloved young woman, co-starring Montgomery Clift and a brilliant Ralph Richardson.

Tennessee Williams' most sensitive play, *The Glass Menagerie* (Warner Brothers, 1950), was effectively filmed with Kirk Douglas, Gertrude Lawrence, Jane Wyman and Arthur Kennedy.

No Respect

They've great respect for the dead in Hollywood, but none for the living.

Errol Flynn
The Wit and Wisdom of Hollywood, 1971

Tragic City

Hollywood is a tragic city of beautiful girls—the girls who mop the floor, the waitresses, the shop ladies.

F. Scott Fitzgerald
Crazy Sundays, 1971

Lonely and Confused

When I came to Hollywood I was lonely and confused. At first I had no friends, no one to really care what happened to me. I was very naive about people and things. Everybody's main interest isn't in you, but in themselves. This is probably true everywhere, but I felt it keenly when I came to Hollywood. I had never worked in films before and it was a rather startling world to be thrown into.

Inger Stevens
The Lonely Beauties, 1971

New Title-Holder

I don't like the title, "Hollywood's Most Glamorous Grandmother." Elizabeth Taylor's got the title now and I don't think she's lucky.

Marlene Dietrich
September 13, 1971

Grew Up on Screen

Hollywood has been very good to me. I was never hurt by the town or the profession. I had all the opportunities anyone could possibly ask for. I spent my teenage years here. I literally grew up on the screen. My first real date was with Tony Curtis. In some ways, I suppose I went through all the glamour bit associated with this town yet without ever actually becoming a real part of the social scene. Then I met Jim (her husband) and that was it.

Ann Blyth
Movie Digest, March, 1972

Something to Sniff At

Hollywood is like a bird dog. When things are going badly, it tenses and sniffs at you. It scrapes away at the camouflage. It knows.

David Niven
The Moon's a Balloon, 1972

★ ★ ★

Freaking Out

I looked around Ft. Lauderdale and realized I was a freak in that society. I suddenly had an overwhelming desire to get back to Hollywood where I could be just another freak among freaks.

Susan Hayward
March 3, 1972

★ ★ ★

Misfit

I can't play the games that go on in Hollywood. Who cares if my pearls are only seven millimeters when everyone else is flashing eleven millimeters? Who cares about dating the most men, or getting the best table in the restaurants? I don't fit in at all.

Janet Blair
TV Guide, May 13, 1972

★ ★ ★

No Time for Glamour

I don't need that awful, unreal, artificial "glamour" that Hollywood devises for people who don't have any personalities. I'm a very happy person.

Claudette Colbert
The Paramount Pretties, 1972

★ ★ ★

Old Chair

Hollywood! It's like an old chair—if it's useful, keep it; if not, give it to Goodwill.

Sylvia Sidney
1972

★ ★ ★

Wonderful Memories

I have wonderful memories of my years in Hollywood. But honestly, it's really a hard life. There are many pitfalls, particularly for young girls. You tend to become so self-centered, accustomed to being the center of things. It's difficult to retain your equilibrium. I'm lucky that I was always part of such a close and devoted family—because, let's face it, it's hard enough just being Irish!

Joan Leslie
Movie Digest, July, 1972

Dead and Buried

If I had stayed in Hollywood, I would have ended up like Alan Ladd and Gail Russell, dead and buried. That rat race killed them and I knew it eventually would kill me so I had to get out. I was never psychologically meant to be a picture star. I left to save my life.

Veronica Lake
TV Radio Mirror, December, 1972

★ ★ ★

Torn Wings

Hollywood has always been unconsciously cruel, as children are with frogs and butterflies; it harpoons its victims with ridicule and tears off the wings of the sensitive.

Frances Marion
Off with Their Heads, 1972

★ ★ ★

Cake for Christmas

I'll never forget my first Christmas in Hollywood in that dinky little one-room apartment. We had no tree, no presents and nothing to eat. My mother had sold the car to pay our room rent and we lived on crackers for two days. Our landlady came by and brought us a chocolate cake she had baked as our Christmas gift. I am sure she was not aware that we had no food in the house. But that was our first Christmas in Hollywood, our landlady's home-baked chocolate cake and nothing else.

Ann Miller
Miller's High Life, 1972

★ ★ ★

Pallbearer Pariah

In Hollywood, when you have two commercial failures in a row you are no longer asked to be a pallbearer at funerals.

Billy Wilder
The 1970s

★ ★ ★

One in a Million

I'm one Hollywood star who hasn't tried to slash her wrists, take sleeping pills or kick a cop in the shins.

Ava Gardner
The MGM Stock Company, 1973

Irving Berlin's *Annie Get Your Gun* (MGM, 1950) provided dynamic Betty Hutton with her meatiest role, and she was ably aided by Louis Calhern, J. Carrol Naish, Benay Venuta, Howard Keel, Edward Arnold and Keenan Wynn.

Nancy Davis, two years before she became Mrs. Ronald Reagan, had the female lead with James Whitmore and Gary Gray in *The Next Voice You Hear . . .* (MGM, 1950).

Character / Actress

I think of myself as a stage actress. I never lived in Hollywood. You can say that whenever I was broke I went to Hollywood.

Doro Merande
After Dark, November, 1973

★ ★ ★

Just a Facade

Once photographed, life here is ended. It is almost symbolic of Hollywood. Tara had no rooms inside. It was just a facade.

David O. Selznick
GWTW: The Making of Gone with the Wind, 1973

★ ★ ★

Survival Prescription

The stakes are so high in Hollywood, the competition is keener, and it is so much harder to survive. The only way *to* survive is to be honest with yourself and evaluate what you can give as a person and an artist, and not be involved with all the b.s. of this place.

Laurence Harvey
Pieces of Time, 1973

★ ★ ★

Mental Bag Packed

I detested Hollywood from the moment I arrived and always had a mental bag packed to come back East. Most of my friends were writers; they were the only people I wanted to be with even though in Hollywood they're rated as third-class citizens.

Geraldine Fitzgerald
It Was Fun While It Lasted, 1973

★ ★ ★

On Guard

Out in Hollywood, when they put their arms around your shoulder, look you square in the eye and say, "Remember, kid, I'm with you all the way down the line," that's the moment to be on guard. It's a signal they're getting ready to cut your throat or stab you in the back.

Dore Schary
1973

Sensuous But Serious

All I really want is the respect that is due me, not to be passed off in Hollywood as a yeh-yeh-rah-busty play girl in the girly business whose every move appears to be sensuous. Even when I say something serious people think it's extremely funny and they laugh.

Jayne Mansfield
Jayne Mansfield, 1973

Squat Team

The Hollywood sidewalks were inlaid with star-shaped bronze plaques, each bearing the name of a theatrical "great." For hours I personally have stood on Hollywood Boulevard at the foot of Whitley Avenue, casually leaning near the entrance to a chili parlor which fronts upon my star. I have watched an endless procession of hippies, dopies, prosties, newsies and boozies traipse across my name; all hope of having someone ask me for an autograph was abandoned the day I noted two dogs squatting in business conference directly over my star.

Tay Garnett
Light Your Torches and Pull Up Your Tights, 1973

Women-Weary

I get a little weary of finding notes slipped under my door, saying things like, "I saw you in the bar, do you think we might have dinner together?" In Hollywood it is the biggest bore, because when you've worked your way around the fifteen or so women on offer, there really is little else to do except go back to the beginning again.

Omar Sharif
Some Enchanted Egos, 1973

Sizzling Reports

To have an affair in Hollywood nowadays is no big deal. Attitudes have changed, and besides, the world is not that interested in what goes on with what they call movie stars today. But in the late '30s it was something else. The most sizzling affairs (which were called romances then, no matter what was going on) were the whole world's business. Every move was reported.

Milton Berle
Milton Berle, 1974

Salary Figures

I was already learning Hollywood's caste system, where salary was almost as important as the kind of roles you had and the sort of pictures you played in.

Polly Bergen
Polly's Principles, 1974

One for the Book
If I ever wrote a book about Hollywood and its inner workings, I know what I would call it—
Insincere City.

Mervyn LeRoy
Take One, 1974

Alone in Crowd
Though I was fascinated by the work at the studio, I had trouble becoming acclimated to the town itself. It was a strange brand of loneliness, one I hadn't experienced before . . . relentless and unrelieved. I could walk across town for rehearsals while in New York and see dozens of fascinating visuals. The crowds of people hurrying along, the honking of traffic and the city lights gave New York a tempo Hollywood couldn't match. It took me a while to realize you had to have a home you liked, where you did most of your entertaining, instead of scurrying over to the Mocambo or Ciro's. So many of us were alone in a crowd of impassive faces.

Vincente Minnelli
I Remember It Well, 1974

Children First
Our children were, and always have been, first with us. So, at this point, if Joe (my husband) had said: "I wish you wouldn't go running off to Hollywood and leave me with two kids on my hands," I would have said, "Fine—I'd just as soon pass it up."

Thelma Ritter
Good Dames, 1974

The Human Quality
It took guts to walk out on Hollywood, but it would've been worse to stay. I had a house, seven black Cadillac convertibles and two wrecked marriages. I already had my head turned; turning my back was easy. It doesn't matter if I have a beard or a crew cut. People respond to me because I have a human quality. I know I'll be put down by Hollywood, but I don't speak to anybody out there anyway.

Troy Donahue
People Are Crazy Here, 1974

Rich on Wheels
I did not like Hollywood. There is so much luxury there, the kind of riches and beauty we never dreamed of back home. It is so sad to be that fortunate and have so little communication, though. I found it frightening. I saw no people walking, no children playing. I never even saw people in the windows of those beautiful houses. Hollywood seems to have just a lot of cars living there.

Liv Ullmann
People Are Crazy Here, 1974

No Sad Songs for Me (Columbia, 1950) was the last film of gifted Margaret Sullavan (center) whose co-stars were Viveca Lindfors and Wendell Corey.

Two Weeks with Love (MGM, 1950) was one of the studio's most unpretentious, enjoyable musicals, with Ann Harding, Louis Calhern, Ricardo Montalban, Carleton Carpenter, Debbie Reynolds, Tommy Rettig, Gary Gray, Clinton Sundberg and Jane Powell.

Sex Crimes

Any interest I might have had in a warm climate had been cancelled by those early years in Hollywood. There the hot, dry air stings your eyeballs, prickles your skin, causes wrinkles in teen-agers and brings on aberrations that produce sex crimes of unspeakable obscenity.

Anita Loos
Kiss Hollywood Good-by, 1974

★ ★ ★

No Culture

The trouble with Hollywood is that it ain't got culture.

Vincent Price
Vincent Price Unmasked, 1974

★ ★ ★

Wolf Pack

If you're a young blonde around this man's town, you have to keep the wolf pack off somehow. If you know all those (profane) words, they figure you know your way around and they don't act quite so rough. It's better than having a black-snake whip in your hand.

Carole Lombard
Gable & Lombard, 1974

★ ★ ★

The Quiet Woman

I've always lived a very quiet and secluded existence, finding my pleasures in the normal, wholesome things that don't seem to interest my Hollywood neighbors. Hollywood resents a lady.

Ann Harding
The RKO Gals, 1974

★ ★ ★

No Part of Babylon

I had no desire to come to Hollywood to work in films. I thought Hollywood was for curly-haired pretty boys. My friends and I would sit in Walgreen's drugstore on Broadway and talk lovingly about theater and complain and bitch about movies. I wanted no part of Babylon.

Jack Lemmon
You Must Remember This, 1975

★ ★ ★

Semi-Retired?

There's too much sunshine (in Hollywood), and I don't think your brain can operate as well. With all due respect, I think in a colder climate your brain works better. I think that when you come out here you're really in a state of semi-retirement. It's just too paradisiacal.

Walter Matthau
How to Make It in Hollywood, 1975

Lost Rainbow

Sometimes I feel like I left the rainbow back at MGM. And it wasn't really a rainbow at all—just a Hollywood backdrop that some indifferent stagehands painted.

Judy Garland
Stars in My Eyes . . . Stars in My Bed, 1975

★ ★ ★

Memorable

I've never been in a Hollywood fight or feud. I have the most wonderful memory for forgetting things.

Marilyn Monroe
Don't Get Me Wrong—I Love Hollywood, 1975

★ ★ ★

Roots—Hepburn Style

I've always had roots. That's why Hollywood never quite got to me. I scurried back to the family circle, to my hometown of Hartford, Connecticut, the moment I stopped working. And when I die, I will be buried in Connecticut as well.

Katharine Hepburn
Nostalgia Illustrated, August, 1975

★ ★ ★

Rich Failure

Hollywood dangles a fortune at you, and you get softened. Money seeps through. You begin to step up the pace for more money. Before you know it, you're rich and a failure.

John Garfield
Body and Soul, 1975

★ ★ ★

Sanity Clause

I stopped believing in Santa Claus at an early age. Mother took me to see him in a Hollywood department store, and he asked me for my autograph.

Shirley Temple
Shirley Temple, 1975

★ ★ ★

Fast Exit

I take no pride in the fact, but I was one of the first actors to sense the poison that lurked in the Hollywood air (i.e., smog). I've been back there only a couple of times and get through and out as fast as I can.

William Powell
The Debonairs, 1975

Difficult Choice
If I had my choice between Hollywood and Atlanta, I'd take Leavenworth.

George M. Cohan
Musical Stages, 1975

★ ★ ★

The Unfaithful
It was almost impossible (to have a happy marriage in Hollywood). One evening a big star gave a party honoring couples who had been married more than 10 years. We showed up with about 50 other couples, and everyone that I knew had either been or was being unfaithful to the other. But these were the survivors.

Lilli Palmer
People, 1975

★ ★ ★

The Users
Hollywood has a tendency to drain and discard people, like TV. It uses up people. Luck plays a very important part in everything out there. I think if you like people you like people. You don't put them in categories. Out there everything reminds me of the Tennessee Williams play I was in on Broadway, *The Milk Train Doesn't Stop Here Anymore*, where they hung bells around the necks of the lepers to tell them apart from the rest. In California they categorize you immediately. It's so plastic. They just care if you're groovy or with it.

Tab Hunter
The Washington Post, May 27, 1976

★ ★ ★

Would-Be Cowboy
When I was about thirteen, I said to my sister that I was going to go to Hollywood and become a cowboy. Now, I had no intention of coming to *this* Hollywood. You see, I supposed that Hollywood was where cowboys were. What I wanted to do was work with cows.

Sidney Poitier
American Film, September, 1976

★ ★ ★

Tent with Bath
Hollywood lived the way the Arabs are attempting to live now, and while there is nothing strange about people vying with each other for great landed estates, there is something odd about people vying with each other for better bathrooms.

Lillian Hellman
Scoundrel Time, 1976

Bette Davis (right) was at her vivid best in *All About Eve* (20th Century-Fox, 1950), assisted by Gary Merrill and Anne Baxter, and the film won the Oscar.

Most of the principals involved with *Sunset Boulevard* (Paramount, 1950) were nominated by the film Academy, including Gloria Swanson, unforgettable as the mad, former silent screen star, and William Holden, as her young lover.

Out of Town

I came to hate Hollywood so much that I enlisted in the Army again to get out of town. When I came out in 1945, I decided to get out of pictures.

Melvyn Douglas
Who's Who in Hollywood, 1976

The Big League

In the theatre we had our sharpies, but when you got to Hollywood you knew at once you had arrived in the big league for con men and frauds. My very first impression of Hollywood was the same for any other town I had encountered in vaudeville—just a place to do your job. But after a while, I began to realize how sadly obsessed these Hollywood people were with their careers.

James Cagney
Cagney by Cagney, 1976

Gossip Lovers

Hollywood has a little Chinese wall around it. Inside, it's a world of people who know everybody else and all the gossip about everybody. And do they love gossip! I'm convinced that Hollywood stars and starlets gossip more than anybody else. They claim they hate gossip about themselves, but they do it all the time. And you have to be very careful about Hollywood gossip. It has a way of growing, like crab grass, until ultimately it can choke out the truth.

Tony Martin
The Two of Us, 1976

They Never Leave Home

One of the problems in Hollywood is that people never leave here, unless it's to fly to New York. People sit in their home watching a picture by pushing a button, and if their son or daughter leaves, it's a flop, and if they stay, it's a hit. There's no contact with the public.

Clint Eastwood
Bijou, April, 1977

Can't Take It

Woody (Allen) hates California, and is unrelenting about how much he despises it but to me Hollywood is not California. I couldn't take Hollywood any more than Woody could.

Diane Keaton
Sunday News, May 15, 1977

No Regrets

It was so exciting to be in Hollywood in those days. I don't regret a minute of it, not even when Dorothy kept the ruby slippers. If I had to do it all over again, I'd do the same.

Margaret Hamilton
Films in Review, August–September, 1977

On the Run

Men told me what to believe. I was supposed to be secretly ashamed of acting in movies instead of raising children. There was that constant pull between what felt natural to me and what was expected. I hated Hollywood, and I was constantly running away from it.

Evelyn Keyes
The Village Voice, August 15, 1977

Slim Chance

Hollywood has influenced women all over the world to think about slimming. This is a great service because overeating is unhealthy. But so are extreme diets. Every woman should have an individual approach to losing weight.

Irene Papas
Los Angeles Times, November 20, 1977

Gung Ho Hollywood

In Hollywood we were all very gung ho, and the day after Pearl Harbor, December 8, I was up in City Hall rolling bandages.

Rosalind Russell
Life is a Banquet, 1977

Unemployment Office, Jeeves

The Unemployment Insurance office in Hollywood was, without a doubt, the snazziest one in the land. You would be just as apt to see a scattering of celebrities there as a studio cleaning woman. It is no exaggeration to say that some jobless stars would run in for their weekly check while their chauffeurs waited outside in their Lincoln Continentals.

Sam Coslow
Cocktails for Two, 1977

A Dirty Word
The myopic eye of the eastern seaboard doesn't rate Hollywood very high. They're not oriented to what happens west of the Hudson, and it's been going on for a long time. Film in the rest of the world is either a pillar or the central core of the national culture. Here (New York) Film is still a dirty word and Hollywood is a dirty, stinkpot place three thousand miles away—what good could come out of Nazareth? . . . An amazing thing is happening in Hollywood. These kids from film schools, many of them not thirty, are knocking out great big blockbusters.

Frank Capra
Focus on Film, 1977

★ ★ ★

From Under Her Hat
To columnist Hedda Hopper:
   Why don't you leave Hollywood and move to the world?

Montgomery Clift
Monty, 1977

★ ★ ★

Hello, Peasants
Hollywood was for peasants, I decided. New York was my town. The New Yorkers were sophisticated enough to understand and enjoy my suave, sterling style. Hollywood was hicksville.
   Soon I decided to join the peasants.

Bob Hope
The Road to Hollywood, 1977

★ ★ ★

Cover Girl
Right after the war it became fashionable to knock Hollywood, but I could never find it in my heart to do that. They made me, to a certain extent: I was in there at the end of the big studio star-building publicity machine. Let's face it, I was on the front cover of every magazine from Tokyo to the Fiji Islands.

Deborah Kerr
Deborah Kerr, 1977

★ ★ ★

Money Minded
The name of the game in Hollywood wasn't (Bosley) Crowther, the *New York Times* film critic, it was money.

Henry Ephron
We Thought We Could Do Anything, 1977

An American in Paris (MGM, 1951), with Gene Kelly, newcomer Leslie Caron and music by George and Ira Gershwin, won the best picture Oscar.

Limelight (United Artists, 1952) was the last film made in the United States by Charles Chaplin who wrote, produced, directed and starred in this story of an aging comedian and a suicidal young dancer (newcomer Claire Bloom).

False Values
Hollywood brings out all kinds of fears and guilts and very false values.

Arthur Laurents
Monty, 1977

Down to Business
I've bought a house in Hollywood, which is something I swore I'd never do. I used to think I couldn't live in Hollywood because I'd spend all my time in the pool and believe all the producers when they'd call and say, "Oh, baby, I've just seen the rushes, kid, and you're great." That was when I was in my "dimpling period." You know, smiling pretty and flashing eyelashes for producers and agents. Now I'm in my Joan Crawford period. Very self-assured. Down to business.

Joan Hackett
Flightime, the late 1970s

Ambition: Stardom
I've only got one ambition in my life, and I've had it since I was a boy. I want to be a movie star. I came out here (to Hollywood) when I was a kid and I tried it. I nearly got myself killed as a stunt man and I nearly died of starvation. I went back East with my tail between my legs. Now I got another chance, and I gotta make it. I gotta!

Lou Costello
Bud & Lou, 1977

Open Door Policy
If one movie makes money, Hollywood immediately mass-produces 10 more just like it. They need to open the doors more to young creative people.

James Caan
The Los Angeles Herald-Examiner
January 1, 1978

Dreams Shattered
Hollywood destroyed all my dreams and fantasies. They were shattered when I was very young. But I'm still an optimist. I haven't been conquered by despair. I'm simply a realist today.

Ricardo Montalban
Daily News, January 14, 1978

Double Indemnity
Christmas in Hollywood was unreal. Presents were doled out like popcorn at a circus. At the studios, stars were expected to give every member of the crew a respectable gift, not only at Christmas, but at the end of shooting as well. A double indemnity for those unlucky stars who were filming in December.

Joan Fontaine
No Bed of Roses, 1978

★ ★ ★

Dynasty of Backbiters
It was back to bitchy, backbiting Hollywood, where I had to kow-tow to Hedda and Louella and the studio heads—watch my dress, my manners and morals, and be aware that the newspapers were avid for snide gossip about me.

Joan Collins
Past Imperfect, 1978

★ ★ ★

Horse Sense
See, my first real name was Marilyn. Don't think I haven't thought about *that*. I believe in seagulls and my horse and my goat who butts those tourists for me. Hollywood isn't me. A movie set isn't me, and it never was. All my animals—I mean, they love *me*. Kim Novak—who's that to my horse? Nobody.

Kim Novak
Films in Review, February, 1978

★ ★ ★

Memory Bank
I remember what it was like when I was a young actor in New York and then here (Hollywood). The guy who's only got two lines doesn't get to eat with the character actors and the star. And the directors treat you as if you're . . . *nothing*. As you go up the ladder, the treatment changes until you get to be a star, and then they're giving you hugs and kisses on the cheek. I despise that kind of thing, and I will not treat people that way.

Burt Reynolds
American Film, June, 1978

★ ★ ★

Showing Off
Oh, certainly the extravagance today in Hollywood is on par with what it was in the old days. Everybody still lives in mansions. Our home has 20 rooms, and we are not showoffy. We had a Rolls-Royce, but we had a family meeting and decided to get rid of it, so we sold it to Lucille Ball. It was her third Rolls-Royce. Right now we have an orange Cadillac. It has a telephone, a TV, a bar and orange velvet curtains and pillows. We take it to every premiere and every time we want to show off.

Jayne Meadows
The New York Times, July 21, 1978

Blight Symptom

I used to fear falling under the cultural blight of Hollywood. My only warning came when I went shopping and began to think that the dresses looked chic.

Anita Loos
The Talmadge Girls, 1978

★ ★ ★

Star Abuse

They completely abused me. I had no say at all. I wish I hadn't been so young. Hollywood is a terribly difficulty place for a vulnerable person.

Luise Rainer
People, July 31, 1978

★ ★ ★

Gloria of Graustark

I left California in 1938 and since that time I've lived in New York or Europe. But no matter where I turn up these days, I'm asked about that mythical kingdom called Hollywood. When I explain that I don't live there, *never* lived there when I could help it, and I've had an apartment in New York since 1938, the next question is: How is Greta Garbo?

Gloria Swanson
Close-Ups, 1978

★ ★ ★

Make-Believe World

I have a soft spot for the Hollywood that once shed a light on our nine-to-five lives. The old stars had a mystique and they clung to it even after everything else was gone. I mean, if they went out the back door to carry out the garbage, they dressed as though they were going to a charity ball. They dressed and lived and fed on that image of glamour. It may have been a make-believe world, but at least they worked at it.

Gene Autry
Back in the Saddle, 1978

★ ★ ★

Just Visiting

The reason I stay young is that I don't live in Hollywood, never have.

Elisha Cook, Jr.
1978

Aquatic star Esther Williams had a superior vehicle in *Million Dollar Mermaid* (MGM, 1952), the biography of Australian swimming champion Annette Kellerman with production numbers by Busby Berkeley.

The Quiet Man (Republic, 1952), co-starring Maureen O'Hara and John Wayne and photographed in Ireland, earned director John Ford an Academy Award.

Similar Attitudes
The attitudes of London and Hollywood toward each other are remarkably similar. Hollywood actors have said to me, "Working in London must be a wonderful experience—there are so many excellent actors there." Quite true. On the other hand, British actors have said to me, "Working in Hollywood must be a smashing experience—you have so many great actors there." Also true.

Edward Dmytryk
It's a Hell of a Life But Not a Bad Living, 1978

★ ★ ★

Through the Mill
When you've been through the Hollywood mill, you've been through the mill of mills.

Joseph L. Mankiewicz
Pictures Will Talk, 1978

★ ★ ★

Life Like Flicks
I've had many ups and downs. But so have old chums back in Stockton. I can't blame Hollywood. I sometimes think life is like one of my old flicks because I'm determined there will be that happy ending.

Janet Leigh
Films in Review, January, 1979

★ ★ ★

Lordly Positions
Vivien (Leigh) and I were both in good, strong positions, but we were miserable being away from England. It was the war which stopped us from being sucked into Hollywood. We were probably naively patriotic, so into my uniform I went. Still, for a while I was sucked into the Hollywood system against my will, and I confess that I had a slight resentment about everything there. However, I couldn't be angry with Vivien for signing with Selznick. Who could have turned down Scarlett O'Hara? Besides, she had a few glasses of champagne before she signed with him.

Laurence Olivier
The New York Times, the 1970s

★ ★ ★

Casting Couch
I had heard in New York that the casting couch was a way of life in Hollywood: it posed no threat to me. For one thing, my mother was a constant chaperone, hovering over me like a Secret Service agent. For another, I had been brought up to believe that you only went to bed with the man you married.

Gene Tierney
Self-Portrait, 1979

One-Track Mind

Hollywood: it only ran on one track, and that track was the motion picture. Any and everyone was obsessed with movies. All you ever heard wherever you went were words such as grosses, below-the-line, above-the-line, precentages, negative costs, reruns, spin-offs and scarcely a word to indicate that anything at all was happening in the real world other than the making of movies.

Sophia Loren
Sophia: Living and Loving, 1979

★ ★ ★

Waiting, Ever Waiting

At night there is nothing to do (in Hollywood), nowhere to go, it's like being in the Foreign Legion at Sidi-bel-Abbès, waiting for one's enlistment to run out.

Alexander Korda
Charmed Lives, 1979

★ ★ ★

Graves Filled

The graves of Hollywood are filled with the bodies of men who have reluctantly accommodated their studios.

John Houseman
Front and Center, 1979

★ ★ ★

One Big Cash Register

Hollywood is a frontier town in lotus land ruled by fear and love of money, but it can't rule me because I'm not afraid of anything and I don't love money. People around here are trapped by success and wealth. You can't get inspired here. Hollywood is like one big cash register ringing up the money all day long.

Marlon Brando
Brando for Breakfast, 1979

★ ★ ★

Terrible Twosome

Another Hollywood thing I hated was the power of those two women, Louella Parsons and Hedda Hopper, the gossip columnists. Their power shocked me, and I thought it very wrong that the film industry had allowed them to build up to such an extent that they could ruin people's careers and lives.

Ingrid Bergman
My Story, 1980

Alcoholics Meet

My wife and I used to say, we'll just have one . . . make it a double . . . 'stead of buying a pint, buy a quart. Us Hollywood alkies (alcoholics) used to meet at Bob Young's house. One famous actor wouldn't come, saying everybody'd say he was an alkie. "Everybody says it now but you," we told him.

Dana Andrews
The Hollywood Reliables, 1980

Wig City

In Hollywood everybody wears wigs. Wigs and hairpieces. Dietrich has dozens of wigs, even for the street. Men, too—not just toupees, mind you, but bits and pieces to cover a bald spot here, a thinning spot there—they call them rugs. And the little pieces? They're called doilies.

Gypsy Rose Lee
More Havoc, 1980

Stands Alone

I never go to Hollywood if I can help it. And as for writing a book about it all, I'm going to be the one who doesn't.

Van Johnson
September 21, 1980

Fangs a Million

Everybody in Hollywood has such gorgeous teeth, not a crooked fang among them. My dentist said capping my teeth would be a waste of his time and my money. He said it wouldn't make that much difference.

Mercedes McCambridge
The Quality of Mercy, 1981

Everything Gone

Hollywood? The whole thing is over for me there. My husband is gone, my home is gone and my picture career is gone.

Claudette Colbert
Time, September 14, 1981

Change of Life

I almost fell victim to the Hollywood tragedies. I could have wound up like a lot of other unfortunates. But I stopped my drinking and I got my whole life changed.

Lana Turner
The Globe, October 8, 1981

Marilyn Monroe and Jane Russell were at their busty best updating Anita Loos' 1920s-set stage musical *Gentlemen Prefer Blondes* (20th Century-Fox, 1953).

A No-No
In this silly town of ours
One sees odd primps and poses
But movie stars in fancy cars
Shouldn't pick their famous noses.

James Cagney
Sunday News Magazine, November 22, 1981

Success Revered
That was typically Hollywood. When a man was down, avoid him like the plague . . .
Khrushchev was visiting Hollywood and being feted as if he were God almighty. Khrushchev
was a success and Hollywood reveres success no matter how it's attained.

Stewart Granger
Sparks Fly Upward, 1981

★ ★ ★

Succinct Definition
Hollywood:
   Bridgeport with palms.

John Barrymore
The Barrymores, 1981

★ ★ ★

Me Tarzan, You Black
All they knew about blacks in Hollywood was what Tarzan told them. And Tarzan was not the
bright one in that outfit!

Lena Horne
People, December 28, 1981

★ ★ ★

Nobody There
In Hollywood, you might have the beautiful clothes and the beautiful car, but when you leave
your dressing room, there's nobody there but the guy who drives you.

Raquel Welch
Family Weekly, November 7, 1982

Strong Husbands
Let's play a game. Let's think of all the Hollywood women who were casualties. Of booze, drugs, no money, no man. Or they had men who drank and spent their money. No, I'm blessed and I know it. It's because I have a good man, darling. Both my husbands have had strength. They gave me a backbone, not a wishbone.

Vera Ralston
Los Angeles Times, November 28, 1982

The Red Carpet
A Hollywood premiere was a gala even in those days. Movies opened to a select audience resplendent in tuxedos and stunning evening gowns. A long red carpet was rolled out to the curb for the film's stars and studio personalities, who swept up in sleek limousines. The press turned out in force, and cheering crowds of fans greeted the arrival of each celebrity.

Lana Turner
Lana: The Lady, The Legend, The Truth, 1982

The Good and the Bad
So many movies (in the 1950s) had to do with the ''bad woman, good woman'' syndrome. Either Hollywood was concocting dreams of the ideal woman that the average woman in ''real life'' could not live up to, or they were concocting dreams, wet dreams at that, of the hot, scorching, sinful, seamy, slithery side of feminine nature according to the popular mythology.

Lily Tomlin
The Movies, July, 1983

Enjoy!
I remember as a young actor fresh to Hollywood wondering what I could give Norma Shearer and Irving Thalberg as a gift. They'd been very kind to me and I wanted to repay them. So I bought them six rather horrible handkerchiefs for Christmas, with ''I'' and ''N'' in the corners. You know what they gave me? A Studebaker.

David Niven
Los Angeles Times, August 7, 1983

Too Much Showbiz
All anyone in Hollywood talks about or reads about is showbiz, and then it begins to matter a little too much. It's suddenly like a life-or-death situation. I don't like that feeling. It's counter-survival.

John Travolta
Us, August 15, 1983

Ignored by Oscar

Why does Hollywood always ignore me at Oscar time? I genuinely don't know. It can't just be that I live and work in New York, though. Look at Woody Allen, who's a complete "New York" director and won an Oscar anyway. No, more than the New York it's the independence. Woody has his own kind of talent that's like no one else's. I haven't. I make commercial pictures. I'm in the marketplace. I could almost be one of them, which is what gets under their skin in Hollywood, I think. But I've got no complaints. I've done a lot of what I wanted to do, and it's a nice feeling.

Sidney Lumet
Sunday Star-Ledger, September 18, 1983

★ ★ ★

Unfounded Fear

Everybody is in awe of everybody before you get here (Hollywood). You're afraid everyone is going to be snotty. But I've never met anyone who was.

Michael Caine
The Tonight Show Starring Johnny Carson
September 21, 1983

★ ★ ★

Warm Treatment

I've always been treated so warmly here by the community. I still feel very kindly about my associations with Hollywood. Both *Zandy's Bride* and *The Abdication* were sponsored by Hollywood, and I'm very proud of them. I think they compare favorably to anything I've done in Sweden.

Liv Ullmann
The Hollywood Reporter, October 6, 1983

★ ★ ★

Theater Preferred

Hollywood seems very long and and far away. I was there for almost twelve years, scooting off to New York or Europe every chance I got. Somehow I was never really at home there— I always preferred the stage and live TV to movies. Today I am very active in theater here in my Florida home: I serve on three executive boards of the Asolo State Theater and am on the advisory board of SKAJ, another equity company nearby. However, I am still very close to some of my Hollywood friends, especially Ann Savage, who is even more beautiful today. So Hollywood was after all a very important part of my life.

Janis Carter
October 7, 1983

James Stewart portrayed orchestra leader Glenn Miller and June Allyson his wife in the hit film chronicling the life of the late musician, *The Glenn Miller Story* (Universal, 1953).

Nina Foch received a supporting actress Academy nomination for her secretary role in the boardroom drama *Executive Suite* (MGM, 1954), co-starring Fredric March.

Great Expectations

In 1939 I arrived in Hollywood with great expectations. I was a top New York model brought out by Howard Hughes to be an actress. I woke up fast.

Hollywood Boulevard, for instance, in my dreams a glistening thoroughfare of golden telephone poles with diamonds on top, actually looked like any other small town street. I was told it was appropriate to stay at the Beverly Hills Hotel; I stayed at the Knickerbocker because I could walk to the shops. There has always been too much emphasis on status in Hollywood. I was told who *not* to go out with, but I went out with them anyway. I was determined to keep the values I came with.

Still, today's young actors don't have the training we had. The studios would groom us, and there were all sorts of advantages. To quote Bette Davis, "Actors used to work to become stars, but today stars work to become actors." There was discipline in Hollywood then— when we got our scripts, we *worked*: no parties, no nothing till afterward.

Now, the discipline is gone, and so are the glamour, the grace, the sense of tradition. I miss the "old world" feeling of the lovely dinner parties that today are just a memory.

Marguerite Chapman
October 11, 1983

★ ★ ★

Unimaginable

No one loves making movies more than me, and no one hates the fringes of the business more than me. If life itself is a compromise, you can imagine what Hollywood is like.

Kim Basinger
Asbury Park Press, October 16, 1983

★ ★ ★

Fantasy World

Lots and lots of people in Hollywood are simply trying to impose their fantasies on everyone else, prove that they are great artists or producers or know what will make money. Whoever's fantasy is strongest wins. So you'll see a producer control one meeting and then go into another meeting and completely deflate in the face of a stronger fantasy.

Lawrence Kasdan
Rolling Breaks, 1983

★ ★ ★

First Lesson

I was so incredibly naive about what was business and what was caring in Hollywood. It turns out it was all business. *King Kong* took one year, including a six-week publicity tour around the world. And then it was over, and I was all alone at the Pierre Hotel in New York, and everybody had gone and left me. It was finished. I got my first lesson in the expandability of the human spirit in Hollywood.

Jessica Lange
Rolling Breaks, 1983

Ordinary Dream Capital

Many people visiting Hollywood for the first time are in for a big disappointment: it is not what one might expect—it's totally ordinary! For years the Chamber of Commerce has been trying to correct this impression, but without a great deal of success. I stood on the corner of Hollywood and Vine, that magical-sounding location which stirs the imagination of people all over the world, and was deflated by its utter mundaneness. I could have been standing on a street corner in Greensburg.

Carroll Baker
Baby Doll, 1983

Equestrienne

I go horseback riding a lot. I'd rather shovel horse manure than listen to that Hollywood b.s.

Mary Crosby
New York Post, October 24, 1983

Bad Trip

In Memphis, they think of women as children, but they treat them well. In Hollywood, they think of them as children, but treat them badly.

Cybill Shepherd
Daily News, November 1, 1983

★ ★ ★

Not That Important

I feel very lucky that I was part of that golden age of movies—especially the Metro musicals. But I remember the times that my husband, Larry Parks, and I would go East to do Broadway, or go out on the road with a play, or to England to play at the London Palladium, and we would suddenly look at each other and laugh and say, "What d'you know? Hollywood is *not* the most important place in the world!" The publicity departments of the studios, the Harry Cohns and L.B. Mayers, the Hedda Hoppers and Louella Parsons, all seemed to try to make you feel it was.

Betty Garrett
November, 1983

What is So Rare

Sincerity in Hollywood is as rare as virginity at Malibu High School.

Hal Kanter
The Hollywood Reporter, November 16, 1983

Prime Cut

In Hollywood, a woman is a piece of meat. It's *worse* than any Bob Guccione fantasy you might have. That's not my world; I'm appalled by it.

Brian De Palma
American Film, December, 1983

★ ★ ★

Saved by Cassette

Hollywood: It's like Sodom and Gomorrah, only the names have been changed. Men loving men, women loving women, drugs running rampant. And everyone wants to be a star. I always carry my cassette with me. Not to boogie-boogie, but to listen to my religious tapes.

Mr. T
Us, January 16, 1984

★ ★ ★

Squirms of Endearment

When I was a young actress working in Hollywood, I was always aware of the prostitution of girls in the film business. Today, it's all so homosexual—the boys having to sleep around with other guys to get places. At my acting school, I say to my male students, "It was the girls for a while. Now it's your turn, boys!"

I came out in 1942 from the New York theater. My mother was an actress and my father an orchestra conductor. I only came here because I had a test contract with Warner Brothers. They liked the test, so I got a six-month option and was immediately put into a WAC training short with Eleanor Parker and Faye Emerson. I was just a kid with baby fat who furthermore had a strep throat and was very sick throughout the shooting—a well-bred young lady didn't complain. Consequently, my face looked like a pudding on screen, with two raisins for eyes, so Jack Warner fired me.

On the strength of my earlier test, however, the next day I signed a seven-year contract with Columbia Pictures, going on to do many features there. Some were pretty good, like *A Song to Remember, My Name is Julia Ross, Undercover Man* and *The Dark Past*.

Harry Cohn, the legendary "King Cohn" who ruled Columbia, was a truly common, crass, uneducated boor with the most beautiful blue eyes. The first time I met him, he said to this virginal young thing, who had been educated in the best schools and whose grandfather was then the Prime Minister of the Netherlands, "Look, honey, if you're going to f--- anybody at this studio, it's going to be me and don't you forget it!" I was probably one of the very few people who didn't sleep with management while I was there, and it was *very* hard not to. I'm amused by these books written today by former Columbia actresses who claim Cohn never laid a hand on them, when short of being in the bedroom at the time I *know* he laid plenty on them.

Eventually, I did learn a grudging respect for Cohn. That famous quote he gave on how he evaluated films is quite apt: "If my ass squirms, it's bad. If my ass doesn't squirm, it's good." I learned, too, that if he gave his word he stuck by it. Another time, we were discussing something in his office when his secretary interrupted us to tell him that Robert Rossen, who was a top director, had been waiting for a while to see him. "Let him wait!", Cohn barked. "If he sits there twenty more minutes he'll forget what he came here to complain about." I never forgot that.

For years, Harry Cohn said variations to me of "Look, you have no sex appeal but you sure can act." He knew I could act because while at Columbia I had done a successful Broadway

Alfred Hitchcock is shown directing the James Stewart–Doris Day–Paramount film *The Man Who Knew Too Much* in 1955.

play called *John Loves Mary* and *The New York Times* told him I could.

After re-signing with Columbia at the end of my contract, I went to New York again and played *The Respectful Prostitute* on stage. Mary Hunter, the director, convinced me that I was a much better actress than I knew or had had the chance to show at Columbia, so I went back to Cohn and—with forty weeks of pay facing me there—asked him to let me out of my contract. I told him, "You can find any number of girls to replace me. I'm not the American ideal type that movie audiences automatically warm to, but I can go to New York and become a really fine actress." He said he understood and would let me go. I told him he would get preference if Columbia ever wanted me for anything. My very next film was MGM's *An American in Paris*, which won the best picture Academy Award—did *this* piss him off.

During World War II, I lived in my car, kept my clothes there. I would pull into one motel and then another. Columbia didn't protect you—it was a terrible place. They didn't give a damn what you looked like. There were a few artists there, people like the writer Sidney Buchman, couturier Jean Louis and some others, but only here and there.

In the early fifties, when I went to work at MGM it was so different. They cared about *everything*. They brought so many skilled people over from Europe for each department. Once while making *Scaramouche* there I needed a rare antique perfume prop for a scene we were shooting that very day. In ten minutes I had five of them! Metro was incredible! To this day, when I go back to MGM I burst into tears remembering the wonderful care you received in every area of that fabulous studio.

I did a game show on the Columbia lot not long ago, and the dressing rooms are as dirty as they were back in the forties. Also, when I go into the recording studio there with my student, Barry Manilow, the place is also still filthy, though I noticed recently that they are trying to clean it up a *bit*.

Yet, some things are much better today. The cameras are better, the film is faster—we're just beginning to learn about this medium. When I was a girl in Hollywood, a script would have pages and pages of talk. We forgot that we were in *moving* pictures.

The seams started to unravel out here right after World War II, when the politicians promised that we would all be equal, that everything would be the same for everybody. So everything became debased and slothful. And it's ridiculous. We are not all equal. Artists are different; they are elite and know something others don't know.

I came out from the snobbish world of Europe and the theater. I found Hollywood appalling—as Gertrude Stein said of Oakland, it's just not there. I wouldn't live here now, except for the lovely weather, my beautiful home and my work. There is no culture.

I never felt at home anywhere, much less here. I never really went to Hollywood parties until I was at Metro and then did attend some given by John Houseman and his wife—he produced *Executive Suite*, which won me an Oscar nomination. I was always more comfortable being with intellectual people. Wild parties? Never saw any, though they probably happened. I would have been too chicken anyway. I've only seen one porno film, at age fourteen, and I watched one scene, became ill and left. A friend of my mother's showed it to me, which says a lot for Mother's friends.

A while back my mother, who as Consuela Flowerton had been in pictures and worked with Rudolph Valentino, came out and I showed her my star on Hollywood Boulevard.

"Isn't all this appalling?", I asked, looking around at the tackiness. "It must break your heart to see it like this."

"No," Mother replied. "Hollywood was always like this."

Nina Foch
March 27, 1984

Fiberglas Fun

Being part of that madness, you can't say you're glad you did it, you can say you're glad it's over with. Living here in Hollywood, being in the *Enquirer* every other week. You can also say it was awful. It was sort of like Fiberglas underwear—interesting but painful.

Robin Williams
April 22, 1984

Companies vs. Cohns

Hollywood is probably the one city in the world that is ahead of everyplace else. Every fashion that ever amounted to anything started in Hollywood. I don't care what they say about Paris. It started in Hollywood. Clothes fashions—punk fashions—fashions that nobody ever thought of before started here. It's a fast life, and an expensive place to live. I'm not really *in* Hollywood, in a sense. I am so far on the edge of that, although I own and run a business here, Beverly Garland's Howard Johnson Resort Lodge, which in itself takes a lot of time and perseverance and work.

Some actors write exercise books, or open boutiques. I fold sheets.

I am not a girl that goes to Hollywood parties, never did. I go to big charity things, at times, most having to do with California's Governor Deukmejian, or Peter Schabarum, who is on the County Board of Supervisors, or Robert Philabosian, our District Attorney. So my role in Hollywood is fairly political and also business-oriented.

Although I am an actress, I have never gone around with the Hollywood group of people. My best friend is an actor, Ed Nelson, but I know very few actors and actresses. You meet actors and you love them and just think that they're the best things in the world while you do a picture and then you go back to your own life. This is because I'm married to a man who is not in the entertainment business, so we have a whole life away from that.

Hollywood has changed radically over the years. Recently, I did a TV show with Virginia Mayo, who was a big movie star in the forties and fifties. She was so great to talk to. She raved about the old Hollywood, explaining how wonderful it was to be taken care of. I was just starting out then and didn't see much of that era, but Virginia Mayo was *there*. Mrs. (Samuel) Goldwyn would pick her up and take her to parties. And she misses it all desperately. It's awfully hard to be in a cocoon and be loved and cared for and then thrown out. It's tough. It's very difficult to be a survivor in this town. To have had the glory, the fame, and to have nothing today is, I would imagine, very hard.

Under the old studio system, you were a little doll wrapped in a gauze package. You were picked up and set down and told where to go and told how to walk and told what to see and told what to say and told what to wear and how to do your hair and told how to do your eyebrows and told how to make up your lips. You were told everything. You were a commodity and they owned you lock, box and sock.

You didn't have to think. The limousine would pick you up at home and put you on the set and from that time on you were taken care of. It's not that way anymore. The studios are not run by the big Louis B. Mayers, Jack Warners or Harry Cohns, and they are not the bosses. The insurance companies are the bosses and the banks are the bosses. And there are lots of independent theater people out there today—actors who have taken scripts and finally got the money together and have gone out and really tried to do something.

Today, you are not graduated into a star. Let's look at Clark Gable, who was one of the biggest stars in the world. How do you know that he would be a star today? You don't know that, because every single thing he did was planned. He did a picture and then they said, well, the people liked him in this, or they liked him in that. Take Gary Cooper: was he really that incredible an actor, or was it that he was given properties that brought out what people loved about Gary Cooper? Gary Cooper played Gary Cooper, John Wayne played John Wayne, Jimmy Cagney played Jimmy Cagney. And that's how it went. And they became stars. Jean Harlow played Jean Harlow, Constance Bennett played Constance Bennett, Carole Lombard played Carole Lombard.

There were a few people that broke out of this mold, and they went through *hell* getting out of it. Like Bette Davis, who said, "I'm not going to play these stinking scripts," and I think for a couple of years she didn't work and had to sue.

It's all different now. Your workshops today are television. Especially daytime television, which hires a lot of very pretty young people. They don't really care whether those people can act. They learn to act on *Capitol* and soap operas like that. When you get into nighttime soaps, you have got to pretty well know how to act—they don't usually hire you unless you are a capable actor. *Depending.* I mean, if the public likes you and you can't act, so what, the public is going to buy you and so is the insurance company and that's the way it's going to be.

Today's stars are stars because they've done a television series and sometimes you never hear of them again, or they're a star in a picture and you never hear of them again, because they can't get another picture. In the old days you'd have so many pictures a year planned for you. Now that's all changed. There is probably a better opportunity for kids today, though, because you've got television and television commercials. Years ago you didn't have that—all you had was radio, and it was a very closed shop. Nowadays you can get your foot in by getting a small part on television, and who knows, you might take off from that.

The transition from television into movies is very difficult for an actor; not many have done it. Once you're a television actor, it seems like you're a television actor. Once you're a movie actor, you're a movie actor. Sometimes because you're doing a television series you're not hired for a movie, because you're so identified with that television show that the thinking is people might not accept you away from it, so that makes it very difficult. And actors have to work. So sometimes you take a television show and say, if I get a picture, okay; if not. . . .

Hollywood is more sprawling today, it's not the little community, it's grown, it's huge. The studios are not the friendly, wonderful little places they used to be with the commissaries and everybody knew everybody else. People come, people go. Producers come, producers go. The old studios are finished—over and done.

To me, though, Hollywood is still a small town, because I've lived here all my life. I think anybody coming here and looking at L.A. and looking at the crowded freeways and looking at Hollywood Boulevard would say, "Oh my gosh, Hollywood Boulevard is a disaster. Rodeo Drive is for the rich and the Arabs. The pace is too fast. There's every kook in the bloody world here."

People like myself *would* like to move out. I'd like to get out of here, go to Seattle, someplace. I don't need all this. I'm lucky that I have a wonderful house on top of a hill; that's my haven.

But there's no use kidding yourself: the opportunities are here. If you really want to work (and although you love New York and may be a great New Yorker), where are you going to get the jobs, where are you going to be seen, where are you going to go? Right here, good old Hollywood, California. And that's why thousands of kids come out all the time and end up on the streets, because we have every kind of kook and con-man alive. But if you ever do make it, and you *can* make it, the glitter is here. This is *it*.

Beverly Garland
April, 1984

Hit the Deck (MGM, 1955) was a starry nautical musical with Jane Powell, Vic Damone, Ann Miller, Tony Martin, Debbie Reynolds and Russ Tamblyn.

The winning musical version of *My Sister Eileen* (Columbia, 1955) gave talented Betty Garrett (second from left) her best screen chance, assisted by Kurt Kasznar, Janet Leigh and Dick York.

Intrigue Time
Hollywood, where an intrigue and a victim are born every time two people meet.

Terry Moore
The Beauty and the Billionaire, 1984

Conversation Over
The quickest way to end a conversation in Hollywood is to mention cocaine. Suddenly everyone remembers he has to be somewhere else. What's their problem? I'm no threat. I'm not a narc!

Cliff Robertson
TV Guide, June 16, 1984

Lying in State
Hollywood columnists: All day long they lie in the sun, and when the sun goes down, they still lie.

Frank Sinatra
Hot Times, 1984

Cutting Remark
Hollywood is a lovely place to get knifed in.

Jackie Coogan
Films in Review, June–July, 1984

Hanging Lucky
Hollywood. People think you gave up your private life to the studios. Not true. If you were a big star and you got out of line—you drank, say—they protected you. That was true in many cases. But someone like me—I was never that big a star. I didn't have to give up anything. I was just lucky to hang in there.

Lucille Ball
Parade, June 24, 1984

Funereal Flamboyance
Hollywood funerals, like most of its milestones, are accompanied by the same flamboyance and flashbulbs that glamorize gayer occasions like parties and premieres. Here, even death is larger than life.

Candice Bergen
Knock Wood, 1984

Wilder Notion

Just as the whole world hates America, America hates Hollywood. There is that deep-seated notion that we are all phonies. Making ten thousand dollars a week and no taxes. Banging all those tall dames. Indoor and outdoor swimming pools. Sixteen in help. All driving Jensen Interceptors. Well, it's all true. Eat your heart out.

Billy Wilder
Things I Did . . . And Things I Think I Did, 1984

★ ★ ★

Disenchanted

I'm not enchanted by Hollywood's mystical golden path to fame. Fame is sometimes painful, tragic.

Jamie Lee Curtis
Parade, September 9, 1984

★ ★ ★

Community Publicity

Hollywood is the only place in the whole world where an amicable divorce means each one gets 50 percent of the publicity.

Lauren Bacall
National Enquirer, September 11, 1984

★ ★ ★

Prickly Heat

Being in Hollywood is like making love to a porcupine—it's a thousand pricks against one.

Anonymous Screenwriter
Niven's Hollywood, 1984

★ ★ ★

Hear No Evil

In Hollywood film circles, everybody lies, but it doesn't really matter because nobody listens.

Jim Backus
The Hollywood Reporter, September 14, 1984

PLAYING

No Freedom
I was bowled over by studio life. I was drunk on what, at first glimpse, appeared to be its utter freedom and lack of restraint, and what I learned later is the most delusive thing about it. There is no real freedom in Hollywood.

Gary Cooper
Photoplay, the 1920s

★ ★ ★

Female Casanova?
Hollywood's gossip-mongers have gleefully reported me as being in the arms of first one lover, then another. Anyone who habitually reads the fan magazines and newspaper chatter-columns might well conclude that I am a female Casanova, and that I cry my loves from the housetops.

Constance Bennett
Screen Book, the 1930s

★ ★ ★

So-So City
Hollywood is all right for a while, but it's not my idea of a good time.

Ethel Merman
The 1930s

★ ★ ★

Close Call
Reading about the glamorous night-life of Hollywood is the closest I ever get to it.

Linda Darnell
Modern Screen, May, 1940

★ ★ ★

High Light
The highlight of the movie industry every year is the Academy Awards Dinner, at which time a committee, composed of none of my relatives, presents various acting awards. All the actresses and actors in Hollywood gather around to see what someone else thinks about their acting besides their press agents.

Bob Hope
They Got Me Covered, 1941

They're Unreal!

Hollywood girls are *too* beautiful—so beautiful that you can't actually believe they are real! And how in the world could a person fall in love with anyone who is unbelievable?

George Sanders
Screenland, March, 1942

★ ★ ★

Men More So

Hollywood men are the same as men everywhere—except more so. They've got a little more looks, a little more money, a little more ego. But they can be handled.

Betty Hutton
Motion Picture, February, 1944

★ ★ ★

Attention Getter

I made it a point to be seen at Hollywood showcases; Ciro's, Mocambo, wherever the producers went. I spent hours designing unusual gowns and hats that would oblige everyone to look at me when I entered. I went to Max Factor's and consulted with Fredericks the hair stylist for unusual coiffures . . . My name was unknown and this was my method of attracting attention to me—for the sake of publicity and for the sake of acquiring the interest of the producers.

Maria Montez
Screenland, August, 1944

★ ★ ★

Bari Taste

Here in Hollywood, it seems to be the smart idea to let everyone know you're carrying the torch. Publicizing a private life is considered *the* thing. To me, that's bad taste. If I ever had a broken heart, I wouldn't tell anyone about it, not even my mother. I have too much pride to want to air my problems publicly.

Lynn Bari
Silver Screen, August, 1945

★ ★ ★

Good Listeners

A lot of girls you see at Hollywood parties work like mad to be witty. They worry about small talk and the kind of impression they are making on others. I'm always amazed to discover how few of them really know how to listen. Any girl can be a good listener—whether she's pretty or plain or too tall or too short or whatever. And how men appreciate that quality!

Helmut Dantine
Motion Picture, October, 1945

Once is Enough

You take a girl to dinner (in Hollywood). That's in all the columns. But that's not all. The photographers take pictures. The pictures are printed. Now they're not printed once. They're sent to magazines and syndicates, all kinds of publications. The printing gets spread out over six months. You've dated a girl once—but it looks as though you'd taken her out every night for months!

John Hodiak
Silver Screen, November, 1945

★ ★ ★

Good Night's Rest

I'll admit Hollywood bachelors are very attractive—but we just don't hit it off! Even if they gather around at first, they drift away pretty soon, because I don't drink and I don't like to stay up late. Actually, I don't see how anbody can stand a diet of three nights a week at Ciro's or Mocambo or places like that! I'd much rather get up early in the morning and play tennis when I'm not in a picture—and when I'm working, there's no question at all about getting a good night's rest!

Joan Caulfield
Silver Screen, November, 1946

★ ★ ★

Fireside Chat

As for the so-called Hollywood night life, neither Will (Price) nor I care for it. We work hard at the studios all day long and by evening we're ready to slip into something comfortable and relax by the fireside.

Maureen O'Hara
Screen Stars, February, 1947

★ ★ ★

Friendly Place

I do like Hollywood. It's a friendly place and is great for anyone who lives an informal, outdoor life as I do. The only thing I don't like about it is its social aspects. I'm definitely anti-social. Oh, I don't go about sticking my tongue out at people on the street, but I just don't like to stay up late and I loathe such dialogue as "How nice you look tonight, Minnie, in that cheesecloth dinner dress."

Richard Haydn
Motion Picture, June, 1947

Joan Collins, twenty-five years before her sensation on TV's *Dynasty*, played the title role in *The Girl on the Red Velvet Swing* (20th Century-Fox, 1955), opposite Ray Milland.

The principals in *The Second Greatest Sex* (Universal, 1955), a musical re-working of *Lysistrata*: Mary Marlo, Kathleen Case, Keith Andes, Mamie Van Doren, George Nader, Jeanne Crain, Jimmy Boyd, Edna Skinner, Bert Lahr, Kitty Kallen and Cousin Emmy.

Rush Act

There's a rush act in Hollywood but when you first arrive you don't know that. You're excited by the glitter and you think you must go to every party that's given. You tell yourself that you must be seen here and there. The races call you. Palm Springs calls you. Home becomes a place where you phone the cook and say you won't be back for dinner.

Dick Haymes
Photoplay, June, 1947

Urges

Hollywood is very hard on romance. You go out with someone once or twice, and the startled gentleman picks up his morning paper to read where somebody says he's going to marry you. Then he's scared off. And so, in a sense, are you. You worry about whether he thinks you are in any way responsible for the match-making urges columnists have.

Joan Caulfield
Photoplay, July, 1947

The Eyes Have It

That's the key to the Hollywood situation. To realize the ever-prying eye of publicity and be careful. Something can happen to two other fellows in a night club that's twice as bad as an incident with a star, but no one pays any attention. Hollywood is constantly being watched.

Irene Dunne
Screenland, August, 1947

Moppet's Morals Clause

I think Hollywood is very aware of morals. In my contract—as I'm sure is in all Hollywood star contracts—there is a clause which states that if I or any member of my family becomes involved in a scandal, the contract can be broken.

Shirley Temple
Screenland, August, 1947

Friends Suffice

I have never given a party to get publicity or to "dent" Hollywood society. I'm the type who doesn't think you have to be in society in any town. A lot of good friends are enough for me.

Lon McCallister
Screenland, September, 1947

Ego Beavers

Hollywood men have too much ego. They're spoiled. They treat actresses like working girls. Which, heaven knows, we are. They expect us to be amusing, don't bother to be fun themselves. Hollywood is a man's town, so they can get away with it.

Marie McDonald
Screenland, October, 1947

★ ★ ★

Party Trick

Someone once said that the trick was to throw a Hollywood party before it throws you.

Cobina Wright, Sr.
Screenland, October, 1947

★ ★ ★

Small Affairs

Harry (James) and I would rather spend an evening at home than go to the glitter spots that seem to be so popular. For instance, we take very little part in Hollywood night life, and we have yet to go to the Mocambo for the first time! We attend parties now and then, but they're usually small affairs given by our close friends. Besides, a heavy night life doesn't make early morning rising any easier, nor does it improve the disposition.

Betty Grable
Silver Screen, December, 1947

★ ★ ★

Lukewarm Welcome

I thought Hollywood would be mad and hectic. Big parties. Red mink carpets rolled out for me. Lights in the sky. Nobody rolled out even an imitation-rabbit carpet, or so much as turned on a flashlight.

Barbara Bel Geddes
Modern Screen, April, 1948

★ ★ ★

Date Grove

One of the reasons that the Hollywood "date" grove is so overpollenated is because the percentage of presentable, eligible and available men is so small. No bachelor is safe from either bobby-soxers or bel-dames. Consequently, the male citizens in these parts get overstuffed opinions of themselves. Since they have such a bevy of beauties to pick from, because the most attractive girls in the country seem to migrate here, the men can practically go out with whom they please every night.

Marilyn Maxwell
Screenland, July, 1948

Male Trouble

There are plenty of men in Hollywood who suffer from several vocational handicaps. Most of them are conceited. Others get dates with actresses simply because they want to be seen in public. And some of the males around Hollywood are ultra-materialistic! Another thing! Men in the film industry are so concerned with their work they don't spend much time with women.

Lizabeth Scott
January 24, 1949

★ ★ ★

Hollywood Romance

Hollywood has the reputation of being an impossible place to find a husband. But you can't prove it by me. I not only met my husband, Glenn Ford, at a Hollywood party, but an actor introduced us. Our first date was on a movie set. Hollywood columnists tagged us "an item." And for two years Glenn courted me between pictures until we were married in nearby Beverly Hills. Ours was a Hollywood romance from beginning to end.

Eleanor Powell
Screen Guide, February, 1949

★ ★ ★

Revolving Social Life

All social life in Hollywood revolves around six major studios and one restaurant.

Evelyn Waugh
The 1940s

★ ★ ★

"Dignity—Always Dignity"

I do enjoy Hollywood parties, but, unfortunately, the term "Hollywood" when tagged on to social gatherings becomes something entirely different to the public from a mere pleasant evening. Society in Hollywood is not made up, as some believe, of questionable antics. Far from it. Those I've attended have been dignified and perfectly managed. The best parties here are given by Joan Bennett, Mrs. William Goetz, Mrs. Alfred Bloomingdale, Mrs. Tom May and Joan Dozier—also known as Joan Fontaine. As for the hosts, Billy Haines is just about tops.

Joan Crawford
Screenland, May, 1949

★ ★ ★

Her Bill

I see so many of the genuinely successful girls in this town come to these parties alone, and leave alone, that I'm thrilled beyond words and thankful to the core to be going home with my Bill (Holden). Nothing else matters.

Brenda Marshall Holden
Silver Screen, November, 1949

East of Eden (Warner Brothers, 1955), director Elia Kazan's emotion-charged drama of youthful alienation, co-starred Julie Harris and James Dean, who died in September of that year at twenty-four.

Rodgers and Hammerstein's enduring musical play *The King and I* (20th Century-Fox, 1956) was superbly realized on screen by Rex Thompson, Yul Brynner (repeating his stage characterization and winning the Oscar) and the exquisite Deborah Kerr.

You Don't Meet People
I've never married but hope to, eventually. In ten years in Hollywood you don't meet people you want to spend the rest of your life with.

Patricia Morison
1949

★ ★ ★

Dating Doldrums
Actresses meet very few men outside of the motion picture profession out here. If you do meet them, they seldom feel they can compete with actors. This is unfortunate and I am certain we miss knowing some very worthwhile men. (In addition), if you make good in Hollywood while you are still young, a woman makes more money than a man does, as a rule. So the young men of your own age have a great deal less than you, which spoils it somehow, no matter how hard you try to equalize things.

Patricia Neal
June 10, 1951

★ ★ ★

The Poor Souls
I've been lucky. When I see the kids who hang around the studios after the day's work, because they don't have any other life—unless someone asks them for a dinner date to Ciro's or some Hollywood party—well!

Jane Russell
Screenland, November, 1953

★ ★ ★

Pointless Wing-Dings
Frankly, we're not members of the Hollywood party set. I don't see much point to those big wing-dings filled with noise and smoke. As far as I can see, they're run on the basis of taking your wife and losing her for the evening. In the meantime, you shout across the table to strangers. That's not for me.

William Holden
Modern Screen, September, 1954

★ ★ ★

Funny About Boys
Too many phonies and frightened people in Hollywood. Certain factions even tried to choose my dates. I'm funny, I don't go out with boys I don't like. I don't even like the climate out there—give me the change of seasons.

Shirley Jones
Newark Sunday News, March 11, 1956

Always On

I turn the other way whenever an opportunist of any sort crosses my path, and believe me, the Hollywoods are full of them. I also try to avoid actors who are "always on," who never seem able to forget they're in the public eye—even in small gatherings. I'm the first to admit that very often they become very successful in the profession because they're so absorbed in themselves . . . and I often wonder, in my quiet moments, if I shouldn't display a little more of this quality myself.

Rhonda Fleming
Screen Parade, March, 1957

Shop Talk

In Hollywood, your social activities are restricted to the people you work with. You meet the same people at party after party. The cast is always the same—and the dialogue doesn't change much, either. Always shop talk.

Tyrone Power
The Seven Deadly Sins of Hollywood, 1957

Other Side of Paradise

Hollywood with all its jazziness and razz-ma-tazz is one of the world's lushest paradises. Glamorous as all get-out, it has fabulous nightclubs and gourmet restaurants. But Hollywood also has a lot of selfish, conniving people who take the edge off everything once you get to know them.

Sal Mineo
Modern Screen, August, 1958

Segregation

Hollywood is a segregated community. The top people—producers, directors, stars—make up the "A" Group, a tag which some members aren't too modest to hang on themselves. On other rungs of the social ladder you find the lesser breeds, who can be categorized as the "B" Group.

Keenan Wynn
Ed Wynn's Son, 1959

Party Protocol
Those Hollywood functions, which look oh-so-glamorous, are hard work. It's not play at all when you go to a party. Producers and directors are there with their wives, looking at you. You must look your best, and behave beautifully, and so must your escort. Your escort is *extremely* important, must not drink too much, must have good manners, must *not* say anything to offend. Hollywood actors know the rules about these functions, the little techniques, whereas a date who is a lawyer doesn't understand the importance.

Martha Hyer
August 4, 1959

Hot Pursuit
Before I got to Hollywood, I had gone along on the assumption that it was the role of the male to pursue the female. I discovered that women know far more about seduction than men. Maybe it was the air around Hollywood, the competition among women to get places. It made some of them wild.

Errol Flynn
My Wicked, Wicked Ways, 1959

Guadalcanal & Vine
Hollywood was like Guadalcanal with houses. It had palm trees and strange natives, and there was lots of fighting going on. The big difference was the beautiful homes.

Jack Paar
I Kid You Not, 1959

Out for One Thing
There isn't a decent man in Hollywood. They're all out for one thing. They don't even bother romancing you. Some of them are good-looking and they think that's enough. The hell with that.

Marilyn Monroe
Marilyn Monroe, 1960

On the Clan
(The Clan's) a figment of someone's imagination. Naturally, people in Hollywood socialize with friends, as they do in any community. But we do not get together in childish fraternities, as some people would like to think.

Frank Sinatra
1960

Charles Laughton excelled as the foxy defense attorney in *Witness for the Prosecution* (United Artists, 1957), with Tyrone Power and Henry Daniell.

Frank Sinatra, Eddie Albert and Beverly Garland brought conviction to the film about bibulous nightclub comic Joe E. Lewis entitled *The Joker is Wild* (Paramount, 1957).

Rumors Are Lying
Rumors here in Hollywood have me going out with people I never even met. Even though I've grown up in Hollywood I still can't get used to all the gossip.

Natalie Wood
Modern Screen, December, 1961

Social Whirl
Hollywood's social whirl is, for the most part, pretentious and politic. There were a few who gathered fascinating people together at a well appointed board groaning under excellent food and wine. Certainly Basil Rathbone's wife, Ouida, was a magnificent hostess as was Joseph Cotten's wife, Lenore. The David Selznicks and the Jules Steins also entertained brilliantly. But most of Hollywood who decorated their homes like Scottish shooting boxes and sent the ladies off to the powder room while the gentlemen stayed at the table sipping brandy didn't know a cadenza from an arpeggio.

Bette Davis
The Lonely Life, 1962

Scantie Mame
A cynic said Hollywood's a place where, if you don't nail it down, someone will steal it—and if you do, someone will steal a hammer to pry it loose. I don't fully believe that; but I don't wear panties any more—this startles the Hollywood wolves so much they don't know what to pull at, so they leave me alone!

Mamie Van Doren
My Naughty, Naughty Life!, 1964

Numbers Please
In my early Hollywood days I was too busy and too scared to collect phone numbers.

Ronald Reagan
Where's the Rest of Me?, 1965

All Wet in Washington
I feel everybody in Hollywood is much more serious about their work. You don't read any more about people getting tossed into pools at parties. I read they're doing that in Washington now.

Martha Raye
The 1960s

Pubic Wars
It is not really a triumph to be a success with these Hollywood ladies, because they have so little opportunity with men.

Richard Burton
Richard Burton, 1965

A&P Nuts
People think that because a few actors out there were nuts, we *all* were. Nothing but wild parties. What wild parties? We all went to bed at 11. I've seen parties in New York that make Hollywood look like the A&P.

Ann Sheridan
TV Guide, the 1960s

Green Kid
I was a green kid as naive as you can be, from Ohio, when I first arrived in Hollywood. I had no ugly things put to me. Never. I've never seen a bad Hollywood party. I've been abroad and been shocked. I don't say it doesn't exist. All I can say is Warner Bros. couldn't have been a better place for kids to grow up in. If you want to be a lady you'll be treated like one.

Eleanor Parker
Los Angeles Times, April 24, 1966

Invitations Guaranteed
Being an extra man in any town attracts invitations. In Hollywood, with its plethora of temporarily unattached females, it guaranteed them.

George Oppenheimer
The View from the Sixties, 1966

The Uninvited
A lot of people say to me "How about the parties and the orgies in Hollywood?" and I say "I don't know. I guess then never invited me."

Patsy Kelly
Film Fan Monthly, February, 1968

Grown Up Now
I had a ball in Hollywood when I was younger—but what do I want with it now? I guess I've grown up.

Victor Mature
Whatever Became Of . . . ?, 1968

Animal Farm

Hollywood gives a young girl the aura of one giant, self-contained orgy farm, its inhabitants dedicated to crawling into every pair of pants they can find.

Veronica Lake
Veronica, 1969

★ ★ ★

Loathsome Activities

I loathe all the peripheral activities that go with being a Hollywood actor—the green room teas, the parties and the "we-must-get-together" cracks that flow so insincerely.

Anthony Quinn
January 29, 1970

★ ★ ★

Olympic Nights

The philosophy of Hollywood publicity was built on the idea that almost any news was good news, and the result was an incredible accent on trivia. Over two dozen fan magazines and countless syndicated columns, aided by platoons of press agents, magnified the smallest details of movie-making and movie folk. If nothing of particular interest unfolded to feed the insatiable publicity machine, then it was invented. Glamour was made remote and unapproachable. There was no such thing as the girl or boy next door, and the nightlife of the gods was reported from Olympus, sheathed in a mysterious, rosy glow.

Joan Bennett
The Bennett Playbill, 1970

★ ★ ★

All-Day Item

If a star came to New York from the West, he could have dinner in a restaurant like everybody else, leave quietly and get lost in the city. In Hollywood, wherever I went, it was: "How do you do, Mr. Wanger. So glad to see you. Want your usual table?" There's a whole dream-world attitude about everything. For instance, in the morning, no work is done until everyone has read the gossip columns in *Variety* and *The Hollywood Reporter*. If anything is reported that's scandalous about the studio, nobody works. They talk about that item all day long.

Walter Wanger
The Real Tinsel, 1970

★ ★ ★

Not as Sociable

One Hollywood custom which impressed me is the habit of entertaining in the home. In France, we do not do this. Actors in Paris go to the studio, do their work, get along as well as possible with the co-workers, then return home to one's private life. We do not socialize as much as you do here.

Jeanne Moreau
June 13, 1970

Susan Hayward received the best actress Oscar for her shattering portrayal of executed murderess Barbara Graham in the Robert Wise-directed *I Want to Live!* (United Artists, 1958).

Divine Madness

In 1952, Hollywood didn't strike me as a place to settle and continue my career. I was rather snooty about it then. But looking back, I'm terribly glad I was there during that period, because it was just toward the end of baroque Hollywood. They hadn't pulled down the Garden of Allah yet. I went and had a look at the swimming pool and heard all the tales about (John) Barrymore pushing people in. And stars were still driving about town in cars lined with tiger skin. I went to some mad Hollywood parties. At one there was a Russian who said, "I've got a new trick—I can eat glass." And he picked up a wine glass and crunched it and immediately he was covered with blood and we all had to take him off to the hospital. I was younger then and a little too serious about life, and I thought all that was dreadful. But now I realize how lucky I was to have seen it before Hollywood became the Ivy League accountant's department.

Peter Finch
Films and Filming, August, 1970

★ ★ ★

A Slipper of Champagne

I was never part of any wild Hollywood scene. My best friends were my stand-in and my movie crews. I never had a man drink champagne out of my shoes or anything like that. That all happened during the Gloria Swanson era. When I got there, it was all over.

Alice Faye
May 2, 1971

★ ★ ★

Crowds Gathered

I've remained friends with Bette (Davis) to this day. Not long ago, we both had to travel to Hollywood for something, so we decided to take a train and catch up. In every town, crowds would gather around her, and she was like a queen, pretending not to notice all the excitement. She'd keep talking, asking about every man on the old Warners lot, and I'd say, "Well, I never had an affair with him" and she'd roar, "Well, you're the only one who didn't, Fitzie!"

Geraldine Fitzgerald
Sunday News, May 9, 1971

★ ★ ★

Scared to Death

Marilyn (Monroe) followed me from room to room at a party at Clifton Webb's one night in Hollywood. "I don't want to get too far away from you," she said, "I'm scared." I told her we were all scared.

Judy Garland
Weep No More, My Lady, 1972

On the Town
Hollywood was gay, glittering and exciting. Everyone went out on the town—dinner at LaRue's or Romanoff's or Victor Hugo's or Chez Roland at the beach . . . And then to the Mocambo or Ciro's to dance, dance, dance.

Ann Miller
Miller's High Life, 1972

★ ★ ★

Press Agent Glamour
Hollywood hasn't changed. Oh, it's had its phases and its times of stress, but movie-making is basically the same as it ever was. They don't make movies anyplace in the world with the efficiency and the know-how that they have right here. As for the glamorous side of Hollywood, it never was, really. That was all press agent stuff. For the most part we were working too hard to live a life of constant parties and revelry. The jet-setters are the party people, not actors.

Bette Davis
Movie Digest, May, 1973

★ ★ ★

Resilient Fun
Party fun in formal Hollywood would reach a high point when the butler brought in a rubber hot dog, and all gathered around to watch the patsy try to eat it.

Phil Silvers
This Laugh is on Me, 1973

★ ★ ★

Nobody Home
In Hollywood a party is not a party unless it is one of those "Everybody who was anybody was there" affairs. What a God damn crushing blow it must be to 159,890,000 Americans to find out that they're not anybody!

Robert Taylor
The Life of Robert Taylor, 1973

★ ★ ★

Honest Opinion
Hollywood . . . I can honestly say that for fun I would rather go to Fort Sill, Oklahoma.

Robert Benchley
Starring Robert Benchley, 1973

Lobby Lies

The postpremiere lobby is one of the falsest things about Hollywood. The people who have made the film—the producer and director and stars—stand there as their friends file by and solemnly tell them how great they thought the film was. Even if it's terrible, you hear the same ridiculous comments—"A wonderful film" or "I was never so moved in my life" or "You've got yourself a sure Oscar winner there."

Mervyn LeRoy
Take One, 1974

★ ★ ★

Kind to Strays

Every year from the time I came to Hollywood I have given a Christmas Eve party. I have it for all the strays. I was alone, very lonesome and homesick for my family, so I had people in that were in the same situation. When I married Freddie (Brisson), he had his strays and the party has gone on traditionally every year. Of course, there are dropouts because many of the strays would marry and have children. This party became quite famous.

Rosalind Russell
Hollywood Speaks!, 1974

★ ★ ★

Nobody Cares

In Hollywood today, the old stars never get invited to parties because we're not box office. Everything goes in cycles, and I was never in a cycle to begin with. My best friends are my dental hygienist and a man who works at the Sands Hotel who used to be a bell captain. I don't even think you could organize a reunion of the old MGM stars. Everybody is gone from the old studio and nobody cares.

Jane Powell
Sunday News, February 10, 1974

★ ★ ★

Word to Wise

Wise Hollywood hostesses never invited columnists to their parties, because once you did you could never leave them off your list for future parties or they would crucify you.

Ray Milland
Wide-Eyed in Babylon, 1974

Margaret O'Brien, Eileen Heckart, Anthony Quinn and Sophia Loren headed the cast of *Heller in Pink Tights* (Paramount, 1959), detailing the trials of itinerant actors in the 1880s.

Elizabeth Taylor won a best actress Oscar as the tragic, sometime model in *Butterfield 8* (MGM, 1960), adapted from the John O'Hara novel and co-starring Eddie Fisher, her then-husband.

Party a Night

In those days (the 1940s), there was a party every single night in Hollywood. We listened to Hoagy Carmichael or Eddy Duchin at the piano, to Bing Crosby, Judy Garland or Frank Sinatra sing or to Charlie Chaplin reminisce. But soon people got bored and started playing "The Game," a form of charades with very complicated rules. Stars like Gable, Bogart, Tyrone Power, James Stewart and Henry Fonda made funny noises, hopped around on one foot and generally enjoyed behaving like children.

Lilli Palmer
People, 1975

Opportunity Knocks

A lot of people said, "Oh, you don't want to go to that terrible place (Hollywood)." My family particularly—other friends: "I hear wild parties and stupidity and other things." "Well," I said, "that's a great opportunity for somebody that maybe would not be too much interested in wild parties."

King Vidor
The Men Who Made the Movies, 1975

Pendulum

Christmas parties! New Year's parties! Birthday parties! Parties to celebrate the end of a picture or a marriage, the signing of a contract, or the birth of a baby! There was always an excuse for a party in Hollywood. And at the end of a strenuous six-day week Saturday night was dedicated to letting off steam. The needle measuring Hollywood parties swung between orderliness and orgies.

David Niven
Bring on the Empty Horses, 1975

★ ★ ★

Playing for Keeps

Hollywood invented a macabre party game called Airplane. This concerned a sizable transport which, owing to some mechanical defect, was destined to take off and never again to land, its crew and passengers doomed to fly around and around forever. The game consisted of providing tickets for those the players felt they could well do without. Hedda Hopper and Louella Parsons, unassailably the two most powerful gossip columnists in the world, had no difficulty whatever in finding space and, a refinement of torture, were usually allotted seats next to each other.

David Niven
1975

Record Holder

I was in Hollywood a week before I got laid. I don't know, that just may be a record.

John Garfield
Body and Soul, 1975

★ ★ ★

Lonely Ladies

Outsiders, I believe, have a distorted view of Hollywood habits. They assume that every actress is automatically popular, has a date book filled weeks in advance. I find actresses are often very lonely people. The public assumes them to be popular and so neglects them. Men will leap to the conclusion that it would be pointless to ask them for dates, because they are sure to be busy, and so don't bother. And I know of many great ladies who spend night after night alone.

Cyd Charisse
The Two of Us, 1976

★ ★ ★

Maelstrom

I got caught up in the fast life of Hollywood. The most important thing to me at the time was living like a star was supposed to live. I never worried about where the money went—I was too busy making movies and enjoying life to care about good solid investments.

Dana Andrews
National Enquirer, the 1970s

★ ★ ★

Casting Call

I knew nothing about cards, and if you don't play poker in Hollywood, well, poor fellow, because that's where the pictures are cast and the deals made.

William Dieterle
Close-Up: The Contract Director, 1976

★ ★ ★

Pasta with Ernst

My idea of a Hollywood party—to which I didn't go very often—is one where I, seated on a staircase, finish eating cold spaghetti with Ernst Lubitsch.

René Clair
American Film, September, 1976

Getting Gertie's Gadget

Among the cream of Hollywood, being intelligent and talented is not enough. You have to be successful and rich. You can spend entire evenings in Hollywood talking about money or gadgets—the gadgets you have or the gadgets you're going to acquire. It's so boring.

Leslie Caron
After Dark, October, 1976

★ ★ ★

When Stars Were Stars

Parties aren't like they used to be. Let's face it, we both remember what Hollywood was like when stars were really stars, and glamour was truly glamour. I can remember planning what I was going to wear to a big social event weeks before it happened. Clark Gable and Carole Lombard, Norma Shearer and Irving Thalberg, Joan Crawford, Jeanette MacDonald, Myrna Loy would be there to light up an exciting evening. It's so different now. Large groups of dissociated people seem to show up in anything from denims to loose robes—even the males. And they seem to have so little in common. Why go?

Lana Turner
October 24, 1976

★ ★ ★

Business as Usual

I hadn't been in Hollywood for a long time and Kirk Douglas' son got married so he gave this huge party at the Beverly Wilshire. People kept asking me, "Has Hollywood changed?", but I couldn't see any difference. They were all there. Name the star and there he or she was.

Evelyn Keyes
Interview, 1977

★ ★ ★

Lamarrland

I never worked hard, as hard as Bette Davis, perhaps, but I enjoyed it. I played in the greatest glittering playground that anyone ever created. You think Disneyland is something? Nothing compared to Hollywood in those years. I wasn't ambitious with my career, I was just ambitious to live, live, live.

Hedy Lamarr
The 1970s

★ ★ ★

Stratified Soirées

Hollywood was rigidly stratified. Every Saturday night there were the ten-thousand-dollar-a-week parties where nobody who made under eight thousand were invited. Then there were the five-thousand-dollar parties, the two-thousand-dollar parties, etc.

Jean-Pierre Aumont
Sun and Shadow, 1977

Director Joseph L. Mankiewicz (right) at work with Elizabeth Taylor, Rex Harrison and Richard Burton on *Cleopatra* (20th Century-Fox, 1963).

Katherine Anne Porter's best-selling novel *Ship of Fools* (Columbia, 1965) was filmed with Vivien Leigh, Simone Signoret, José Ferrer, Lee Marvin, Oskar Werner, Elizabeth Ashley, George Segal, José Greco, Michael Dunn, Charles Korvin and Heinz Ruehmann.

Not-So-Marvelous Party

Sue Mengers, who's my agent in Hollywood, invited me to a party she was throwing. She assured me it was going to be a wonderful party because all of hers were. So I went. Afterward she said, "You know, I'm so sorry you had to come to this party. It was the only one I've had in a long time that wasn't a good one." It's always ahead or just behind (in Hollywood).

Woody Allen
American Film, May, 1977

Tracy Tops

Those who know say that nobody—but nobody—could drink or fight or cause more trouble than Spencer Tracy in the early days of Hollywood.

Stanley Kramer
Close-Ups, 1978

The Exception

A woman may go with whomever she pleases in any other town but Hollywood.

Loretta Young
Tyrone Power: The Last Idol, 1979

Party Lists

This town does something to performers who tend to be sensitive. Your worth in this town is determined by your degree of success. It's a horrible fact. You make the party list once you are in the limelight and you are recognizable. Every other town in the world, if someone said what do you do, I'd say with pride I'm an actor. People ask you in Hollywood and you muffle your voice as you answer, 'cause you know the next question is going to be, "What are you doing *now*?"

Peter Strauss
Rona Barrett's Hollywood, the 1970s

Caviar, Cocaine, Anyone?

You go to almost any Hollywood party, and there's a little booze left on the side for the alcoholics. Nearly everyone else is standing around the table, dishing into two big bowls. One carries the caviar, the other, cocaine.

Sammy Davis, Jr.
Hollywood in a Suitcase, 1980

See No Evil

I'm so happy that I arrived in Hollywood in time to get a taste of the Golden Era. Until I met Ronnie, I had no really serious romance in Hollywood, but, of course, I dated. I went to the sneak previews and parties—sometimes at famous actors' homes or in well-known night-clubs. My first date with Ronnie was at Ciro's, a nightclub which is gone now, as is most of that way of life. The Sunset Strip doesn't have the glamour today that it had then . . . I never saw the Hollywood I often heard about—the heavy drinking, pushing starlets in pools, etc. I suppose it existed, but I never saw it.

Nancy Davis Reagan
Nancy, 1980

★ ★ ★

Above the Title

I had become as bad as all the other people in Hollywood when I went to parties; I forgot everybody who wasn't above the title as soon as I shook his or her hand and thanked him or her for the kind remarks about my pictures.

Gloria Swanson
Swanson on Swanson, 1980

★ ★ ★

Bathroom Bound

Now it's cocaine. You go to a Hollywood party now and all during the party, there's this conga line to the bathroom. You hear sniffling behind the door, like everybody's crying. And nobody's at the party anymore. Hollywood should build large bathrooms and forget about living rooms.

George Hamilton
Rona Barrett's Hollywood, October, 1980

★ ★ ★

Loss of Status

It was an accepted fact in Hollywood at that time (the 1940s) that producer Sam Speigel gave the definitive New Year's Eve party. That meant that if you weren't invited to his party, your entire coming year was ruined as far as your status in the industry was concerned.

Shelley Winters
Shelley, 1980

★ ★ ★

Target for Tonight

The true objective of your typical Hollywood Don Juan is not so much the lady's bedroom as a story in the gossip columns.

Philip Dunne
Take Two, 1980

Vital on Set
Kids today reading fan magazines must have thought Robert Taylor and I did nothing but attend premieres in furs and jewelry, but we never went out. We were younger, but our vitality was used up on the set. I don't know where they got the idea Hollywood was a never-ending round of parties. Most people were working then, so if you were under contract the studios got their pound of flesh, so you never had time to go to parties. Today, they're all unemployed so they've got nothing better to do than stay up all night. Now they write books about everybody that read to me like fairy tales.

Barbara Stanwyck
Daily News, April 13, 1981

★ ★ ★

I Was a Lousy Lover
You know what it was to be out here in Hollywood? Christ! You'd go to dinner at Chasen's. There'd be Tyrone Power at one table with a knockout of a girl, and Bob Taylor at another table with Barbara Stanwyck. Those guys gave me a complex. They *looked* like lovers! Sure I had to kiss girls in pictures, Bette Davis, Barbara Stanwyck, Joan Crawford, Joan Bennett, but I wasn't any good at it.

Henry Fonda
Fonda: My Life, 1981

★ ★ ★

Scenic View
Hollywood and the movie studios were a spectacular place to grow up. When I was 16 and at Paramount, one of us kids discovered the Paulette Goddard scenic view. Pretty soon we all knew about it. Somebody had noticed that there was a vantage point with a direct, unimpaired and total view into her dressing room. Furthermore—and this was the juicy part—Miss Goddard liked to loll around her dressing room topless.

Jackie Cooper
Please Don't Shoot My Dog, 1981

★ ★ ★

Swearing Off
I thought I ought to go out with everyone who asked me and become a part of the Hollywood night life. I was stunned by it. After about two weeks of going out with the men there, I said I'd never go out with anybody again.

Claire Bloom
Limelight and After, 1982

★ ★ ★

One Hand Washes Other
I went out with every big male star in Hollywood. They wanted my body and I needed their names for success.

Barbara Payton
Hollywood Studio Magazine, June, 1982

The Group (United Artists, 1966) from Mary McCarthy's novel, traced the lives of eight college friends (Joanna Pettet, Mary Robin-Redd, Candice Bergen, Jessica Walter, Shirley Knight, Elizabeth Hartman, irreplaceable Joan Hackett and Kathleen Widdoes).

Down to Earth

I was absolutely fascinated by Hollywood but I was also very wary of it all. I'd been told fame and glamour could go to your head, so I took it all with a sense of humor. At my first party there, (given for me), I overheard someone say, "Who the f--- is the guest of honor?" That brought me down to earth for a few minutes!

Michael Caine
Raising Caine, 1982

★ ★ ★

TV Town

Hollywood is a television town now, not a movie town, and it's less crazy and, maybe, less fun because of it. The town makes more *sense* now, and there's a sort of a gray flannel shadow of Madison Avenue that's fallen over it. It's more respectable and less screwball. I kind of liked it at its worst.

Orson Welles
From Where I Sit, 1982

★ ★ ★

Hot Numbers

The Hollywood gossips were persisting in their notion that I was a hot number. There were so many rumors by now that I was the playgirl of the western world that I simply gave up denying anything. I confided in Lana Turner at MGM and she consoled me by saying, "After reading about the twentieth new romance I'm supposed to be having this month, all I can say is I only wish I had the time."

June Allyson
June Allyson, 1982

★ ★ ★

Rolling Revelers

The big Hollywood parties were unbelievably true to their reputation—a sheer joy if you were in a mocking vein. Those glamorous creatures, with their entrances and descents down the staircase, were quite magnificent in their grace and stateliness and their confident composure —so soon to disappear without trace. After a couple of bootleg shots, and in as few minutes, all that majesty was sprawling and rolling about unable to utter a sentence that could be understood.

Laurence Olivier
Confessions of an Actor, 1982

★ ★ ★

Homebody

I'm a very ordinary person who lives in fear of being stuck at a Hollywood party. I'd much rather be at home doing some restoration work.

Harrison Ford
Us, June 20, 1983

The Working Class

Hollywood has a very strong caste system. There are the workers and the ones not working. There are the ones who have five lines and more, the ones who have featured parts, the ones who have co-starring parts, the ones who are stars and the elite, the so-called superstars.

I was once invited to a party attended by all sorts of celebrities from a popular television series of the day. I asked about some other people I knew in the area, from that same associated group, wondering why they weren't at the party. I was told it was because those people were not working. It was explained to me that the people I asked about would not have expected to be invited, nor would they have wanted to be, because they were not working.

Harry Goz
October, 1983

New Rage

Tennis is the new rage among Hollywood stars now—since adultery's been accepted, they need a new pastime.

Phyllis Diller
New York Post, October 10, 1983

Disillusioned

Hollywood parties not only confuse me, they often disillusion me. The disillusion comes when I meet a movie star I've been admiring since childhood.

Marilyn Monroe
Marilyn Monroe: In Her Own Words, 1983

No Party Girl

When I first came to Hollywood I came late to the party because I was frightened. All the big movie stars were there—Paul Newman, Marlon Brando, etc. I sat in a corner. The next day the papers said "Barbra Streisand—aloof, unapproachable."

Barbra Streisand
20/20, November 17, 1983

The Land of "LA"

When a person with a lazy nature like me moves from New York, where the energy is palpable, to Hollywood, which is so laid back, well, it's not a good move.

I was doing my television show *Coke Time* when I moved to Hollywood around 1955. I didn't know it was the Land of "LA." I was looking forward to it. I had been there in 1949 with Eddie Cantor, and couldn't get the *smell* out of my system—the sunny warmth, the healthy, wide open spaces, all those palm and coconut trees. For a poor kid from Philadelphia, it was very heady stuff.

I think almost everybody in show business dreams at one time or another of going there to live and be a part of Hollywood. But you go and it really doesn't exist. It's a state of mind, it's in your imagination. You can make a movie anywhere today.

When I moved out there in the fifties, the big studios were no longer making the musicals that would have been right for me. If you're going to Hollywood with any hope of making it, you have to have a great script and a great director. I got *Bundle of Joy*, co-starring with my first wife, Debbie Reynolds, which was a cornball musical remake of an old David Niven–Ginger Rogers comedy called *Bachelor Mother*. Eddie Fisher as David Niven?! Our director was the veteran Norman Taurog, who made sort of a specialty of directing films with singers-turned-movie stars.

Bundle of Joy was made at RKO, a studio then on its last legs, and was consistently frustrating. I suggested to Bill Dozier, RKO's head of production, that we find another title, one more appealing to our young audience, but he said no. I suggested cutting down on the overabundance of songs; he said no to this, too. His attitude was, I was just a kid, what did I know about movies? Debbie, furthermore, was pregnant with "Princess Leia" (our daughter Carrie) and showing it more each day. Also, my old friend, Joey Forman, had been set for a featured part until Dozier promised it to Tommy Noonan at a party. Joey and I were estranged for years because of this.

I owned 65% of the picture. Howard Hughes, who owned the studio, got 35%. What I *really* got was a doozey!

I was rushed into the picture to capitalize on my recent "storybook" marriage to Debbie. She was then getting $1250 a week at MGM, whom we had to pay $125,000 for her services (which she was well worth, let's add).

Afterward, I went to Lew Wasserman about making a film of the book *What Makes Sammy Run?* No, he said, it's very anti-Semitic. Then I saw Dore Schary, who wanted to do a musical remake of *Dead End*. This time *I* said no, not another remake!

All anybody cared about in Hollywood then and now is making a deal. The money is everything. You're just a piece of meat. This is true in every medium, even in the book world, which I discovered when I wrote my autobiography a while back. I wasn't able to tell the whole story in that, but I'm going to do another book and in this one *will* tell all.

When I was married to Elizabeth Taylor, we appeared together in *Butterfield 8*, for which she deservedly won the Academy Award as best actress of the year. I also got an award—from *The Harvard Lampoon* as the worst actor of the year. I think I deserved mine, too.

It was really an awful script. Again, we tried to make helpful suggestions. Elizabeth had her friends Joseph L. Mankiewicz, Paddy Chayefsky, Daniel Taradash and Tennessee Williams—pretty fair talents—all secretly writing scenes for us which we had to pass off as our own ideas. But the producer, Pandro S. Berman, said, "No actors are going to tell me how to do a script." He went with the screenplay by Charles Schnee and John Michael Hayes. There was a lot of wonderful footage left on the cutting room floor written by Mankiewicz, Chayefsky, Taradash and Williams—our producer was true to his word.

The party scene in Hollywood was certainly, shall we say, interesting, and I was there all right. But that's not what it's all about. I was ignoring my work. Elizabeth and I had vowed to be together twenty-four hours a day, never to be separated. All we did was have fun. Sure, you've got to have fun but I also wanted to work. My desire to be in the movies had sidetracked me—I was still a singer. Then I had to take care of Elizabeth, who was sick for a very long time. So I worked less and less.

As for drugs in Hollywood, I didn't see much of it going on. I haven't been there for a while, so I don't know about now. But I don't think it was so out in the open then. Oh, some ladies would go into the ladies' room now and then for that purpose, and there were wise guys once in a while who would flaunt it. Recently in New York I've been to some parties where cocaine has been used, but I would always leave. With my history, I suppose I'm the last one

Barbra Streisand received the Oscar for the film version of her Broadway hit *Funny Girl* (Columbia, 1968), also starring Omar Sharif.

Julie Andrews, producer Saul Chaplin and director Robert Wise on the set of *Star!* (20th Century-Fox, 1968), in which Andrews essayed the late actress Gertrude Lawrence.

who should point a finger at anyone. In my own case, I was responsible for the length of time that I was into drugs, and that's where I was the victim and then my own worst enemy.

I forgot the word "sustaining." Once you're a star you've got to work to sustain it or it goes away. I live in New York now, but I lived in Hollywood for about twenty-five years. While I don't think I ever really belonged there . . . I still can't forget that *smell*.

Eddie Fisher
March 22, 1984

★ ★ ★

Madland
I love living here. From the first, I was attracted by the climate, parties, people and money. Hollywood is a wonderful madland.

Dudley Moore
National Enquirer, April 10, 1984

★ ★ ★

German Invasion
The really disgusting thing at that time, before Pearl Harbor, was that Hollywood was full of Germans, and I remember one at a cocktail party proposing a toast to the fall of France, so I threw a lot of glasses at him and they told me to leave because America was still supposedly neutral.

Anna Lee
Tales from the Hollywood Raj, 1984

★ ★ ★

Everybody into the Pool
I was a young actress in the 1930s, just getting started in Hollywood. But I recall that Ouida Rathbone, wife of Basil Rathbone (who played Sherlock Holmes), was a formidable hostess there well into the forties.

Ouida gave spectacular affairs, spending Basil's money like—well, water seems appropriate. She once gave a pre-Christmas party for British War Relief at the Beverly Hills Hotel and had snow machines cover the lawn with a wintry white blanket. We were all to draw up in rented sleighs, while Sonja Henie was supposed to skate on man-made ice. Alas, it rained that evening, creating floods. Ouida wisely came down with the flu and remained at home to take everybody's insincere calls of congratulations that Basil insisted we make from the soggy party.

Ria Langham Gable, Clark's wife in the thirties, gave parties that were usually white tie, as did the Robert Montgomerys. There was more striving for elegance during that decade, I think.

Everyone wanted to make Hollywood very upscale in those days. Even the Academy Awards were initiated very cunningly by the men in power to elevate the industry. They had just been through the Fatty Arbuckle and William Desmond Taylor scandals of the twenties, and they were afraid of censorship, the women's clubs, the religious organizations, and, finally, the (Will) Hays Office. They were out to improve Hollywood's status.

The first big party that I gave was soon after I became Mrs. Brian Aherne (whom I married in 1939). It was a Christmas party for the English group in Hollywood then. One whole veranda of our home was done in flats, like an English pub, with dart boards, holly and ivy, flaming English pudding, steak and kidney pie, seasonal music, all the trimmings. I gave many more.

The parties were deductible, you know; still are, of course. You only invited business people—they were all you knew, really—although occasionally there would be a distinguished visitor from abroad. William Randolph Hearst and Marion Davies were fantastic party-givers, and the David O. Selznicks were enormously extravagant entertainers as well.

You must realize that we're talking about people who were fabulous showmen. Because of this, the party had to have a great motif and theme to it.

In the late forties, Nunnally Johnson, who had just shown the new picture he had written and produced called *Mr. Peabody and the Mermaid*, gave a party for which a huge tent was rigged with fish nets and those big shiny reflecting globes and there was a great treasure chest with gifts for everybody. Atwater Kent gave a famous circus party with elephants and camels.

As for the wild, promiscuous Hollywood parties of legend, I never saw that and I wouldn't have been invited. I did attend a party at Errol Flynn's once where everybody suddenly jumped into the pool fully clothed and my mother said, "You're going home now."

Later on, at one of my parties we all jumped into the pool dressed, too. That was always being done in Hollywood. You didn't need much of an excuse. One afternoon we were all by the pool when my butler Theodore came along with this great tray of hors d'oeuvres and accidentally fell in. There was poor gurgling Theodore, surrounded by all these floating canapés, so we all jumped in and nibbled the hors d'oeuvres right there in the water. That was about as wild as my parties got.

Actually, the party scene hasn't changed that much out there. When I went back to Hollywood at the end of 1968, the Jack Bennys were still doing it. They had tents and flowers flown in from San Francisco, but naturally it was all no longer the same for me. I had become a New Yorker.

No, I don't miss it; I still go to great parties. Only last night I went to a lavish affair at Monmouth College in New Jersey for the New York Opera hosted by Jerome Hines. Lucine Amara sang, and there was an elephant outside. Just like Hollywood.

Joan Fontaine
May 6, 1984

★ ★ ★

Sexual Undercurrent
I rarely saw past the facades that the Hollywood dream machine had created for the superstars. The undercurrent of drug abuse, bizarre sexual practices and the myriad of affairs in the inner circle seemed to pass over me. I'm amused at my naiveté as I look back, remembering how flattered I was that some of my celluloid heroes took the time to pick me out at parties, complimenting me on my skills as an actress. I thought they were just the nicest people in the world and was never aware that their kindness and attentions were, in actuality, sexual advances. At least Howard (Hughes) said they were.

Terry Moore
The Beauty and the Billionaire, 1984

Fast and Furious

Hollywood is a pretty fast town and the women are terrible. Some actresses do this whole number, proposition me, right in front of my wife, and sometimes I am so naive that I don't get it until maybe ten minutes later. I cannot believe the gall of these people.

Pierce Brosnan
TV Guide, June 9, 1984

Where There's Life

For excitement at night in North Hollywood, George Burns, Lawrence Welk, Vincente Minnelli and I sit around and watch to see whose leg falls asleep faster. Then we try to contact the living.

Bob Hope
New York Post, July 2, 1984

Dateless Angel

I don't date very much in this town. Luckily. I wouldn't want to be one of those girls who've dated actors and producers. I'm glad I can actually walk into a Hollywood party and say hello to everyone and not have to go, "Oh, my God. . . ."

Farrah Fawcett
Us, October 8, 1984

Neil Simon's Broadway comedy *The Odd Couple* (Paramount, 1968) was made into an equally popular film with Iris Adrian, Walter Matthau and Jack Lemmon.

Jack L. Warner (center), one of the founders of Warner Brothers Pictures, was given a testimonial dinner circa 1970 attended by more than a thousand guests plus Ted Ashley (left), his successor as head of the Warner studio, and Frank Sinatra, master of ceremonies.

POLITICKING

What Next?
I tell you Hollywood's coming into its own—I'm a great defender of Hollywood—and they're even going to put out political pictures.

Irene Dunne
1939

★ ★ ★

Democracy in Action
The big-shots in Hollywood are Democratic. Look at Spence Tracy over there. You heard him stop before and ask about my mother and everyone. You saw him chatting with extras and technicians. Would the stodgy head of a business firm be so considerate or thoughtful?

Robert Stack
Modern Screen, May, 1940

★ ★ ★

Commies Under Control
Why single out Hollywood? As Bob Montgomery and Ronald Reagan said, we have a minute percentage of Commies, but they are under control. Why didn't Washington single out the auto industry, or the coal industry, or the Newspaper Guild? Why smear Hollywood?

Humphrey Bogart
Photoplay, the 1940s

★ ★ ★

Believable Ism
The only "ism" in which Hollywood believes is plagiarism.

Dorothy Parker
The 1940s

Everyone's Pigeon

Hollywood is every man's pigeon. There is no editorial writer so dull that he can't straighten out the movies on the average of four times a year. There is no preacher who can't get at least three rousing sermons annually out of Hollywood. There is not even a congressman so benighted he can't speak with confidence on what ought to be done about the business out there. Surely somebody ought to talk back.

Nunnally Johnson
Hollywood without Makeup, 1949

★ ★ ★

Burning Desire

I have a burning desire to produce or direct, but women in Hollywood just don't get the same opportunities men do. It isn't fair but that's the way it is. These things should be equal. After all, ideas have no gender. Of course, I welcome the freedom I have—it's more than women had in past generations—but it still isn't enough!

Ginger Rogers
September 19, 1958

★ ★ ★

Gutless Wonder

Hollywood is gutless. You can't make an honest, forceful picture here. Hollywood is the whipping boy, the natural target for all kinds of pressure groups, and the movie industry does not stand up to them. Hollywood is to blame for everything that has happened to it.

Mark Hellinger
The Fifty-Year Decline and Fall of Hollywood, 1961

★ ★ ★

Citizen Webb

Hollywood has done an important thing for me and a lot of other actors. It made citizens of us, who during tour travels never stayed in one place long enough to be able to cast a vote. Though I have made a couple of pictures abroad, I've made most of them right here. I think it's about time I took some active interest in community, state and national government, and I'm grateful to Hollywood for the opportunity of exercising my rights as a citizen.

Clifton Webb
Studio Biography, 1962

★ ★ ★

Another Blacklist

It was the late forties in Hollywood. Politics during the war had run like a mad cloudburst through the studios. I have spoken of the far left and the claims of blacklisting of the Unfriendly Ten and their friends. Some, it would later seem, very unfairly. Now somehow I had gotten onto another kind of blacklist, made up of people of the center and the right. For the left remained powerful in the studios, and actors like the late Adolphe Menjou lost out on a couple of dozen film parts because of his vocal voicing of his far right opinions. I was against Communists. But I hadn't made a full-time crusade of it. Yet here I was with a score of my films playing all over the world, and soon to flood over into television, an unemployable actor to the motion picture studios. *Why? Who?*

Pat O'Brien
The Wind at My Back, 1964

Communist Takeover?
The Communist plan for Hollywood was remarkably simple. It was merely to take over the motion picture business. Not only for its profit—but also for a grand world-wide propaganda base. In those days before television and massive foreign film production, American films dominated 95 per cent of the world's movie screens. We had a weekly audience of about 500,000,000 souls.

Ronald Reagan
Where's the Rest of Me?, 1965

★ ★ ★

A Friend in Greed
During the McCarthy era in Hollywood, friend informed on friend not to save their lives but to save their swimming pools.

Orson Welles
The 1960s

★ ★ ★

Some Genuine Patriotism
There was a great deal of patriotism in Hollywood during the war, much of it even genuine. The stars were busy on bond-selling tours and entertaining troops through the USO; "back home" there was the Hollywood Canteen (chairman, Bette Davis), which was, of course, made into a feature film by Warner Brothers. (And in one or two scenes, if you looked fast, you could discover that there were even handsome, light-colored Negro soldiers in the war, for they could be seen dancing in the background with extremely beautiful, light-colored girls.)

Alvah Bessie
Inquisition in Eden, 1965

★ ★ ★

Believers
When I came to this country, the Big Powers—England, France, too—tried to appease Hitler . . . Some of us saw it coming, but the only ones who were really opposed (we *thought* they were the only ones) were the Communists. That was one of the reasons why so many people here in Hollywood turned to the Communists—because they *believed* that the Communist Party was the only group really fighting the Nazis.

Fritz Lang
Fritz Lang in America, 1969

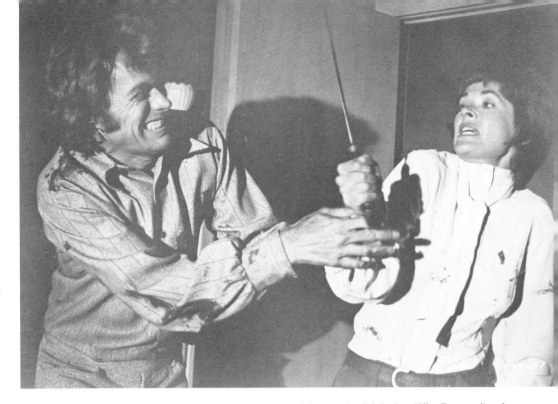

Play Misty for Me (Universal, 1971) was the suspenseful story of a disk jockey (Clint Eastwood) and a homicidal fan (Jessica Walter).

Marlon Brando (second from left) won a best actor Oscar for his portrayal of the Mafia patriarch in *The Godfather* (Paramount, 1972), with Al Pacino, James Caan and John Cazale.

Connected with World

We became, as they said, "politically conscious." And by the next time I went out to Hollywood they were organizing the Hollywood Anti-Nazi League. This was in '35 and Hitler had come to power. I worked with the people at the head of the League—there were Dorothy Parker, Oscar Hammerstein, Freddie March and his wife, Herbert Biberman and other people. And we really got Hollywood connected with the world for almost the first time politically.

Donald Ogden Stewart
Focus on Film, Winter, 1970

Organizer

We music people have had our problems in Hollywood. For a long while we weren't getting paid for our background music, so in 1942 I organized the Screen Composers' Association.

Max Steiner
The Real Tinsel, 1970

Rally for Attention

The trouble with Hollywood is that producers and agents are the aristocrats . . . which made actors who make their living in Hollywood usually feel they are some sort of scum. They looked for other means of showing off and were great on rallies for political candidates.

James Mason
Los Angeles Times, August 10, 1971

The Kiss-Off

They keep telling me out in Hollywood to keep my nose clean. People are always saying, "Why take a chance? It can't help you to get involved." My response is, "Kiss off!"

Paul Newman
Movie Digest, March, 1972

Reactionaries

Almost everybody in Hollywood was rather reactionary. (Director John) Ford, like most of the others, was very conservative indeed. But he wasn't as bad as (Cecil B.) DeMille. DeMille was a petrified old man. And I think his pictures are petrified.

Douglas Sirk
Sirk on Sirk, 1972

Divided Community

About 1946–47, you could feel this cold wind blowing into Hollywood from the East, chopping the city into factions. There was a clash between the liberals and the conservatives.

All you had to do was know someone of questionable political persuasion and you were labeled a Commie. There were perhaps six or seven hard-core Communists in Hollywood then, and they were not very dangerous people. But at that time a terror had seized the whole country, and in Hollywood the terror was that the Communists would take over. So the right wing organized. They engaged in a witch hunt. If you were a staunch Democrat like me and were politically involved, and a friend of Eleanor Roosevelt's, as I was, you were labeled a Commie sympathizer.

Myrna Loy
The MGM Stock Company, 1973

★ ★ ★

Smoke Scene
Lobbyists were constantly at work in Hollywood attempting to get stars, male and female, to smoke; sometimes to get men to smoke cigars instead of cigarettes. I was offered a handsome gift if I could induce Ginger Rogers to smoke a cigar in one scene.

Garson Kanin
Hollywood, 1974

★ ★ ★

More Than Willing
If I were given the responsibility of getting rid of the Communists, I would love nothing better than to fire every last one of them and never let them work in a studio or in Hollywood again. I believe firmly that the producers, the heads of the studios in Hollywood, would be and are more than willing to do everything they can to rid Hollywood of Communists and fellow travelers.

Robert Taylor
Hanging on in Paradise, 1975

★ ★ ★

Lost the Knack
The bottom was falling out, not just because of the (Communist) blacklist, but because of television as well. Hollywood lost its knack then and they haven't had it again since!

Anne Revere
Los Angeles Times, June 20, 1976

★ ★ ★

Learning Experience
I learned more about communism in the three-and-a-half years I was one of the "Hollywood Ten" than I ever learned when I was actually a party member. And what I learned wasn't good.

Edward Dmytryk
Who's Who in Hollywood, 1976

National Shame

The Communist witch-hunt during the 1940s and early 1950s was a wretched period in this country's history, truly a national shame. The "Red Menace" hanging over Hollywood—and eventually over the entire country—gave rise to a miasma of fear, hysteria and guilt. There was a Communist under every bed, and everyone seemed eager to drag him out. It was brother against brother, friend against friend. Innocent people were hustled off to jail. Many lost their jobs—even their lives—simply because they believed in and exercised what they knew to be their Constitutional privileges: freedom of speech and political affiliation.

John Huston
An Open Book, 1980

★ ★ ★

Liberalism Spreads

Nowadays there is a huge liberal influence spread over most of the country, and much of it is coming out of Hollywood. It certainly wasn't always like that. In the old days, during the studio system, all politics was taboo.

Sammy Davis, Jr.
Hollywood in a Suitcase, 1980

★ ★ ★

Collective Effort

What's so wonderful about movies and so frustrating if you're working in Hollywood is that film-making really is a collective effort even though the director has the final control. That's what seems exciting about film-making in a socialist country. Film-making is a socialized process. When it is working right, everyone is participating . . . The alienation of the technicians from the process in Hollywood is particularly sad. Most of the time, they are not given the script to read. They don't understand why the film is being made or what is being attempted in any given scene. I've never heard of a film-maker sitting down with the crew to tell them how the film has been conceived and asking their opinion. So the technicians' (general) attitude is: who cares? And who can blame them?

Jane Fonda
Cineaste, Vol. VI, No. 4, the 1980s

★ ★ ★

The Real Thing

The blacklisting that took place in Hollywood was slightly different than how you hear of it today. There was a genuine Communist threat in this country, and there were Communistic actors, directors, screenwriters and producers in Hollywood trying to grab control of the motion picture business and use it for their own end, which was to spread Communist propaganda throughout the country and the world. The system used to get rid of the Communists was bad. Joseph McCarthy and his methods were a little cruel and drastic. But the Communist danger was there. And it has grown.

Virginia Mayo
Focus on Film, March, 1981

Laurence Olivier and Michael Caine had tour-de-force roles in the film version of Anthony Shaffer's stage thriller, *Sleuth* (20th Century-Fox, 1972).

The cast of the Burt Bacharach–Hal David musical version of *Lost Horizon* (Columbia, 1972): John Gielgud, James Shigeta, Michael York, Olivia Hussey, Peter Finch, Liv Ullmann, George Kennedy, Sally Kellerman, Bobby Van and Charles Boyer.

Enough Irrelevance

I remember my business manager and my public relations people saying, "Oh, Jane, don't do that. You're going to ruin your career!" But I thought to myself, What has my career meant to me at this point? Am I all that happy with my career? I've lived in Hollywood long enough to know that all the mansions and swimming pools also mean psychiatrists; it means having your children alienated from you; it means not necessarily a great deal of happiness. I felt that I had spent enough time being cynical and irrelevant and apathetic.

Jane Fonda
From Where I Sit, 1982

Good Movies Only

I'm a Hollywood director who wants to please a mass audience. I don't believe in selling personal beliefs—just in making good movies.

Fred Zinnemann
Films in Review, January, 1983

Blacklist Lesson

The blacklist years had done something to me, shown me how insecure anyone's footing in Hollywood could be, how easy it was to be in and out of favor as an actor or director.

Paul Henreid
Ladies' Man, 1984

Politics in Paradise

The question is always asked:

Do Hollywood actors have the right to be visible and vocal on politics?

I don't view actors as being any different type of citizen from bankers or laborers or housewives. As do any citizens, actors not only have the *right* to speak out politically, they have a responsibility to do so. But, as with any citizen, they also have a responsibility to learn about the issues and/or candidates before spouting profundities that others may take as gospel—especially from celebrities.

Yes, there are hazards in Hollywood for the politically active, as there are for non-celebrities. The main hazard, of course, is having people disagree with you who are in a position to affect your livelihood. Most thinking people don't act in an unseemly manner even if they *do* disagree, but there are those who will—perhaps subconsciously. It's harder to separate your "political life" from "career" because, of course, a well-known person speaking out has a much louder voice than a "regular" citizen: when we speak out on an issue, it's broadcast.

I don't think any of the hazards come from the public. I never let my own differing views stop me from seeing John Wayne movies, for instance. Humphrey Bogart had the same opinion: the public likes good acting and will continue to patronize the good actor, no matter what his or her politics are.

I tend to feel that Hollywood politics are more liberal than in many other industries. Certainly there are those for whom the bottom line is "money," but our business depends on, indeed can only *survive* in an atmosphere of creative freedom. So even in the pursuit of money, our industry people see the necessity for democracy and freedom. We actors, especially, have "walked in the other man's shoes" through our different roles—we can sympathize with the poor, disabled, oppressed. We tend to speak out for the people more than big business might, for example.

To indicate the extent to which Hollywood has influenced politics there is the campaign manager's slogan: "No camera, no candidate." Politicians since Nixon's televised "Checkers" speech have realized the power of the media and the power of having a visible celebrity speak for them, and they use that power more than ever. In some ways, that's good, if it's used to disseminate information more widely—in some ways it's bad, if it's used to spread deception or rely only on slick surface appeal rather than substance. I like to use the figure that more people watched the last episode of *M*A*S*H* than voted in the past Presidential election. TV can reach people that can't be reached by any other method.

Hollywood is more politically active today. After the bad taste of the McCarthy era wore off, celebrities slowly began to speak out again without a lot of fear. I think candidates are turning more to celebrities for endorsements, using them more for fundraising and visibility, and the celebrities are responding. I wouldn't know about the behind-the-camera people as much, but many of my personal acquaintances are getting involved who weren't previously. Naturally, given the current (Reagan) administration in Washington, there's much to speak out against, many that need educating and prodding to do their own speaking. If a celebrity can command that kind of respect and possibly imitation from his fans, then by all means he should use it.

What is Hollywood NOT doing politically?

If anything, we're not coordinating our efforts enough. It seems a sort of random and spurty political functioning at times—although there are more and more committees forming, such as the Committee of Concern for Central America, made up of groups of industry people who are sharing information and efforts to get the widest possible effect. But that random effort is understandable, given the nature of an actor's work and schedule.

Our biggest goal should be to be as informed as possible, to speak responsibly and consistently.

Ed Asner
April 4, 1984

★ ★ ★

Exit Cue

I never thought I'd be in the movies for long. When I signed my contract with David O. Selznick, he had to agree that I could go back to Broadway whenever I wanted to. I didn't like Hollywood at all at first. It was very cliquish. You'd go into someone's living room and talk about voting for (Franklin Delano) Roosevelt for President, and two people who were Republicans would get up and leave. Thank God, that kind of stuff is long gone.

Gene Kelly
August 13, 1984

★ ★ ★

Nightmare Time

The McCarthy years in Hollywood?

I remember them too well, though I didn't have much time then for political involvement myself. I was busy bearing and caring for four daughters, acting in a weekly radio show (*Dr. Christian*), fulfilling a Warner Brothers movie contract and appearing with Jackie

Gleason in a short TV series (*The Life of Riley*). I also spent twelve years on the Screen Actors Guild Board.

The SAG Board negotiations for residuals (or payment for re-use) took two years and were difficult for producers as well as those of us who participated in the arbitration. As I recall, none of us who sat around the bargaining table with the major producers ever worked in a major studio feature again.

The McCarthy era preceded the above and overlapped, at least in effect. It was a complicated and ugly period. There were so many groups opposing each other, hiding from each other and spying on each other that some of us shut our eyes and ears and hoped we'd wake up from the nightmare. The blacklist was real enough, though probably never written down. It was a rumor mill spreading vague smears about Communist involvement that took years to erase. Most of the opposing groups were totally sincere in their "patriotism." Many were real victims. Some clutched at martyrdom. A few named names to buy respectability.

Years later when the Freedom of Information Act was publicized as being open to all, I wrote for my dossier. It was a joke—several dollars a page and the only mention of my name was from a bookstore in Burbank that I had never heard of. My husband was amused and sent for his, as he had been up for a Federal appointment. It came with a huge bill and was loaded with comments about him. All the names, however, had been blacked out, as in a censored letter.

Hollywood survived but since then has never been free from the fear of government pressure— through IRS audits—refused bank loans—and network slurs. Most of this was re-played during the Nixon years for a different reason: campaign contributions.

We can only hope that none of this comes around again—because of peace activism—or praying in the wrong place to the wrong God.

Rosemary DeCamp
September 10, 1984

The Poseidon Adventure (20th Century-Fox, 1972), with Jack Albertson, Shelley Winters and Red Buttons, involved an upside-down ocean liner and was one of the most lucrative of the 70s' rash of disaster films.

CHANGING

The Wild West

Hollywood has changed. There isn't the old wickedness. Which is why my folks have no objection to my working in pictures.

Jeanne Crain
Photoplay, December, 1944

★ ★ ★

Abracadabra

I'm working on a new disappearance act. When I perfect it I'll just give one wave—and Hollywood will disappear.

Orson Welles
Screenland, January, 1946

★ ★ ★

Tractor Factor

I, Charlie Chaplin, declare that Hollywood is dying. Hollywood is now fighting its last battle, and it will lose that battle unless it decides, once and for all, to give up standardizing its films—unless it realizes that masterpieces cannot be mass-produced in the cinema like tractors in a factory.

Charles Chaplin
1947

★ ★ ★

Increasing Gain

Recently, Hollywood has been criticized for its portrayal of the Negro on the screen. I have been censured by some of my race for not joining in the denouncement. Many of those loudest in their condemnation are newcomers who do not remember the days when no Negro player was given a dressing room, when there were no hairdressers on the sets for Negro actresses, when no studio hired a Negro wardrobe girl. I have seen many changes in the film city and the trend has been one of increasing gain.

Hattie McDaniel
The Hollywood Reporter, September 29, 1947

★ ★ ★

Gossip Power

Hollywood is done for. Hollywood and I have no future in common and I don't know if Hollywood has any future at all. It's top-heavy in its internal and financial economy. It is so egocentric it doesn't know the rest of the world exists, and its social life is one of simply incredible, preposterous boredom. Hollywood is seriously ill. It is run by a coterie of moronic gossips and it would hardly be going too far to say that Hollywood is in their power.

Rex Harrison
The 1940s

★ ★ ★

Public Be Polled
The Oscars? I think it's time Hollywood let the public in on the voting. Let the industry pick the technical awards but leave the major selections to moviegoers.

Ida Lupino
March 22, 1950

★ ★ ★

Exit Stagedoor Johnnies
Nowadays in Hollywood, an actress scrapes off her makeup, ties a bandana around her hair, leaps into her convertible and heads for home. No eager ogles from handsome men at any stagedoor and no roses or diamonds. I'm sure that Mary Pickford and Gloria Swanson used to ride through the gates and throw kisses and rose petals at the throngs. But years of discouragement from studio gatemen have dispersed this kind of following, and anyway most actresses with their covered heads and dark glasses aren't recognizable when they whiz by in high-powered autos.

Jane Wyman
Movie Play, November, 1952

★ ★ ★

Dethroned
It was obvious, even before the advent of television, that the Golden Age of Hollywood was over. With box office returns moving steadily downward, production costs were going higher, and the problem of high costs *versus* low returns had to be faced. New picture schedules were becoming shorter; everyone was talking economy. Studios were laying off great numbers of their employees, and the very few pictures going into production were being assigned to lower-salaried contract directors. Then the dark specter of television descended, confirming a fact already apparent—Hollywood had lost its royal position.

King Vidor
A Tree is a Tree, 1952

★ ★ ★

Now You See It . . .
Hollywood's going to vanish like the amusement parks, and that's just about what it deserves. For many years there's been more talent and genius within five miles of Romanoff's than in any other place on earth. It could have meant a Renaissance of the first magnitude. But Hollywood has succeeded in ruining almost everything it's ever touched.

Ben Hecht
Cue, July 18, 1953

Mommie Dubious
They like to whisper that Hollywood distorts you—turns you into a drunk, a tramp, a bad father or mother. But look at me. It has also been said that I am a typical Hollywood creation. Now am *I* so bad? Don't believe everything you hear.

Joan Crawford
Press Conference, "21," New York, 1955

Resembles Philly
Old Hollywood was a Never Never land that hadn't been paralleled since the red-hot days of Rome. The parties were lush, and so were most of the guests. Hollywood today is one of the stuffiest and most dignified communities in the United States. Most everyone hits the sack by midnight, either to be on the set bright and early the next morning, or to meet their tax man to learn the latest gimmick in capital gains. It's getting to be just like Philadelphia.

Groucho Marx
Groucho and Me, 1959

Unrecognizable
Men were being killed all around the world, and women were mourning for them. So actors were ordered to play charades in the cause of Happy Families, the idea being that we could prove Hollywood people were clean-living and public-spirited. Glamour queens were presented as contented housewives bent over kitchen stoves. Lana Turner baking apple pies, Ginger Rogers scrubbing floors, Joan Crawford hoeing her victory garden. Theda Bara wouldn't have recognized the place, but the fan magazines lapped it up.

Keenan Wynn
Ed Wynn's Son, 1959

Pleasant Memories
Yes, the place has really changed since I was under contract here. That was just after the war, when the boys were coming back . . . Hollywood seems much quieter now. There seem to be no big parties anymore, no real colony at all. But I like it here. I have pleasant memories of Hollywood on the whole.

Rex Harrison
1960

Pressure On
I went to Hollywood in the last of the really fabulous years—the time of Big Entertainment pictures. But now the economic structure has all changed—even in the theater you can't put on the smallest production without tremendously high costs. This leads to a hectic atmosphere and a time pressure . . . all the experienced actor can do is burn the midnight oil by himself! I certainly do, for you no longer get the time to create on-stage or on the set.

Agnes Moorehead
The Christian Science Monitor, November 14, 1961

The Last of Sheila (Warner Brothers, 1973), a mystery, starred James Mason, Raquel Welch, James Coburn, Joan Hackett, Ian McShane, Dyan Cannon and Richard Benjamin.

Woody Allen and Diane Keaton were likable lovers in *Annie Hall* (United Artists, 1977), which won the best picture Oscar as well as best director and best actress designations for Allen and Keaton.

Shirley Frankenstein

Hollywood and the stars and agents have created their own monster. I'm as guilty of it as anyone. Many times when a star is on his or her own, freelancing with no contract, they can charge an exorbitant amount of money for their services. It's open to question whether or not a star in a bad picture will pull in the public; a star in a good picture, yes, but I think maybe a nobody in a good picture will pull in the public, too . . . not the nobody, of course, but the picture. The audience is becoming critical. It's not necessary to bank so much on a star.

Shirley MacLaine
Films and Filming, February, 1962

End of Era

When I came to Hollywood, the great era of silent films was over. The village was not "gay and reckless" anymore. The studios operated like any other establishment—one had to clock in at a certain hour and heaven help you if you failed to do so. It remained like this all through the rest of the thirties until I left to join the army. Today, when so few films are being made, Hollywood harbors more television actors than film actors. "Hollywood" is dead.

Marlene Dietrich
Marlene Dietrich's ABC, 1962

Shame on Moneybags

So look at Hollywood. It's a place of shame, and it is a shame that we see so little talent emerge. I really think we are in a mess. The moneybags think that anybody can write or produce. They also think they know what the public wants. They obviously don't.

Viveca Lindfors
New York Post, May 27, 1962

In Slugging

When television killed comedy and love stories, the movie makers went in slugging. They offered the downbeat, the degenerate as competition. This seems to me to be a sad campaign for Hollywood to use to combat box office disaster.

Joan Crawford
Motion Picture, the 1960s

Dim View

Another thing that's changed in Hollywood is on accounta the smog. In the days of Garbo and Harlow, you could always tell a star by dark glasses. Now, on accounta of all the smog, everybody wears sunglasses and nobody sees nuttin'.

Jimmy Durante
Hello, Hollywood!, 1962

Hollywood Hotel

When I was in Hollywood recently, well, that was most depressing. The studios are practically shut, and when you see half of 20th Century-Fox, which was my alma mater, occupied by a big hotel and there's so little left . . . it's very depressing. Oh, it was delicious (in the 1930s and 1940s).

Arthur Treacher
The New York Times, the 1960s

★ ★ ★

Monsieur Dodo

The whole of Hollywood deserted silent pictures and I was the only one left. I had been lucky so far, but to continue with a feeling that the art of pantomime was gradually becoming obsolete was a discouraging thought.

Charles Chaplin
My Autobiography, 1964

★ ★ ★

Living in Present

What a wonderful change has come over Hollywood! Ten years ago it was a very depressing place to work in. Everyone was living in the past, and the whole attitude was one of dust. But now, Hollywood seems to have come to terms with the past. The city is living in the present now, and it is a comforting thing to see it and be a part of it.

Olivia de Havilland
December 26, 1964

★ ★ ★

"Oomph Girl" Indignant

What have they done to the place (Hollywood)? I don't know it any more. The lots are chaotic. TV has turned everything into big, ugly factories. I'm indignant!

Ann Sheridan
TV Guide, the 1960s

★ ★ ★

Serious Groups

Hollywood is changing. Many of my friends are serious actors who meet in small groups at somebody's home and talk for hours.

Diane Baker
The Star-Ledger, the 1960s

★ ★ ★

Time of Lunacy

The early years of the twenties were a time of lunacy. You could throw rocks on Sixth Avenue in New York and not hit a cloak-and-suiter. They were all in Hollywood, along with the fast-buck characters from everywhere, the con artists, the real estate chiselers, soda jerks, writers who never wrote, call girls with agents, hoodlums, gamblers and touts. They all wanted a piece of the movie gold mine, and it was an inexhaustible vein.

Jack L. Warner
My First Hundred Years in Hollywood, 1964

Noblesse Oblige
It was 1923, the recent war had crumbled one empire after another, and members of the nobility had become doormen in Paris, cab drivers in New York and extra players in Hollywood.

Josef von Sternberg
Fun in a Chinese Laundry, 1965

Grand Illusions
Currently, Hollywood is on a binge of superrealistic super-sexy pictures. Why? Because these days superrealistic, super-sexy pictures make money. It is, generally, a bad time for illusions. We used to have the illusion of the great star, someone who was remote, someone who was oddly different from ourselves. He, or she, was glamour. The illusion of the star was a big thing in Hollywood. Look at TV today. There's the great Harry James. He's playing Kleenex. There's the great Edward G. Robinson. He's out in the kitchen making Maxwell House Coffee.

Mickey Rooney
i.e., An Autobiography, 1965

All Business
They've lost the tinsel and glory of Hollywood that had all the glamour. Now it's business. "I want a slice of the picture," and the actors hiring directors. The man with the long beard (Uncle Sam) has had a lot to do with it. You don't want to do that many pictures.

Pat O'Brien
Bogey: The Good-Bad Guy, 1965

The Golden Goose
They take an unknown little broad who can't speak her name and have to convince the public she can act, that she loves children and wants to get married. In doing all this, they have killed the glamour of Hollywood. They try to convince people that Tony Curtis is just like the kid next door. But why pay money to see the kid next door?

Humphrey Bogart
Bogey: The Good-Bad Guy, 1965

Paul Clemens and gravely-ill Kathleen Beller were high school sweethearts in *Promises in the Dark* (Orion, 1979), produced and directed by Jerome Hellman.

Nine to Five (20th Century-Fox, 1979), the very funny story of rebelling secretaries, starred Jane Fonda, Lily Tomlin and Dolly Parton.

Humor, Vitality Needed

Hollywood is becoming too middle-aged, too complacent, too much involved with money. American films should return to the humor and vitality that was *purely* American as shown in many early films.

Gregory Peck
The Miami Herald, March 25, 1966

★ ★ ★

Prosperity Around Corner

I think we've got some great actors on the screen—Paul Newman, Steve McQueen, Warren Beatty. They are the expression of the age and the time. Hollywood has changed as everything has changed, as the world has changed. But it doesn't mean it is finished. I think pay television is just around the corner, and then this town will be prosperous as it never has been before. It won't be the same business we know, but it will be very exciting.

Rosalind Russell
March 17, 1968

★ ★ ★

Bring Back Hollywood

We've got to bring Hollywood back to Hollywood. Our homes and families are here, so why should we leave? Besides, I've heard from friends who have gone overseas on pictures that the going was great the first couple of years, but now the prices are going up and up so that you could almost make the same features here for the same price. I hope they find an answer to this problem before we're the only people left in town.

Ida Lupino
The Hollywood Reporter, April 8, 1968

★ ★ ★

Gone to Pot

Both my husband (Richard Denning) and I feel Hollywood has completely gone to "pot"—in more ways than one. He and I—Dick especially—have both turned down scripts for movies and plays because we felt they had been written under the influence of LSD.

Evelyn Ankers
June 20, 1968

★ ★ ★

Humorless Robots

When I arrived at Metro, Esther Williams was keeping the studio going by diving into a pool. Now, Metro is so sad. There's not a soul there. Everyone's gone. Los Angeles has become one huge robot. Hollywood is a little sadder. The same friends are there having the same dinners, except that everyone is a little older and grayer. Maybe I'm getting older, but the young stars don't seem to enjoy being stars. They don't have any sense of humor.

Deborah Kerr
Newark Sunday News, June 8, 1969

A Proper Farewell

If the time had come to leave Hollywood, I wanted to feel that I could do so with dignity—like Norma Talmadge who, a few years after her retirement from the screen, came out of the smart restaurant of the day in Beverly Hills to find the usual crowd of fans, pushing forward for autographs. With a wave of the hand, she said to them pleasantly, "Run away, dears. I don't need you now."

Brian Aherne
A Proper Job, 1969

★ ★ ★

Beverly-Bound

Hollywood is dying as a film capital and a system. That's all to the good because it's been corrosive and destructive: It's been occupied by too many people who didn't belong there, fattening up on the payroll. Young people who had ideas, who were much more in tune with what was happening in the world, were not given a chance to express themselves. The system had been led by people who never ventured beyond their Beverly Hills mansions.

Robert Redford
September 11, 1970

★ ★ ★

Pandering

In the great Hollywood days, movies pandered to the matron just as today's movies pander to youth.

Orson Welles
Newsweek, December 7, 1970

★ ★ ★

Deviated Scepter

Practically all the Hollywood filmmaking today is stooping to cheap salacious pornography in a crazy bastardization of a great art to compete for the "patronage" of deviates and masturbators.

Frank Capra
The Name Above the Titie, 1971

★ ★ ★

Important Resource

What has anyone done to leave the movie industry here in Hollywood healthy? Everybody keeps pointing a finger at everybody else—the stars, the unions, the runaways . . . maybe the government should do something. Moviemaking is an important resource of the country. Movies were *once* synonymous with America.

Kirk Douglas
March 4, 1971

Life and Death
I saw Hollywood born and I've seen it die.

Mary Pickford
TV Radio Mirror, July, 1971

Workaholics When
That's all gone now, the old Hollywood. They worked all the time. I don't. I can't function that way. I've never made very many movies. There's no point in making a movie just to be making a movie.

Warren Beatty
Long Island Press, August 8, 1971

Death Exaggerated
Hollywood is not dead or dying. It's time for us to reexamine our position and stop making this garbage and start making pictures the audience can take wives and children to see. I've never been faced with the problem of being offered pornography. I don't like to watch it, either. I don't want to sit and watch something on the screen that I know I can do better.

Glenn Ford
October 26, 1971

Collectors to Rescue
Hollywood has never preserved its own history. If it was not for private collectors, most of the great masterpieces would be gone forever. I asked for some of my early films and they told me to go . . .

Roddy McDowall
Sunday News, November 21, 1971

Great Time
It was a great time when I was a star. It was "Bohemia" at its best—all the great authors and composers were here (in Hollywood) and the most beautiful women and the most handsome men. But that world doesn't exist now. Today the poets are the scientists. If I were young today, I think I'd try to learn everything I could.

Paulette Goddard
1972

Richard Gere and Hector Elizondo were conspicuous in a slice of sleaze from director Paul Schrader entitled *American Gigolo* (Paramount, 1980).

Harrison Ford played intrepid Indiana Jones in *Raiders of the Lost Ark* (Paramount, 1981), a breathtaking series of adventures directed by Steven Spielberg.

Cheap Shot

After the early fifties—after television folk inundated the area—using "Hollywood" as an epithet became a critical cop-out, really. Some critics still do, of course. When they can't, or won't bother to, analyze their dislike for a film or its creators. Calling something "Hollywood" today is just a cheap shot. Whipping a horse that's not only dead but disintegrated.

Joseph L. Mankiewicz
More About All About Eve, 1972

★ ★ ★

Ghost Town

Nobody ever imagined Hollywood'd be a ghost town. It was so beautifully run, by such genuinely capable people. There were silly ones, I admit, but the majority knew their business and protected it.

Joan Blondell
Films in Review, April, 1972

★ ★ ★

Berserk Studio

I filmed something called *The Pleasure Seekers*, and that's when it occurred to me how really drastically Hollywood has changed—for actors. One afternoon we had just about completed shooting and I was sitting there in the studio when I heard this music coming from one of the dressing rooms—real roof-shaking music and it was coming from the dressing room of that girl—the one who has all the long blonde hair and talks so soft—yes, Ann-Margret. Well, presently, she came out snapping her fingers and wearing a leather suit and she hopped right on a motorcycle and roared off into the wind. And I just sat back in amazement. The studio would have gone berserk if any of us had done that! Back then!

Gene Tierney
After Dark, July, 1972

★ ★ ★

Damn Bursts

Everything was fine in Hollywood when we had the code that governed what actors said and did, but when they let the cast use "damn" in *Gone with the Wind*, they let everything go. Nothing can exist without laws.

Ruth Donnelly
Dallas Times Herald, October 19, 1972

Floored by Beauty

I am a realistic person. I don't look back to the Good Old Days in Hollywood. Yet—it *is* sad. The glamour is gone, and I am in a position to compare. When I first came to Hollywood, I was floored. I used to die when I was all those *beautiful* women. But today none of them cares how she looks!

Merle Oberon
March 24, 1973

★ ★ ★

No Future

Hollywood has no future. All we have out here is the past. And God knows, it hasn't much present.

Lewis Milestone
July 15, 1973

★ ★ ★

Incomparable

I was lucky being in Hollywood before it began to dry up, about a dozen years ago—the atmosphere has changed incredibly since I left and it's dead compared to what it used to be.

Deborah Kerr
September 12, 1973

★ ★ ★

Paging Irene, Norma, Greer

Everything they say about Hollywood is true. It's a walled-in city bounded on all sides by arrogance. What's more, the people in Hollywood who make motion pictures simply do not know about people, or, often as not, about making motion pictures. Forty pictures I was in, and all I remember is, "What kind of bra will you be wearing, honey?" . . . There was a time once when Irene Dunne and Norma Shearer and Greer Garson all played strong, unsick women. But today everything has to be *Butterfield 8*. I'm sick of this kind of misfit role, and I think the public is, too.

Donna Reed
The MGM Stock Company, 1973

★ ★ ★

For the Better!

Hollywood is just like anyplace else. You find the best and the worst here. I don't like the way Hollywood is used as an adjective. I think things have changed for the better out here. We've progressed like everything else. Take a look at the old pictures sometime, and you'll realize we've progressed just as much as the aviation industry.

William Wyler
Pieces of Time, 1973

Maturity

Hollywood now is like the rest of the world—disturbed and frightened. In the old days Hollywood was young and the country was young. They are both mature now.

Mary Pickford
Sweetheart, 1973

★ ★ ★

Crumbled Pyramids

Hollywood's like Egypt, full of crumbled pyramids. It'll never come back . . . there might have been good movies if there had been no movie industry. Hollywood might have become the center of a new human expression if it hadn't been grabbed by a little group of book-keepers.

David O. Selznick
GWTW: The Making of Gone with the Wind, 1973

★ ★ ★

They Were Expendable

Who needs Hollywood anymore? What's the use of shooting a New York street scene on a lot out here when you can do one for far less right on location in New York? Or, for that matter, if you're doing a movie in England, Mexico or Italy. Maybe they don't have quite all of Hollywood's skills, but they're learning fast.

John Wayne
It Was Fun While It Lasted, 1973

★ ★ ★

Legacy of Looting

Hollywood? Don't speak ill of the dead. Who have we got? Elliott Gould, Richard Benjamin and Dustin Hoffman. If those guys had been my roommates in college, I couldn't have got them a date. Sure, we've got a crisis in Hollywood. But what do you expect? The producers left a legacy of thirty years of stealing. They robbed the place blind.

Mort Sahl
Some Enchanted Egos, 1973

★ ★ ★

Manure and Moguls

Horse manure and the moguls killed off the old Hollywood. They were like ostriches putting their heads in the sand and fingers in their ears hoping the crisis would blow over.

Tony Curtis
Some Enchanted Egos, 1973

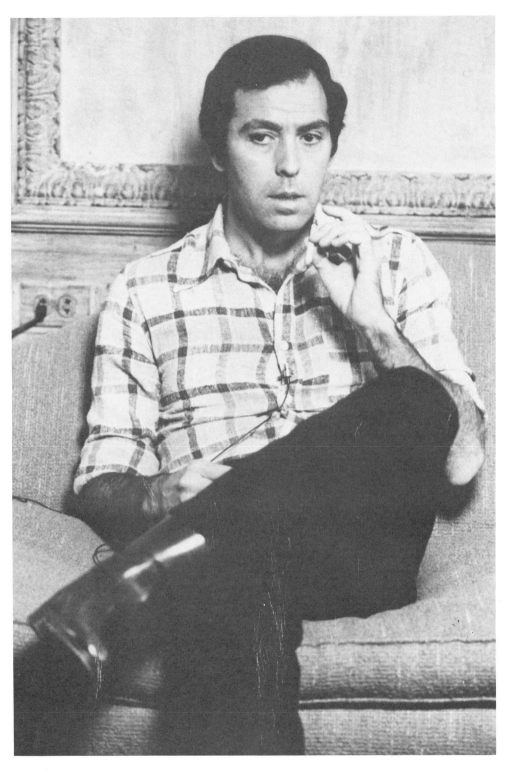

Robert Getchell wrote the screenplays for *Alice Doesn't Live Here Anymore*, *Bound for Glory*, and *Sweet Dreams*, and is creator of the TV series *Alice*.

Suffocating Costs

I am very pro labor. I am a member of three unions myself, but I'm afraid things have gotten to the point that labor costs are suffocating what little film production is still left in Hollywood. Our technicians are the finest in the world, the best trained and with the best experience, but the "below the line" part of a film budget which they represent has become too heavy.

Rosalind Russell
Hollywood Speaks!, 1974

★ ★ ★

The Smell of Success

Bring back the cult of the personality! Today the people who control Hollywood don't give a damn about that! A studio's owned by an underarm odor company or a car park or the arm of some big industrial complex.

Laurence Harvey
The National Bulletin, January 21, 1974

★ ★ ★

The Disenchanted

I am convinced that Hollywood's decline from glory is in no way the result of senility. On the contrary, it is a relapse (temporary, I hope) into the immaturity of adolescence . . . vocational misfits swarm into the industry, mining not gold but mountains of garbage. Their odiferous product has disenchanted millions of customers from the marketplace, who, I predict, will begin to come back only when we give them good films.

Raoul Walsh
Each Man in His Time, 1974

★ ★ ★

Old-Fashioned Way

And if we have to tell Hollywood good-by, may it be with one of those tender, old-fashioned, seven-second kisses exchanged between two people of the *opposite* sex, with all their clothes on.

Anita Loos
Kiss Hollywood Good-by, 1974

★ ★ ★

Gone with the Goldwyns

I am often asked what the difference is between the Hollywood of yesterday, my Hollywood, and the Hollywood of today. There is one fatal change. Gone are the gamblers: Zukor, Goldwyn, Mayer, Warner, Cohn, Thalberg, Zanuck and countless others. They gave us our careers—sometimes they won, sometimes they lost millions in promotion of a script and a star. People of my era—the 1930s, 1940s, 1950s—owe these men our careers. They were our fathers. This is the big change in the Hollywood of yesterday and today.

Bette Davis
Mother Goddam, 1974

Ashes to Ashes

Hollywood is a town of ashes. The excitement is gone. Today, Hollywood doesn't know what the word glamour means. Those mad, crazy days are gone forever.

Shelley Winters
National Enquirer, April, 1975

Always Changing

I was at a party with a lot of film people the other evening and heard a great deal of grumbling and dissatisfaction about how Hollywood has changed, that the good old days were better. But I don't recall a time out here when people weren't talking about the good old days. There was always change and dissatisfaction. Silents into sound was quite a change, wasn't it? People in the industry complained that sound was going to ruin the business. People in Hollywood or anyplace else are generally afraid of change.

Douglas Fairbanks, Jr.
You Must Remember This, 1975

Like Lincoln

Hollywood has gone to hell. It's like talking about Lincoln. He ain't here anymore, and neither is Hollywood.

George Jessel
You Must Remember This, 1975

New Route

In the old days in Hollywood, when you went on location they sent a limousine to your home to take you. Now they give you a map.

James Stewart
Great Movie Heroes, 1975

That's Style!

It was great getting together with all those wonderful people from MGM on stage after the premiere of *That's Entertainment!* That's really my style—but there isn't that kind of style going in Hollywood anymore. It's a new trend, a new generation. And that's as it should be, even though I violently disapprove of so many things going on today—drugs, alcohol, no morals, no inhibitions—some of the very young really putting themselves into an early grave.

Fred Astaire
Motion Picture, November, 1975

Basket Case

Today it would be impossible for a Ginger Rogers to happen. There's no Hollywood left. Hollywood is like an empty wastebasket. It made me sad to watch the movie business change, but there was nothing I could do about it. The joy has gone out of picture-making. That little box over there (the television set)—that's the handsome villain.

Ginger Rogers
Sunday News, March 28, 1976

★ ★ ★

Like a Morgue

Hollywood? I visit there occasionally—though I never see the people I worked with—and I'm really glad I'm out of there. I visited MGM about three years ago and it was just like a morgue.

Jackie "Butch" Jenkins
Who's Who in Hollywood, 1976

★ ★ ★

Dirty Doings

The war changed things. Other people came in who weren't qualified, magazines started giving our Hollywood tricks away and foreign films came into play after the war and grabbed much attention. I have never minded foreign films, but who needs *dirty* foreign films? We can do better dirty films ourselves.

Mae West
Motion Picture, October, 1976

★ ★ ★

Four-Letter Land

The glory of Hollywood will return when they make four-star films, and eliminate the four-letter words in the scripts.

Richard Greene
Hollywood Players: The Thirties, 1976

★ ★ ★

Atmosphere Looser

In the old Hollywood, acting was fun. The atmosphere was looser. We used to play practical jokes on each other. Once I went with a film crew into the High Sierras. After I finished my part, I fell asleep under a tree. When I woke up, I was all alone—the whole company had picked up and gone. I spent half the night trying to hitch a ride back to Los Angeles.

Rod Cameron
Hollywood Players: The Forties, 1976

Fort Apache, the Bronx (20th Century-Fox, 1981), found Paul Newman and Ed Asner as policemen in one of New York's toughest battle zones.

Katharine Hepburn and, in his last film, Henry Fonda touched the heartstrings as an aged married couple in *On Golden Pond* (Universal, 1981), and both won Academy Awards.

Batty Belles

The dames I started out with (in Hollywood) are mostly batty today. They had their looks and when that passed they were finished. Reality has always meant my home and friends and children.

Yvonne De Carlo
Films in Review, April, 1977

★ ★ ★

Sorry!

The reason I left Hollywood is because they wanted me to play Elvis Presley's mother. Not that I have anything against Elvis Presley. But that just wasn't my cup of tea.

Joan Fontaine
Asbury Park Press, April 21, 1978

★ ★ ★

Going—Going—Gone

The lush Hollywood, the ripe Hollywood, the Hollywood of the big studios with the biggest and most beautiful stars under contract to them, the Hollywood of Louella Parsons and Hedda Hopper, the classic Hollywood, is gone.

Joshua Logan
Movie Stars, Real People, and Me, 1978

★ ★ ★

Not His Bag

Sometimes I think I should have died about twenty years ago. Today these actors with their hippy-dippy cocaine bag—I don't know. Don't get me wrong. I love Hollywood. I just hate what's being done to it. And I love pictures. I'd like to make three or four good ones before I croak.

Robert Blake
American Film, December–January, 1979

★ ★ ★

Catering to Children

As for contemporary Hollywood, it is a little crazy, with an air of amateurism about the whole thing. In the old days the industry was kept going by a group of Jewish studio bosses who really knew what they were doing. Today, more than ever before, Hollywood is a huge one-armed bandit. With *Jaws* and *Star Wars*, it's like we were catering to children and the unemployed.

James Mason
London Sunday Telegraph, April 15, 1979

Seen the Best

The years in Hollywood had, in Samuel Johnson's words, been a "heyday: an expression of frolick and exultation, and sometimes of wonder." I had, I believed, seen the best of the heyday—the laughs, the art, the motivation, position, honors, satisfactions. It had been right for me to turn a corner and head away from Hollywood. I had seen it all.

Dore Schary
Heyday, 1979

★ ★ ★

Dirty Linen

Today's Hollywood? It's Sodom and Gomorrah. The drugs, the corruption drag down an industry—and a nation. The sad thing is that most of the people involved don't see their own dirty linen. They're not going to get my money to see the junk that's being made today. No way.

Ginger Rogers
People, the 1980s

★ ★ ★

Women of Wit

When TV came, panic hit Hollywood. The studios began to close down. People who had been under contract for twenty-five years were fired. Lesser films were being scheduled. Nobody cared about the quality. Many of the European artists who had lived in California as refugees decided to return to Europe. McCarthy was around the corner. One began to sense the danger of fascism. Within a year or two, he succeeded in cutting off the balls of the gutsy, radical writers and directors. Then the women's image went down the drain. Gorgeous women, women of intelligence and beauty, integrity and wit, like Joan Crawford, Irene Dunne, Greta Garbo, Claudette Colbert, Katharine Hepburn, were slowly replaced with the girl-next-door or the sexpot image. Only a few of the real actresses survived, mainly those who dared to return to the theater.

Viveca Lindfors
Viveka . . . Viveca, 1981

★ ★ ★

Closed Shop

When the doors of Hollywood shut on minorities and blacks at the end of the '70s, a lot of black artists had been enjoying the exploitation for 10 years. But one day they found the shop had closed down. Now I find some of them working in department stores, in restaurants, in little offices where you might expect them to be selling music services, but instead they're selling fertilizer.

Harry Belafonte
The New York Times, August 28, 1981

They Stood Alone

There aren't any big stars today in Hollywood who are like the stars they had then. Nowadays, there is so much emphasis on youth and trends. Whatever bastards those moguls were, they encouraged women.

Faye Dunaway
The Village Voice, November 4, 1981

★ ★ ★

In the Past

Actresses who live in the past are always suspect; people in Hollywood drench themselves in nostalgia and it doesn't work, because things aren't like that anymore.

Patricia Morison
The Village Voice, November 4, 1981

★ ★ ★

Still Life

The old Hollywood that I knew is dead. It only exists now in still photographs and a few people's memories.

Olivia de Havilland
The Films of the Thirties, 1982

★ ★ ★

Bad Effect

Times have changed. These days Hollywood has gone too far toward the shock-horror cult—showing all the lurid details, the blood and the gore. It has a bad effect on people, I believe, especially on the unbalanced in society.

Vincent Price
Los Angeles Times, December 26, 1982

★ ★ ★

Weird Harold

Hollywood is not as glamorous as it used to be. People go there expecting to see stars on the sidewalk. Did you ever see Weird Harold on the corner of Hollywood and Vine? For a dollar, Weird Harold will show you his version of *Flashdance*.

Johnny Carson
The Tonight Show Starring Johnny Carson
September 15, 1983

Mommie Dearest (Paramount, 1981), the story of movie star Joan Crawford as alleged child abuser, presented Harry Goz as a Crawford husband and Faye Dunaway as the necessarily late lady in question.

Dustin Hoffman triumphed as an actor who masqueraded as a woman to get work in *Tootsie* (Columbia, 1982), with Jessica Lange as his girlfriend in her Oscar-winning supporting performance.

What Becomes a Legend

After 70 years of multimillion-dollar profits for California, that income is now threatened by runaway production. And that's Hollywood's fault—it's taken those resources for granted when others have not. A current list of films now in production shows twice as many movies being done outside California as in . . . Elizabeth Taylor once said, "You're only a legend when you're dead." If California doesn't change its course, Hollywood is soon going to be a legend.

Ed Asner
October 12, 1983

Smog Alert

I hope to leave Hollywood and move back to New York, because the heavy smog from the deal-makers' cigars is beginning to choke me. They don't have what it takes anymore, and they're all in, you know, the deal-making business. It has nothing to do with the product itself. They throw the stuff out in the marketplace, most of them, and just pray.

Bette Midler
October 13, 1983

Pause That Depresses

I started using Coke in 1975, at the point when it became epidemic in Hollywood. I stopped pretty quickly. I was making *Bound for Glory* and I became short-tempered. I'd get cross at (cinematographer) Haskell Wexler for things that weren't his fault. It's not my nature to be curt and quick-tempered. I saw what was happening and stopped using it.

Hal Ashby
Rolling Breaks, 1983

More Freedom

Changes in Hollywood? The movie industry is more open now for new people. All kinds of independent films are being made and shown. And the loosening of the ratings system has been very good. Even though I don't approve of everything that goes on in today's films, I'm pleased to see the changes. It means more freedom, in the last analysis, for the serious film-maker.

Martin Ritt
October 20, 1983

Question of Priorities

The deal-makers have taken over the business. I got a lot of laughs during the recent Hollywood strike when I pointed out to my fellow writers that five of my former agents had become studio heads. Now the number is seven. In the old days at least, L.B. Mayer and (Irving) Thalberg saw the script as a commodity; they tried to get people like Dorothy Parker and William Faulkner to work for them; *then* they'd mess up the writing. Now, people see scripts as talking papers to get a hot star or director interested in a package. It's a question of priorities.

Waldo Salt
The New York Times Magazine
October 23, 1983

Warmth Missed

What I miss most about the old Hollywood is the warmth and camaraderie among actors then, the sense we all had of belonging to the industry, of contributing something, big or small. Now everybody is more concerned with making deals. Hollywood has become a town of transient people, nobody stays for too long at any level.

Cesar Romero
Hollywood Studio Magazine, October, 1983

Unconvinced

I don't think anybody is quite able to figure out where Hollywood is going. We don't make glamour movies today, we don't build images. Everything now is very realistic, artistic—and depressing. When is the last time you saw a wonderful musical or a fabulous fantasy. Nobody is going to convince me that Hollywood is going to continue like this.

Edith Head
Edith Head's Hollywood, 1983

A Fixer-Upper

The old Hollywood: Your eyebrows were plucked, your teeth were fixed. You were not allowed to keep any of the features you came in with.

Helen Hayes
Live at Five, November 8, 1983

Took It and Ran
If you've noticed in Hollywood where millions and billions of dollars have been made, there aren't any kind of monuments or museums—and I don't call putting your footprint in Grauman's Chinese Theater a monument—all right, this did mean a lot of sentimental ballyhoo to me at the time. Gee, nobody left anything behind, they took it, they grabbed it and they ran—the ones who made the billions of dollars, never the workers.

Marilyn Monroe
Marilyn Monroe: In Her Own Words, 1983

Smilin' Through
Though interesting and productive for me personally, the years during which I was active in Hollywood were stressful for the industry as a whole.

I signed my contract with MGM only weeks after Pearl Harbor and I remember the anxiety of the executives—knowing that many of their young actors and technicians would be drafted and wondering if the studios would be able to cope without them. During the war, we in the film industry, like others across the nation, endured losses of loved ones. When the war was over the threat of TV consumed the conversation of studio personnel. Shortly after that, the horrifying tactics of Senator Joseph McCarthy anguished the artists of the industry and forever prevented many talented members from working.

In those golden years we wore the smiling mask of our profession and hid the tragic symbol. The show must go on. It did.

Ann Richards
November 27, 1983

Popcorn Premium
No one rehearses any more in Hollywood, so how do you know what to do? They just do takes 100 times over. Now, distributors make more money on popcorn than on the film—and deservedly so.

Lillian Gish
Asbury Park Press, December 1, 1983

Heirs Apparent
The old Hollywood's all gone now. I'm glad I was part of it and knew about it, but when I go out there now it's a different town. I'll tell you what does exist. The children and grandchildren of the great movie moguls are still Hollywood society. That's all there. But not the rest.

Angela Lansbury
On Cable, January, 1984

RKO Pictures players and personnel held a reunion in Hollywood in 1982. Top row: Lizabeth Scott, Martha Scott, Joan Leslie, Joel McCrea, Frances Dee, Helen Mack, Mary Brian, Dorothy McGuire and Rudy Vallee. Second row: Janet Leigh, Jane Wyatt, Hermes Pan, Susan Strasberg, Jane Greer, Pandro Berman, Mala Powers, Harriet (Hilliard) Nelson, Ralph Bellamy and Guy Madison. Bottom row: Fred Astaire, Laraine Day, Ginger Rogers, Rhonda Fleming, Fay Wray, Sam Jaffe, Virginia Mayo, Anne Jeffreys and Jane Russell.

Divine Rights

It was all so different when I started coming out to Hollywood to film in the early 1940s. You were treated so divinely then. I'd come out from New York and the studio would put me up at the Beverly Hills Hotel, give me a car, arrange for wonderful publicity. And I was not the star. I played Lana Turner's best friend, Hedy Lamarr's best friend, Joan Bennett's best friend. You never worried after you finished a film, "Will I ever work again?"

I remember when my career really began to accelerate in pictures. I was in *The Doughgirls* on Broadway, and L.B. Mayer, the head of MGM in Hollywood, asked me to come to the Coast and play Lana Turner's mother in *Marriage is a Private Affair*. I didn't think I was old enough to play Lana Turner's mother! What next, I thought, Clifton Webb's mother?! But I did it and Mr. Mayer called me into his office one day to get me to sign a seven-year contract with the studio.

"You're a lady," he explained. "We don't have ladies in Hollywood. Please sign."

I told him I was sorry, but I had a lover back in New York and couldn't possibly leave him.

With that, Mayer turned on me, screaming, "A lady?! I thought you were a lady! Get out of here!"

(My lover was the playwright George S. Kaufman, who always seemed to be married to someone; no, I didn't identify him to Mayer.)

MGM hired me from time to time anyway, as did other studios, but I remained a free-lancer. (So did Louis Calhern, to whom I was married in the thirties. He made many MGM films, and most people thought he was under contract there, but he wasn't.)

As for Hollywood parties, they were simply part of your business. The agents would make arrangements for you to go on, and so would the studio, and you'd be seen and meet people who could be important to your career.

In those days, money didn't mean anything. Now they have someone with a watch standing by on the set to tell you when you're through. The director is good because he brings the film in on time. They no longer bring character players like myself in from New York, or anywhere else—the cost of everything is so great today.

When I first came out to Hollywood even the featured players had the same make-up man on each film, which gave you a great sense of security and continuity. I had one make-up man, Keester Sweeney, for years in pictures. When I finally moved out here in 1965 and went into series television with *Gilligan's Island* I asked for Keester and got him again. No make-up men are under contract to the studios today. You have to take whoever is available. At Universal Studios, you are made up right on the set!

The glamour is gone. You have to rely on an agent, and that's difficult for actors "of a certain age" like myself, because agents now are only interested in young people whom they can build. In the old Hollywood, too, everyone looked so great. The stars might arrive at the studio with kerchiefs and no make-up, but by the time they faced the cameras they were dressed to look beautiful. Today's stars arrive the same way but by the time they face the cameras they often aren't dressed at all!

I always say, Natalie, don't live in the past, that's not good. You must live for today. But the old days in Hollywood *were* better—there's no getting around it.

Natalie Schafer
March 4, 1984

Boulevard of Broken Dreams

The word "Hollywood" evokes fantasies, dramas, legends, but the harsh reality is that Hollywood Boulevard, where it all began, has become more onerous than any back street in any bad film ever made. (We should be) replacing the porno shops with little theatre groups, having shops that sell movie memorabilia—simply turn the street into a living memorial to the Hollywood of our dreams and memories.

Mickey Rooney
The Hollywood Reporter, March 5, 1984

Directors? Nein!

The most regrettable change I have seen take place in Hollywood is the deification of the director, a tendency that came largely from Germany. All heil the Herr Director—at the expense of the writer, the dramatist. From the days of Aeschylus, to Shakespeare, to Shaw, to Eugene O'Neill, it has been the man who could invent wonderful characters and put them in exciting predicaments who was essential for public entertainment. Then there was need for actors to impersonate and illuminate them.

Where the *hell* did the director come from?

Before coming to Hollywood, I acted in the London theater (a golden age—1925 to 1939), where the director's job was simply to dodge you around the furniture and see that the star was comfortably upstage for his big moments.

Movies *are* different. However, note this: the director of *The Uninvited*, which I did in 1944 and is probably the best ghost movie ever made, was Lewis Allen. It was his first picture. He previously had been Broadway producer Gilbert Miller's stage manager (because no one else would put up with that bullying shit!). Allen was perfectly adroit at "dodging" one around the furniture. But the film was excellent because of Charles Brackett, who produced it and presented his director and actors with a superb script from the original novel.

That is how good movies are made.

That is the way the esteemed late producer David O. Selznick worked. He bought the best writing talent to produce superior scripts. So did all the great producers.

Too often, the Hollywood director is a disagreeable convenience rather than an artistic necessity.

That the "old Hollywood" method worked best is amply proved by the fact that it's not only the doddering but the kids who see the vintage movies on television and say, "Why don't they make pictures like that anymore?"

To sum up: a director without a good script is like a doctor without a stethoscope. Would-be directors are a dime a dozen, but good dramatic writers are rare and precious.

Alan Napier
March 13, 1984

Trouble Spot

Hollywood got into trouble when the town started making films instead of movies.

Richard Widmark
The Hollywood Reporter, April 17, 1984

Risky Business
If Hollywood keeps gearing movie after movie to teenagers, next year's Oscar will develop acne.

Mel Brooks
Sunday News, April 22, 1984

Kicks About Cocaine
There's an epidemic of cocaine use in L.A. now, but I maintain it's worse elsewhere. One of the reasons I left L.A. was because of excessive drug use there, but it was more the whole collage of people in Hollywood and what's happened to it. And when you sit back and think about it, you realize you got out not because of the cocaine use but because of what the place has become. I don't want to live there.

Jerry Lewis
Parade, April 22, 1984

Paging Professionalism
Today in Hollywood, I'm on the set and these young actors come in and say, "What's the scene?" . . . "What page is it on?" I'm standing there on the set with my forty years of experience and they come along without knowing their lines! How *dare* they do that?

Janis Paige
Woman to Woman, May 10, 1984

The Omen
The day I arrived there to play Franz Liszt, the D fell off the HOLLYWOOD sign.

Dirk Bogarde
Tales from the Hollywood Raj, 1984

Heck Hath No Fury?
Once upon a time in Hollywood *damn* was a four-letter word and the wicked went to heck.

Oscar Millard
Los Angeles Times, May 13, 1984

Mel Brooks and Anne Bancroft co-starred in *To Be or Not to Be* (20th Century-Fox, 1983), the remake of the 1942 Ernst Lubitsch comedy with Jack Benny and Carole Lombard.

Terms of Endearment (Paramount, 1983), a serio-comic exploration of a mother-daughter relationship, brought Shirley MacLaine a best actress Academy Award and Debra Winger a best actress nomination.

Jeanne of Fox

I was born in the Mojave Desert town of Barstow, California, but lived in the Hollywood area since infancy. Acting in movies was never part of my plan, though; it was something that just came about.

When I was signed by 20th Century-Fox in 1943, there were around two hundred stock contract kids there, young people who seemed promising and whom the studio tried to develop. Nowadays, there is hardly anybody under contract to the studios.

World War II was on then, and my peers on the lot and I used to wonder, "Where's the glamour? Where are the Jean Harlows and the Carole Lombards?" I had grown up watching their pictures. Because it was wartime, we had to boost the morale, be the girl next door waiting to welcome her serviceman home. We were photographed in gingham dresses and milking cows, but we yearned for the furs and sequins. Then we reached another era and realized that those days, our days, were indeed great—now they say we were part of Hollywood's "golden age."

Fox was a beehive of activity in the forties. There were so many productions shooting, so many talented people. There was something in the air. We worked six days a week then—we were the last business in the United States to work those hours. And when we went on location to film we worked seven days a week. We shot *Home in Indiana*, the picture that established me, in Ohio and Kentucky—Indiana wasn't the type, I guess; that's Hollywood for you.

When I first started in Hollywood, I *was* that very young girl I played. I married in 1945, however, and began having children as soon as possible. I had my fourth child before my oldest was five. So then I wanted to be Sadie, Sadie, married lady. I wanted to wear the black crepe dress and the pearls. But even though I had become a top box office attraction, the studio still saw me as Margie, the name of the dreamy girl I seemed to play in so many of my early movies.

My first really big starring success was probably *State Fair* in 1945. Everyone everywhere was singing the Rodgers and Hammerstein songs from the Broadway hit *Oklahoma!*, so Fox decided to do its own country musical. The services of Oscar Hammerstein were obtained to re-write the old *State Fair* screenplay that had starred Will Rogers, and the new songs were by (Richard) Rodgers and Hammerstein. Right after it was announced that I had won the lead in it, I met Janet Gaynor who had co-starred in the earlier version.

"I congratulate you," she said, "but you have no idea how I feel."

Years later, when the musical *State Fair* was remade, I looked at the actress who was playing the farm girl and knew exactly what Janet had meant. It was *my* role.

I loved *Centennial Summer*, too, though for some reason it wasn't a big commercial success. It had the great composer Jerome Kern's last score, which was beautiful. Mr. Kern was on the set quite a bit. He was a real Mr. Five-by-Five, a chubby little elf whose face just lit up when you talked to him. Tragically, before the picture came out he collapsed on a street in New York and died.

On the other hand, *Margie*, although it started out to be just a small film, is one of my best-remembered movies. The little high school girl I played was always losing her bloomers, and you would be amazed at the number of ladies I have met over the years—from all walks of life!—who tell me that the same thing happened to them in school!

Henry King, who directed *Margie*, was the most important director on the Fox lot, the favorite of our boss, Darryl F. Zanuck. At this point, he had just finished a big picture, and the studio said, "Don't you want a vacation?" But he was a workhorse and said no, he wanted another film right away. They showed him some scripts from some of the big novels of the day, but when the script of *Margie* came his way, he said, "This is the one I want to do." I think Zanuck tried to talk him out of it. Mr. King did it, though, and that was probably why *Margie* turned out so well.

Mr. Zanuck was like other moguls of those years, a star-maker. He could assess you as a green, awkward colt and see something in you that even you didn't see. Personally, he was like an emperor, like Napoleon. I can still see him walking to his private dining room on the lot, so jaunty with his Tyrolean hat and riding crop and cigar. He never talked to you. And when he called you into his office, which was only about every five years, you were scared to death. It was not like MGM, where, I was told, boss Louis B. Mayer liked to think of his contract players as his children.

I haven't read the new book out about Mr. Zanuck. So many of the books being written about our Hollywood are error-prone because the authors dig up the old "official" studio biographies and publicity releases and believe what they said about us. The facts in these "bios" were often glossed over, even falsified, to make us seem fascinating and perfect.

One of my better parts was in *Apartment for Peggy* in 1948. That extroverted, chatterbox wife was totally unlike me—except for the fact that she was pregnant.

My best acting role, though, came the following year in *Pinky*. I played a black girl who passed for white in a picture that was a courageous undertaking for Hollywood at the time, a dramatic indictment of racial prejudice. The great John Ford, who did *The Grapes of Wrath*, was the original director of the film, and I tested for him with the wonderful black artist Ethel Waters—she would be playing my grandmother. I was very worried that I wouldn't get the part. We shot the test sans make-up ten days after my second child was born, and no woman looks very good so soon after childbirth. I also didn't look black. But there was an instant rapport with Ethel, whom I adored, and for some reason she seemed to return my affection.

"I'll see it in your eyes," said Mr. Ford. It must have been there because I got the part of Pinky.

Unfortunately, Mr. Ford left the production after a couple of weeks' shooting. He had been having terrible battles with Zanuck, who was flooding him with memos. We started all over again with Elia Kazan, a fine director from the New York stage who had just done *A Streetcar Named Desire* there. I learned so much from him. Up to working with Mr. Kazan, a lot of what I had done was for places, cameras and lights and you just hoped that the first or second take of a scene would be it. We never had a free second with Kazan. We rehearsed what we were going to do a week or two before we shot it. That was his stage background. He said, "A thing evolves when you work this way." It was a completely different way of working for me at that point. I have done many plays since then, and you rehearse it and work on it and when you do it, it really GOES!

I would love to see some of the original *Pinky* footage shot by Mr. Ford, though. He was a very foxy gentleman. He knew Zanuck liked to fool around with films in the cutting room, but he shrewdly protected himself by never making cover shots of a scene (which were usually done for protection). This way the studio had to go with what ever he had in mind and not tamper with what he'd shot.

Mr. Kazan was tricky, too. We had this important shanty town cabin set in *Pinky* where we'd worked for weeks. Now Kazan and Zanuck began to fight, too, because Zanuck was at him to re-shoot things. One day we finished everything we had to do on this one set and Kazan, in defiance of Zanuck who still wanted to re-shoot, ordered it torn down. Now we couldn't re-shoot. As pliable and young as Kazan was then, he knew what he had to do.

Pinky won me a best actress Academy Award nomination. So guess what they put me in next? *Cheaper by the Dozen*, in which Clifton Webb as the father of twelve was really the main character. At the time, it was the trauma of my life. The distinguished director William Wyler had seen me in *Pinky* and wanted me for his production of *Sister Carrie*, opposite Laurence Olivier, but Zanuck wouldn't loan me out—he had four or five pictures lined up for me, beginning with *Cheaper by the Dozen*. I went to see him and begged, cried and screamed. I asked, "How could you cast me again as a pigtailed fifteen-year-old?!"

In stentorian tones, he answered, "There will come a time when you'll want someone to cast you as a fifteen-year-old girl and no one will." He was right about that.

Of all the Hollywood producers then, I think David O. Selznick was the greatest. He managed his stars' careers fantastically well. If he didn't have any films for them, he'd loan them out for very carefully selected quality vehicles.

Joseph L. Mankiewicz, who directed two of my better films, *A Letter to Three Wives* and *People Will Talk*, was another director who taught me a lot. With Joe, every comma and syllable and breath had to be exact. Some directors will let you paraphrase the dialogue, but not Joe, perhaps because he also wrote his own scripts. It was excellent training. I remember at the start of *A Letter to Three Wives* I said, "Mr. Mankiewicz . . ." He interrupted and said, "What is this Mr. Mankiewicz. Call me Joe." Not all directors were this informal; many wanted the respect of being called "Mister." They were the absolute rulers on the set, you know.

Once, around 1951, before I did a scene in *People Will Talk*, I told Joe that it seemed very unnatural that any girl would react in this certain way. He replied, "This is not any girl, any ordinary girl—she is unique, a particular girl." I always say that I learned to act in front of a hundred and fifty million people.

There's such a different atmosphere in Hollywood today. All they care about now is the cost. That's why I don't bother to scrounge around for pictures anymore. Years ago, Henry King, although he was even then a gray-haired, older gentleman, told me, "There's got to be some fun to it." Making a movie involves a certain amount of drudgery, but when you lose the fun completely there is a spirit lacking in the finished product. When I was busy in films, there was always fun and by-play on the sets with your colleagues. That's all gone now. GONE!

But you were taught to be a thorough professional. For instance, no one was ever, *ever* late for work—the studio just would not have permitted it. They took a valid point and drove it into the ground. Now *everything* is money. It's all you hear. It's been a cliché for years that the bankers took over Hollywood, and today it must be somebody's mother-in-law deciding what television shows get cancelled—it's often the best ones.

There's no question that the momentum of my career in Hollywood was diminished by my family duties. I have seven children, and now six grandchildren, and I lost any number of good roles because of being pregnant, or because I was needed at home. But you have to have your priorities in life. My family always came first, and I wouldn't do anything differently today.

At the beginning, when my name was just going up on theater marquees, my grandmother was dying. She said to me, "Jeanne, we're all so proud of what you've accomplished. But at the end of your life there is nothing that can take the place of your children." I have always believed that.

Jeanne Crain
May 21, 1984

★ ★ ★

Never So Few
It seems to me we're getting further and further away from what Hollywood set out to do—which is to make people pictures. Look how few are being made these days.

Robert Wagner
Los Angeles Times, August 4, 1984

Jane Greer and Richard Widmark were prominent in *Against All Odds* (Columbia, 1984), a remake of Greer's 1947 film *Out of the Past* in which the actress now played the mother of the character she had played earlier.

Then and Now

Pretty soon after a child star's TV series ends, you don't know who he or she is. But you always know us, even if we don't work anymore. Studios built up names we'll never lose. That's the difference between Hollywood today and Hollywood then.

Margaret O'Brien
Twinkle, Twinkle, Little Star, 1984

★ ★ ★

Everybody's a Star

In my time Hollywood had much more class. There was a glamour, an intrigue. Now the people in pictures all look alike, and everybody's a "star." The word has really been kicked around.

Alice Faye
Family Weekly, November 25, 1984